Don Dedera

A MILE IN HIS MOCCASINS

a mile

by Don Dedera

Edited by Thomas K. Sanford, Jr.
Drawings by Kearney Egerton

in his moccasins

Great Spirit,
let me not judge my brother
before I have walked a mile in his moccasins.

McGREW PRINTING & LITHOGRAPHING CO., PUBLISHER
PHOENIX, ARIZONA

Library of Congress Catalog Card Number 60-16692

Printed in the United States of America
First Edition

For Nancy
and Dian

Acknowledgments

This book is made mainly of columns which originally appeared in The Arizona Republic. I offer my thanks to its editors, and to its publisher, Eugene C. Pulliam, for permission to reprint the material. Orien W. Fifer, Jr., managing editor of The Republic, has given sustaining faith to the column and to the book. I am obliged to William L. Hermann, my city editor through the years of these columns, whose pencil speared a hundred of my major mistakes. I am grateful also to Thomas K. Sanford, Jr., who stabbed some more while editing this book. By no reckoning should others be responsible for boners this book may yet contain. They are my exclusive property.

I wish I could thank, for caring, the late Professor John Girdler. Perhaps his close friend, Ernest J. Hopkins, professor emeritus of journalism at Arizona State University, will accept double measure of my gratitude in their behalf.

I must cite debts to my family of rather retiring folks who, by accident of relation to a newspaperman, have suffered invasions of their homes, their schedules, their private affairs. My mother and father are Mr. and Mrs. Frank Dedera of Tempe, Arizona, and my brother and sister-in-law are Mr. and Mrs. Frank C. Dedera of Phoenix.

Further, I am beholden to a host of friends who not only are curious of mind, but loose of lip. They are tipsters to stories, sometimes trivial, sometimes libelous, but nearly always interesting. In the columnist's recurring nightmare, all his storyfinders are cataclysmically exterminated, and he is compelled to fill his corner unassisted.

Other people's utterances are all neatly bound up in quotation marks, I hope. I am especially thankful for permission of Milo Wiltbank of Eagar, Ariz., to reprint poems and fragments from his *Grama Grass Wisdom*, privately printed in 1958. Mrs. Byron Cummings graciously has given leave to quote from her late husband's brilliant work, *Kinishba*, published in 1940 by the Hohokam Museums Association and the University of Arizona.

Kearney Egerton, Arizona's most versatile cartoonist and illustrator, has won my gratitude for his enthusiasm.

I am further beholden to Irvin (Dan) McGrew, for moral and material support in the publication of this book. I am obliged to him for the opportunity to turn and take words and phrases of the columns as they were transferred from newspaper records to the book manuscript. Every newspaperman has seen emboldened by ink the despised cliche, the misspelled word, the wayward grammar, under his by-line, and he has longed for a chance to rewrite. Changes from the originals are not extensive, but I could not resist the urge to scratch a few old itches.

Conclusions, sequels, and transitions were brought current, here and there, but as a rule, the selected columns fell of substance and order of their appearance in The Republic through the years 1955-1960. The nomadic propensity of Arizonans erodes the accuracy of time-element stories. Let it be said that everybody in this book is a real person, or was when involved in the stories, which are, or were in the time of their telling, true.

D.D.

Conclusions, sequels, and transitions were brought current here and there, but as a rule, the selected columns fell in substance and order of their appearance in The Republic through the years 1958-1960. The nomadic propensity of Arizonans erodes the accuracy of time-element stories. Let it be said that everybody in this book is a real person, or was when involved in the stories, which are, or were in the time of their telling, true.

D.D.

A MILE IN HIS MOCCASINS

Chapter One

At wintry Chevelon atop the Mogollon Rim, Mr. and Mrs. O. B. McGuire invited me into their snug cottage for an hour's conversation.

They owned a Great Dane dog which in 1955 weighed 150 pounds and had not reached his prime. He was as big as a mature doe, and similar in color. In fact, during the deer season they locked the dog away to keep him out of the gun-sights of impulsive flatlanders.

O. B. was telling these things, when my glance wandered over to the dog. He was stretched out nearly the width of the living room, and unless my glasses were broken, the dog was eating a cat alive.

McGuire seemed to be looking at his dog, too, but he continued with his small talk. You should never challenge the customs of host humans or gigantic dogs, I thought. Maybe McGuire fed his dog a live cat every day.

Rudely fascinated, I watched the dog take most of the cat into his mouth. He made grimaces of a bored child retrieving a bubble of chewing gum, until at length only the hind paws and tail tip of the kitten were visable to me and McGuire. O. B. calmly ignored the astonishing procedings, and observed that thanks to a recent snowfall, he and the others of the forest ranger station were burning slash.

"Hold on!" I could contain myself no longer. "Is that dog eating a cat?"

"Sure is," said McGuire. "He'll chew him up and spit him out in a minute."

Presently the dog flung the cat onto the rug. The cat, name of Albert, licked futilely at its matted fur, rolled onto its back, and playfully punched the dog's apple-size nose.

That was their way of having fun, McGuire said.

I had never seen such an exhibition in my life. It occurred to me that I might search Arizona over, from Mananaland to the Strip Country, from its deepest copper mine to its tallest mountain, from the Colorado to the Blue, from Navajo hogans to Tucson motels, from Grand Canyon to the old Town Ditch, by train, bus, automobile, blimp, truck, horse, helicopter, foot, bookmobile, jet trainer, ore skip, snow tractor, airliner, bicycle, coaster, Jeep, steam engine, motorboat, squad car, stagecoach, horseless carriage, snowshoes, and mule—and never again would I see a cat which enjoyed getting itself wet all over, inside the mouth of a Great Dane.

I traveled, in those ways, and in more than five years I've not seen the equal to O. B. McGuire's dog-and-cat act.

But there have been other things. . . .

BLUE POINT—Pop Grayson stuck half a handful of tobacco into his mouth, mashed more into his pipe, scratched a kitchen match, lighted up, and spat.

Then he poured beer from a can into a plastic cup that was about twice the size of a shot glass and had Jack Be Nimble written on it. He blew off the tiny head of foam, took a small sip, and exclaimed:

"There ain't no Lost Dutchman Mine. No more than Jacob Walz was a murderer. The hull blame story is a pack of lies thet the chamber of commerce keeps alive fer the tourist trade."

It was pleasant outside of Pop's dinky, sagging trailer in a glade of mesquite at the Blue Point Picnic Grounds. Rain from the previous night brought smells from the earth. The slanting sunshine seemed to warm Pop to his subject. Counting Fiddlestick and another dog, we were listeners three.

"I knowed Jake in the '80s when I drove a team of oxen. He used to winter down to Yuma, and summer up here. Spring he'd buy up a load of supplies off the river boats at Yuma and a couple time I helped him taken his stuff to Phoenix.

"Gold mine? Jake had a gold mine, all right. He'd pack those supplies up the Verde a ways and trade with miners who was stealin' highgrade from the Vulture over t' Wickenburg.

"That's how he come t' have nuggets to spend. An' that's why he thowed people off his trail. Hi, sure, he had a camp back in the Superstitious (Superstition) Mountains. But he didn't have no gold mine, and that's a fact."

Pop stopped for another sip. That was a long speech for a man who attributed his long life to "keepin' my mouth shut when I got somethin' to say." In his jeans, khaki shirt and baseball cap, Pop might have weighed 110 pounds. He was 93 years old. He rode a mule from St. Louis to Arizona, in 1882, and except for one trip to the Klondike and another to California, he stayed. For most of his life Pop (his real name was Walter) was a gold prospector. He said he found fortunes on the Klondike and at Rich Hill near Wickenburg, and "put it all back in the ground." After he lost his Wickenburg bonanza, he said, he figured that wealth just drives a man crazy. He set up camp on a placer claim near Bumble Bee and took out from $10 to $45 per week for 35 years.

"U-ranium?" he shouted. "Haw. I'll take gold you can trade for cash."

By strict interpretation of the law, Pop was illegally squatting at Blue Point. He said he couldn't live well in town on his $70 per month pension, so he worked out a casual agreement with Tonto National Forest Ranger R. R. Riley of Mesa. Pop camped year 'round on the picnic ground northeast of Phoenix. He kept the grounds clean, and he ran off fools who wanted to shoot at the trash barrels. Every so often a forest service man would drop off a box of groceries and a six-pack of beer and stay long enough to cut Pop a stack of wood.

Pop never married and all his close kin were dead.

"I couldn't see draggin' a woman over them hills," he said. "A woman wants to be goin' to town once a week, and they cost more to keep than they're worth."

Not that he didn't have his chances.

"Ol' woman picnicker up here couple years ago said, 'Pop, whyant you and me git married? I'm a right smart cook,' and I said, 'Hell, woman, you'd waste more with a spoon than I could carry in here with a steam shovel.' "

Within 10 months Pop was dead of a heart attack, and Ranger Riley uttered his epitaph: "I doubt if we'll ever find a replacement."

(And they never did.)

In Arizona, men-of-the-house scramble onto their roofs to fix their coolers.

So does Jess Richie.

Suburban breadwinners drive their cars to work and back home.

Jess does, also.

Many a dad finds time for kids, wife, chores, and maybe a little dreaming about a fishing trip.

That's the way it is for Jess Richie, too. So what is special about Jess, husband of Therese, father of two girls and a boy, and boss of 2416 E. Picadilly?

Not that he is legless. Not that alone, anyway.

"Heck," he said, or something stronger. "It isn't legs that make a man. It's up here." He pointed to what his fellow police officers call his big, fat head.

That is one of the nicer things they say about Jess. Fellow officer Harold DeWitt has been heard to threaten to catch Jess with his wheelchair brake released, and run him around the block.

"He's the best radio operator I've got," said Police Chief Charles P. Thomas. But in the same breath, Thomas spelled a warning to Jess. He said if he ever finds Jess with his feet on the desk, Jess will pound a walking beat. Jess has lost count of the times he has been challenged to a kicking contest.

In other words, at the station Jess is treated like a friend. He takes kidding. He dishes it out. He earns his pay. He knows he would be reprimanded for failure. He wishes it were like that everywhere.

"The toughest thing about this," said Jess, "is the way some people put you aside as something different.

"In trying to spare your feelings, they make you feel bad.

"I was at the doctor's one day, and a kid there was curious about me. The mother of the little girl shushed her up. Now, that little girl was doing okay. She wanted to know. I just spoke up and told her. Nothing wrong with asking. And I thought that mother was gonna fall out of her chair. . ."

Jess was hurt Nov. 19, 1947. An arrested man stamped Jess's feet, injuring blood vessels. Through years of hospitals and operations, as the Arizona Police magazine observed, Jess endured "a penalty of pain and suffering that no criminal is compelled to pay."

The words embarrassed Jess.

He said. "Some guys can do some things I can't do, and I can do some things other guys can't. There isn't a person in the world who doesn't have a handicap of some kind."

Byron F. Hunter swapped his motel for 30,000, cold-rolled nickel-plated concho belts. A year later he had worked his stack of concho belts down to 2,500, and he predicted, "I'll just about break even on the deal."

Hunter, of Tempe, owned the Motel de Manana on E. Van Buren, Phoenix. A friend was Fred A. Rhodes, operator of Southwestern Jewelry Mfg. Co. of Scottsdale.

"We had lunch one day," said Hunter. "I had a motel on my hands. He had nine tons of concho belts.

"One thing led to another, and we traded—my equity for his belts."

A third of the belts Hunter sold outright to curio and department stores.

"The balance I traded for anything and everything," said Hunter, who subsequently acquired an Indian store at 3900 E. Van Buren, Phoenix. "Animal horns. Prehistoric pots. Indian rugs. Other concho belts. I even took an insurance policy in a swap. The agent staggered out of here with 12 dozen belts. His eyes were glazed, and he looked like somebody had belted him one."

Hunter's neatest trick smacked of selling iceboxes to Eskimos.

"I worked out some deals on the Navajo reservation," said Hunter. "I can say positively that there are some Indians up there wearing nickel-plated concho belts."

Among the powerful good reasons for coming to Arizona is Arthur Neckameyer's. He drove 2,800 miles to find a place to park his car.

Two blocks beyond the right field wall of Ebbets Field in Brooklyn was the apartment house where Neckameyer and his family lived.

"On nights when the Dodgers were in town," complained Neckameyer, "I'd have to park 15 blocks from home. I got to hate all those cars, and baseball. That is exactly why I moved to Phoenix."

To begin with, it was the dummy with the knife sticking in its overstuffed chest.

Laid out in the master bedroom, it looked just like a dead man to the returning Russell Wright family of 2002 N. 38th Pl., Phoenix.

"It should have," recalled Bob Conners of 2010 N. 38th Pl. "I spent three days trying to make it look like a dead man. Yeah, I guess that was the first of it. Shortly after the Wrights moved in next door they went on a trip and I decided to put the dummy in their bed. I was going to stand it in a closet—you know, so it'd fall out when they opened the door—but at that time I didn't know how strong their hearts were."

Retaliation was quick in coming.

Wright picked a night when Conners was having in a flock of guests, and sent over a tray of hors d'oeuvres.

"You can imagine," said Conners, "how a tray of chicken claws with toothpicks would take the spark out of a party."

After the dead man-chicken claw exchange, the Wright and Conner families learned to open doors slowly, mistrust telephone voices, and expect, at best, the worst. Lawn furniture and other odd objects were put on the roofs of both homes. Once Wright had to bail out a plastic swimming pool before he could drag it over the eaves.

"Our wives think we're damn fools," said one husband, "but a lot of guys are in that boat, and we are careful never to do anything that would cause harm or destroy property."

In his mining work, Wright used a variety of vehicles which he kept at home. Before taking his family on a week-end jaunt, Wright asked his salesman buddy, Conners, to keep an eye on the equipment. Wright gave Conners all the keys, which was akin to pitching raw meat to a tiger. Conners lined up the two sedans, a pickup truck and a Jeep in front of the Wright home, and hung a bedsheet sign: "Ridiculous Russ Used Cars." With white shoe polish he liberally splattered the windshields with "Make an Offer" and "Must Sell" and "Real Deal" and other slogans. He posted rock-bottom prices.

Fifty eager customers were waiting when Wright got home. Thinking fast, Wright told them, "I'm sorry. It's not my stuff. It really belongs to the man next door, name of Conners.

"Now he's a hard man to get ahold of. He works late, and doesn't get home until after midnight. Best thing for you to do is call him then, or maybe a little later . . . "

For a long time the comptroller of Arizona State University, Gilbert Cady, insisted that he was Tempe's most-telephoned citizen.

A tree would die. Somebody would call Cady. Lost wallet. Call Cady. Stopped toilet. Call Cady. On top of this, he was expected to keep the books straight.

"I am a sufferer of telephobia," he groused.

Cady sought respite from the Bell System by vacationing in Colorado Springs, Colo. One day he visited scenic Cave of the Winds, and followed the tourist trail to a curio shop. A leather jacket took his fancy—then he staggered.

Pinned to the jacket was a card reading:

"Gilbert Cady. Call Operator 91."

A Texas friend, wanting to reach Cady, had learned of Cady's Colorado travel, and reasoned Cady would see Cave of the Winds, would enter the curio shop, might be in the market for a leather jacket.

Cady resignedly reached for the telephone.

Maj. Walter E. Cotten, training officer for Phoenix Air Reserve Center, had his hair cut by a Jewish barber at Sky Harbor Airport. The job was done before Cotten remembered he had no money with him.

"That's all right. Pay me next time," said the barber amiably.

But Cotten returned the next day and paid the bill. As

he turned to go, Cotten heard another customer say to his barber:

"You charge a buck and a half just to walk in here? No wonder the Arabs are warring on our people."

Dick Irvin of Phoenix didn't seem to be the sort of man who could keep going three days and three nights in his struggle to the top of the world.

His build was slight; his complexion, fair; his thick, full beard, blond. He said his strength was less than average.

Yet Irvin had spent a considerable portion of his 25 years clinging to ice and snow and rock at 10,000 feet and higher. For several terrifying seconds he once clung to nothing but the hope that his rope might stop his plummeting body. His head had been split open by falling boulders. He had seen his friends die. He had buried his name on tops of mountains where no man stood before.

His conquests were in Alaska, Canada, the Western states, Central and South America. In mountain climbing, he was a big leaguer.

He did not climb for fame, he said. His adventures had cost him all the money he could put aside through college years, and much of his salaries since graduation. He said he didn't care if others knew about his feats.

"I know what I do," he said. "I'm the only one who needs to know.

"Climbing is a personal thing. Some people say it is ridiculous. But so is hitting a little white ball back and forth across a net, if you want to analyze it closely. Climbing is not getting to a place where other humans seldom, or never, have been. For me, there is no religion involved in it, although I know a man who climbs mountains because he wants to be closer to God. I know another who has an inferiority complex, and must repeatedly prove himself. I am sure another I know is a paranoiac.

"But I like to think that I climb because it is beautiful up there. I become a part of beauty. I am alive up there.

"It is possible that I will die there. That possibility is an essential part of climbing. What is worth gaining if it demands no risk?"

Irvin's first big climb was Mount Ritter, 13,156 feet, in the Sierra Nevadas. Irvin was 15.

Before that he admitted to "some non-technical scrambling." Since, between school years at San Francisco State College where he earned a degree in anthropology, Irvin explored the upper levels of the Western Hemisphere.

He broke his arches packing 110 pounds of wet food off Mount McKinley in Alaska. He climbed nearly every mountain of size in Central Canada, including more than a dozen of the highest. He topped Mexico's tallest mountain, and two of five peaks he reached in the Andes had never been climbed before, including Huandoy, 20,850 feet.

He rated his toughest "lead" as the Praying Monk on Camelback Mountain near Phoenix. To lead, up a mountain, is to find a way for followers.

"That's a 70-degree face," Irvin explained. "It's one finger at a time. I guess there are enough climbing holes and ledges to make it easier now. Arizona is probably the most untouched climbing country in the United States. Somebody is going to come here and have some first-time fun."

One question a mountain-climber hears over and again: What does a man think about when he reaches the top?

"This may be disappointing," said Irvin. "But I generally worry about how the devil I'm going to get down."

It is a daily ritual in Arizona, at about 300 places.

A man (or very likely it is a woman) peers at a set of instruments, then jots down a few figures on a government form. Late in 1955, in Fredonia, it was the postmaster. In Kayenta, a minister. In Lukachukai, a priest. In Holbrook, a railroader. In Aguila, a motel operator. In Sanders, a school principal. In Littlefield, a cafe owner. In Signal, a prospector.

They were weather observers—volunteers in a nationwide system of which the President's science advisory board has said, "One of the most extraordinary services ever developed anywhere, and probably (it) nets the public more per dollar expended than any other government service in the world."

Louis R. Jurwitz, Arizona's weather chief, said the value of volunteers' observations to farmers, meteorologists, doctors and engineers was beyond estimate.

Surgeons at army posts collected Arizona's first weather data, beginning at Fort Defiance in 1851. By 1880, stations were added along telegraph lines and railroads.

E. L. Whetmore of Tucson was Arizona's first citizen-volunteer, in 1884, and by '89 there were 71 in the territory. Some stations became family traditions. Walnut Grove, established by J. O. Carter, had the longest continuous record. Cort Carter, a grandson, inherited the post. Another station, Pinal Ranch above Superior, had continuous records dating to 1891, kept by the station founder, D. I. Craig, until his death in 1954. His son, Gerald, carried on.

For the most part, keeping a station has few rewards. There is no pay, and observers would no more leave their stations unwatched than a mother would abandon a child. But the work has had its moments of excitement.

It was a hellish walk to the instruments in Parker on July 7, 1905. The thermometer stood at 127 degrees—hottest ever recorded in Arizona.

Honors for exposing themselves to the coldest weather were divided between observers at Fort Valley near Flagstaff, Jan. 3, 1912, and Maverick, Jan. 4, 1949. Minus 33 degrees.

The late Mr. Craig sloshed out to his instruments in 1905 to measure Arizona's wettest year. A whopping 58.45 inches fell at Pinal Ranch. One day that year, Jan. 9, he found 5.95 inches in his gauge. Only once before and once since has five inches of rain or more fallen in a single day at a state station.

At the other extreme, Wellton in 1928 shriveled with

.44 inches of precipitation for the year. Down the pike, Yuma proved to be the driest spot, year in, year out. Its average rainfall was 3.02 inches. At Sierra Ancha, the yearly average was 29.91.

Perhaps Arizona's best-remembered weather freak was the Great Phoenix Snowfall. Only twice before in the 20th Century had it happened.

"Some doubted it. Others whooped and tore out into the front yard," the press reported.

That night, telephone operators couldn't handle all the calls. Editors, who had been preoccupied with floods in the Midwest and the second inauguration of President Roosevelt, ordered staff writers out of bed and into the streets of Phoenix.

Radio broadcasters dragged their microphones to open windows. Owners of camera shops were begged to begin their business 10 hours early. There was plenty to talk about, and write about, and photograph. When the sullen sun had set, the city was green and brown and gray. The first light of dawn spread across a city of white.

"School kids could scarcely wait to finish breakfast before dashing toward their classes," reported The Arizona Republic of that day. "So enthusiastic did high school or junior college students become . . . that police were summoned to the vicinity of Seventh and Dennis streets shortly after 9 a.m. after one woman reported two windows in her automobile were broken."

Snowballs, sure. And a snowman in front of every other house. A girl rode a sled behind a car to the top of South Mountain. Another young woman skidded on the snow while driving down the mountain road, and almost killed herself and her passengers. Amateur climbers found Alpine conditions on Camelback Mountain.

Across Arizona's desert southland, similar scenes were repeated in Yuma, Ajo, Florence, Tempe, Mesa. In the north motorists were rescued from blizzard-blocked highways.

Those days of Phoenix's snowfall—Jan. 20, 21, 1937—were cold. The temperature range on the 20th was from 31 to 46 degrees, and on the 21st, from 29 to 39.

"There is," said the executive secretary of the Phoenix Chamber of Commerce, "no snow.

"I've been from a point almost to Wickenburg (snowfall then one and one-half inches) to the South Mountains (an inch on the road) and from Mesa (two to four inches) almost to Buckeye (light flurries) and you may quote me as saying definitely, positively, and finally, there is no snow."

CAMP VERDE—Jeannie Dibbens put a gallon pot of coffee to boiling when she saw she had company.

"I hope you don't mind waiting," she said. "This is the mad hour."

She made a lunch for her daughter, Linda, 7, home from school. She attended to the feeding tube for her other daughter, Patti Jo, 5 months, whose throat was partially paralyzed.

All the while, Michael Dibbens, 2, was asserting himself by reading loudly from an upside-down book, dragging a blanket over the kitchen floor, and tipping over glasses, cups, chairs and visitors. Mike had a shock of independent blond hair, an independent lower lip, and an independent left hook that had earned him the respect of the Camp Verde tricycle set.

"Now," said Mrs. Dibbens, when Linda was off for school, Patti was fed, and Mike was quietly crayoning the walls in another room. "We can have that cup of coffee."

The talk centered on how both Mrs. Dibbens and her husband, Norman, were expected to die years before.

"Norman was a marine sergeant; I was a navy nurse," said Mrs. Dibbens. "He was seriously wounded on Iwo Jima (trying to rescue a wounded buddy), and I met him when his hospital ship docked at San Diego.

"When I first saw him he weighed less than a hundred

pounds, but that night I went back to the barracks and told my roommates: 'Today I met the man I'm going to marry.'

"In the months I nursed him, he was expected to die four times." But Norman lived to ask Jeannie for "the only three dates we ever had. Once he proposed. Once we got the marriage license. On our last date, we were married."

Shortly after the birth of Linda, it was Mrs. Dibbens' turn to confound the doctors. Tuberculosis attacked Mrs. Dibbens when she was under the strain of a new baby, and an invalid husband. During her year of hospitalization, she was given the last rites three times.

Their journey to Camp Verde was 38,000 miles long, by trailer, with detours to nearly every section of the United States. They settled on three acres of the old Fort Verde parade ground. From their kitchen window could be seen the barracks and headquarters buildings of the historic fort.

"We bought it sight unseen," said Mrs. Dibbens. "We should have looked." The walls sagged. The plumbing dripped. The roof leaked. It was hardly a place for a convalescing couple. But Dibbens' strength returned as he mended the house and tended a vegetable garden. His part-time job with the highway department became a full-time job, and he studied highway engineering through correspondence courses.

"As for me," said Mrs. Dibbens, "there isn't time to be unhealthy with this gang of mine. Two more boys, and one more girl, will be all I want."

Bob Holstin, airman stationed at Davis-Monthan Air Force Base, learned that one old wives' tale didn't apply to modern brides.

He wanted to buy engagement and wedding rings for Shirley Zorn of 2608 N. 10th St., Phoenix. Bob didn't know her ring size, so he cast about for advice.

"Easy," said a friend. "Find out the size of her feet. That'll be her ring size."

Bob asked, and was told. And before the wedding, they had to have the rings reduced in size.

"I told him 7, and was fudging at that," admitted Shirley.

When the Alfred Thomas Jr. (he is Arizona State University registrar) family moved into their new home, Thomas's two sons anxiously awaited the ripening of the dates of nine palms.

The trees made "too many dates for us, too few to go into business." The boys insisted on packaging and labeling the dates.

Friends of the Thomas family were sent packages of dates labeled, "Itchy Palms Date Grove."

Ordinarily, Phoenix Post Office would be open on Friday, but it was Veterans Day. The doors were posted with notices, "Closed, 8 a.m. to 6 p.m."

"I was surprised," said Phil Stitt, "at how many people were waiting around for the post office to open at 6 in the afternoon."

Bill Fohl of 7140 N. 23rd Ave., Phoenix, telephoned his young son from St. Joseph's Hospital.

"You have a baby brother," proudly announced Bill.

"That's nice," said 6-year-old Eddie, till then an only child. "Is it a boy or a girl?"

William Patrick Macbeth, in his Belfast, Northern Ireland home, closed his eyes and plunged a pin into a map of the United States.

The pinpoint pierced the map in Arizona, near to Phoenix. He stuck to the stab. Seven months later William Patrick Macbeth had become headwaiter at one of Arizona's more famous resorts, Camelback Inn.

The Chevelon School was one room.

The teacher, Jessie Bellotte, was nearly 70—a tall, lean

widow with graying hair, and a habit of wearing a city hat and gloves when she went calling in the lumber camp. Asthma attacks would drain her color, but she always managed to bring out a smile or a cheering word from some secret reservoir of happiness.

She never knew how many pupils she would teach until she called roll each day. At Chevelon, 41 miles south of Winslow into the pine ridges, housewives would shoo deer from their doors to keep them from dragging down clotheslines with their antlers. In a one-industry town so near to nature, sudden storms and unemployment could halve the school population overnight. At times there were eight children. At others, there was but one.

In the spring of 1955, Mrs. Bellotte's health declined to a point where she doubted she could survive another winter. She resigned and moved to a dream house on the warm desert near Tucson.

That summer she wrote a friend of her delight in cooking in her own modern kitchen.

Before classes were to begin the next fall several young teaching couples investigated and turned down the Chevelon job. The first week of September passed and there was no teacher to open the school.

In the second week, Mrs. Bellotte unpacked her suitcases in the two-room teacher's quarters of the Chevelon School.

"I felt I was letting you down," she told the town.

Her health grew worse, and two months after she returned to Chevelon, she died.

Those who have accused Arizona of being a land of bumpkins never hear of the prince of 40th Street and Indian School Road.

When he was a boy, this prince had private tutors, and he could play hooky in 92 castles. As a young man he was landlord of 1 million acres of farming estates. Later he was a financial advisor in the diplomacy of France and Germany after World War I.

Since he came to Arizona he has worn Levi's while working for a living, and he said he wouldn't swap for the old days.

His life was one of deep contrast—from uncounted wealth to the means of a small farmer; from continental society to Texas cattle roundups; from the regal title, Prince Johannes von Liechtenstein to plain John Liechtenstein, American citizen.

"Call me John," said the prince.

John was born in 1899, a member of the ruling family of the tiny principality of Liechtenstein. The country, nestled between Austria and Switzerland, is 65 square miles in area, the largest of four small sovereign states of Europe.

"I am sure that my family at that time was the wealthiest in all Europe," said John. "Wars had not touched the family's holdings for generations."

John was reared in the luxurious and gentle style of royalty. He saw combat both as midshipman and airman in World War I, and prepared himself to manage the family's land in Czechoslovakia by taking a degree in agriculture at Vienna. For a while he was next-estate neighbor to the late Czech national hero, Jan Masaryk, long before Masaryk's country and the Liechtenstein holdings were taken by the Communists.

He came to Texas in 1933, saw a ranch that he liked, bought it, and ran it for 12 years. He raised Herefords and turkeys on 1,200 acres near Fort Worth. He learned to ride, to brand, to put up fence. He came to Arizona to manage the White Hereford Ranch near Springerville, and there he met his wife, Gean, a Des Moines, Iowan.

John's American castle was a ranch-style home tucked back in a citrus grove. There he tended 4,000 chickens, and delivered eggs to grocery stores.

The Liechtenstein family of Europe was still wealthy, and if he wanted, John could have made a claim, but he renounced his royal title in 1948 to become an American citizen.

"I wouldn't trade," he said, "for a kingdom."

YOUNG—So peaceful, this cattle and sawmill town strung out across Pleasant Valley between the Mogollon Rim and the Sierra Anchas.

Yet within the memories of living men an ugly hatred was upon this valley. Herds went untended. Fruit fell rotting to the ground. Neighbor fought neighbor, and no settler was untouched by a blood feud until one side of the Pleasant Valley War was exterminated.

As late as 1955 Misses Ola and Betty Young were living in their house on the main road near the Young post office. Miss Ola proudly showed a rolling pin she carved of juniper in the 1880s. Miss Betty was still boiling water in an iron teakettle the Young family had used while traveling by covered wagon to Arizona from Texas.

From 19 to 29 deaths are listed in the versions of the Pleasant Valley War.

Of one faction were the Grahams and their followers. In the other were the Tewksburys and many supporters. According to the story of widest currency, bad blood between the two alliances boiled over when the Tewksburys drove sheep below the Rim—into cattle country. How the war began was debatable. But before it ended three men swung from rimrock pines, fathers disappeared, strangers were bushwhacked, bodies were left to be rooted by hogs, and the valley was swept clean of Graham men. Tom, the last of the Grahams, turned over his ranch in 1889 to Silas W. Young, father of Ola and Betty.

"Our father was brave to come here and run Graham cattle," said Miss Ola.

She was Pleasant Valley's first schoolmarm, and her pupils were from both sides of the war. The school was a small log house. It didn't have a window or a floor. The second year Miss Ola established Pleasant Valley's first post office.

She kept the job 50 years, and when she retired in 1940 the government gave her a silver medal which she thereafter wore on a chain at her throat.

The Young sisters recalled when Tom Graham revisited Pleasant Valley in 1892.

"He swore he would never come back to live," said Miss Betty. "He had moved to Tempe, and married, and he just came back here to divide his cattle. There was so much bitterness here, I know he wasn't coming back to stay."

Whatever his intentions, Tom Graham never had a chance to carry them out. While hauling his first crop of grain to market near Tempe, he was mortally shot from ambush. The body of the last of the Grahams fell back upon the grain.

The shooting war was done.

Arizona's most popular talking war broke out.

Chapter Two

FLORENCE — TOM MARKS, who supposedly hadn't made an enemy in 84 full years, celebrated his 21st birthday February 29, 1956.

As was his custom, Tom decorated Florence Women's Club, filled it with refreshments and entertainers, and invited a couple hundred friends to help him whoop it up.

Tom was born Leap Year Day, 1872; he had a birthday no oftener than every four years. He made the most of them all, but he was especially pleased, because by his reckoning, he had finally come of age. He had no birthday in 1900, which was not a Leap Year, but he figured 1956 would make him 21.

Tom's popularity in Florence and Pinal County was by no trick of the calendar. He had done nearly everything, and had done them exceedingly well. With small exaggeration one resident said that if Mayor Richard Fulton had not declared "Tom Marks Day" the populace would have stoned city hall.

Thomas Josiah Marks was born in Peekskill on the Hudson, N.Y., and "as soon as mother and I were able to travel," moved west to Virginia City, Nev. He was brought up there when that silver town was a hell-for-leather boomer, and was graduated from a tiny high school that still stands there.

Tom's character got its first test soon afterwards. He was set on being a general, and his good school grades won him a West Point appointment. Before he could leave Nevada his military career was ended when a snow plow broke his legs.

"There were still three choices," Tom recalled. "Cowboy, miner, or railroader." He chose the railroad, and by 1889 was supporting his widowed mother and brothers with a Southern Pacific job in Tucson. Tom was telegrapher, agent or dispatcher at a dozen Arizona stops. He wooed and won his sweetheart by wire. He was station agent at Casa Grande when he met Fannie Mauk. Miss Mauk's brother, George, was agent at Arizola, a few miles down the track. Mauk taught his sister how to read code, and Tom sent her telegraphic love letters. Because it was the best transportation available, Tom powered his way to their wedding on a railroad handcar. Aug. 9, 1956, Tom and Fannie celebrated their 60th anniversary.

Even when Tom was a railroader, he had a yen for police work. He rode some for the Arizona Rangers, wore a deputy's badge in Tucson, and volunteered as special officer in several towns where he worked. After seven years as assistant superintendent of roads in Phoenix, Tom decided to change careers.

He took a job as chief deputy in Prescott and it lasted 15 years.

"Every time somebody got hurt, it was me," he said. He was wounded in five gun fights. Once he took a posse into the hills north of Prescott to break up a bootlegging ring that was armed with sawed-off shotguns. One blast ripped through Tom's arm. He had to hold an artery with his good hand and ride horseback to help. When the gang leader learned it was Tom Marks who was hurt, he went to Tom's home and surrendered.

Once Tom was tracking an escaped prisoner into an Indian reservation. Because he was armed, Tom was stopped by an Indian. Tom explained he was hunting a prisoner. "No hunting on reservation," coldly ordered the Indian.

Twenty-five years before his 21st birthday, Tom changed careers again when he was elected clerk of Pinal County superior court. Since then, no candidate has had a chance against him. They stopped trying.

He earned his popularity on a dozen counts, including his habit of riding a red bicycle to work. His never-offensive practical jokes on marriage license applicants became a town legend. For years Marks kept a book titled, "What Every Young Couple Should Know." Tom would turn his back, and of course the applicants would sneak peeks at the book, and of course, there was a thing inside that exploded with a bang that could be heard throughout the courthouse. Tom didn't remember how many thousands of licenses he issued, day and night, but again, the stories with a laugh stick best in his mind.

He always had to take pains with Indian couples. Confused by white man's law, some of them thought the license was all that was required. One brave returned with a 2-year-old, unused license and asked Tom to erase his woman's name and write in another.

Tom ran another institution, until he had an eye operation. He had a fixit shop set up in the clerk's office, and he mended free of charge whatever clocks and spectacles and gadgets were brought to him. When he was 75 he built a house for his daughter at the rear of his home.

To celebrate his majority, Tom chose a Gay Nineties theme for his party. He renamed the women's clubhouse The Golden Nugget. Guests wore period costumes.

Those who came to the party were great and small, the white and the brown, judges and janitors, rich and poor. Besides his daughter, Mrs. Alan Johnson, Tom had his son, Thomas G. Marks of Big Bear Lake, Calif., some seven grandchildren, and an uncountable number of great-grandchildren.

Governor McFarland, once a judge during Tom's tenure as clerk, came to the party because he was afraid the statehouse would be stoned if he didn't.

One newspaper or a thousand, it was all the same to Ralph Richardson.

At the beginning of one of the longest newspaper routes in the United States, Richardson dropped off two still-damp copies of The Arizona Republic at New River. Nine hours later he flung a single copy to his last subscriber near Congress Junction.

In that much time he helped speed more than 7,000 copies of The Republic to Northern Arizona readers. His 391-mile loop was part of an interlocking truck, bus, train and mail system that made possible a boast—98 per cent of Arizona readers get their Republics in less than seven hours after they leave the presses.

Richardson's run began at the Republic and Gazette building in Phoenix, where his red stake-body truck was loaded with packages varying from single copies to bundles of 50. In this edition of The Republic were stories that came off the news wires and local typewriters less than one hour before.

By 1:30 a.m. Richardson was rolling northward on Black Canyon Highway. Four papers at Rock Springs, a single to a roadside restaurant, 15 through Black Canyon, and by 3 a.m. Richardson was parked at Cordes Junction, tossing bundles to young Gheral Brownslow.

"Everything from janitor to district manager," was Brownlow's self-description. Each morning he drove to meet the

Phoenix truck. He picked up 1,850 copies for Prescott and Bagdad, and other bundles for dealers along his way.

A cold wind was cutting through Camp Verde when Richardson pushed out fat bundles to two dealers. There he shared a thermos of coffee, and thought of the rolling curves ahead.

At 4:15 a.m. the headlights of Richardson's truck flashed on a Jeep parked at Cornville Junction. "Where you been all day?" jibed Orville Davenport, Clarkdale district manager. "Lookin' for you," answered Richardson. Davenport took 480 papers for Verde Valley subscribers.

A half hour later Richardson slowed his big red truck, rolled down a window, and tossed out a single copy to Grasshopper Flats, south of Sedona. Richardson's tour of Oak Creek Canyon was something out of a circus. One minute he was kicking out a bundle of 75 to a dealer; the next he was throwing singles with the accuracy of a baseball pitcher. A man does not have enough arms to grip a flashlight, lower a window, shift gears, drive through a tight curve, and toss rolled newspapers to both sides of the road—but Richardson did it.

Of major importance to Richardson was getting to Flagstaff and U.S. Highway 66 for train and bus connections. Fred McFall was waiting for the 1,400 Flagstaff papers, and Richard Wishman took 900 more for his Winslow and Holbrook districts. Dozens of bundles were dropped off at the bus station for points east and west on U.S. 66.

The sky was brightening when Richardson left a 45-paper bundle on the roadside for Bellmont, and kicked Big Red down the slope to Williams. Newspaperboys noisily took off 710 papers, and another 200 went to a news shop. Still others were put on a bus (along with 20 tourists) for Grand Canyon.

At Ashfork, where Richardson delivered papers to dealers and the Santa Fe depot, his job was nearly done. Remaining were flurries of small bundles and singles to be cast at

Chino Valley, north of Prescott, and Peeples Valley, to the south.

By the time he deadheaded Big Red into Phoenix, Republic staff workers had been at work for three hours—putting together the skeleton of the next day's editions.

"That's the one trouble with the job," said Ralph Richardson. "You never get a chance to read the paper."

Nothing much was proved at Phoenix's Madison Square Garden, unless it is important that second-stringers in-the-flesh are a better show than the electronic dolls offered on television.

The question was obvious, during an exciting main bout—what's wrong with boxing in Phoenix?

There were Jimmy Martinez, the former Guadalupe tavern keeper of Glendale, and Dick Goldstein, as colorful as a clown at Christmas, meeting for the middleweight championship of Arizona (for that week).

The fight had more action than three out of five television bouts. Goldstein was busier than a one-armed fan dancer with an ankle itch, but much bonier. Despite his bookkeeper's build, he fought like a famished cobra, and it was surprising entertainment just to see such an underweight hold out his arms for 12 rounds.

Martinez was worthy. He was doing the best he knew how, and sometimes that had been pretty good. They said he once whipped the former champion, Bobo Olson, in a non-title contest, even if he didn't get the decision.

With his right, Martinez massaged Goldstein's slim rib cage. With his left, he reddened Goldstein's nose. Goldstein got in the biggest punches, and but for the hasty intervention of Referee Jimmy Flynn, might have had Martinez on the deck in the ninth.

All in all, it was a good, fast defensive fight—according to some fans, the best kind. The decision, a draw, gave everybody something to argue about.

When Goldstein sat down in his corner after the first round he looked first over one shoulder, then the other. He was counting the house, probably, and he needed only two glances. There were enough empty places to accommodate a company of marines in grenade drill.

If Goldstein had taken a third look, he might have perceived the scarcity of women. Women, fairly or not, are calling the shots for family entertainment. The decline of arena boxing seems to be correlated with the disappearance of pool halls and stand-up saloons.

Madison Square Garden's terraces of smoke, balm to men, would be miasma to women. Its dirty floors, unnoticed by men, would soil women's shoes. Being seen in such an old barn would be social suicide.

How to interest the ladies, short of tatting lace to the water buckets and setting rhinestones in the mouthpieces, is quite a problem. Ten-to-one, though, if she doesn't go, he can't go, and if he doesn't go, boxing has had it.

Andy Chuka said our offices are coming to look like boudoirs.

"You see fewer and fewer words to live by in the offices. I guess there is a fear of hurting somebody's feelings. Those things make you stop and think (or nowadays THIMK), and we live in a world where a little stopping and thinking wouldn't hurt a bit."

Andy was Phoenix's foremost sloganeer. A most-time printer and full-time philosopher, he collected slogans, quotations, and bon mots which he printed up and passed out to his friends. A pair of his favorites:

"We Have 35 Million Laws Trying To Enforce 10 Commandments."

"Happiness Is A Perfume You Cannot Sprinkle On Others Without Getting A Few Drops On Yourself."

Arizona State College (now University) had just whipped University of Arizona at basketball.

Police converged on the new student union building where somebody was whanging the college victory bell so vigorously the campus was awakened in an instant.

The police spotted the culprit, then fell back. The bell-ringer was President Grady Gammage.

Clark Shelby, when he became acquainted with his wife-to-be, Wanda, said that he was not ready to settle down.

He had seen the South Pacific as a hand in the navy, and after he finished up at Arizona State University, he wanted to see the other side of the world.

Needless to say, they were soon married.

Clark was graduated in 1952 and began teaching that fall in the Alhambra school district. A year later, with the encouragement of Wanda, he took night work in a service station. Every dollar he earned at the extra job was saved.

By 1954 summer vacation, Clark Shelby had $710, a collection of maps, his passport, a sleeping bag, a knapsack, and the wanderlust. He kissed Wanda and their infant son, Mike, goodby, and set out for the East Coast as passenger in an Alhambra coach's car.

"I had to go fourth class," he said. "There is no fourth class, and I had to invent one." He rolled up in his sleeping bag one night in Washington, D.C., under a hedge by the Department of Labor building. Slept fine. In New York, he tried to save the cost of a cot in a Bowery flophouse, and asked to spend the night in a police station.

Union rules dashed his plans to work his way to Europe, but he found an Italian ship that would carry him for $145. He landed at Bremerhaven, Germany, and bought a motorbike. When that broke down, he took the cheapest train travel available. Across Europe he meandered, through 14 countries, and most of their capitals, setting up camp in Cologne ruins, Italian forests, a London park. He made do without breakfast, and put off lunch until the middle of the afternoon. That meal had to last all day. He lost 15 pounds.

Forty-six days and 18,000 miles behind him, his mad money diminished to 19 cents, Clark was back in Phoenix, embracing Wanda.

"I had to go a long way to learn," he said, and he swore he would be a homebody the rest of his life.

Stabbing a red chili pepper into the air for emphasis, Joe Jordan refused to be drawn into the Spanish-Mexican Food debate.

"One of our signs reads MEXICAN FOOD and another reads SPANISH FOOD," he said. "Order what you want. You get the same thing."

But by any name, Joe said, the stuff has enjoyed a surge in popularity since World War II. Ten years before he had opened the second Mexican food restaurant north of Van Buren. Now there were 40 or 50 such dining rooms in Greater Phoenix.

"Know something?" he asked, and answered: "The things we serve here are not often eaten in the homes of Spanish-Americans. They are feast foods, for holidays and special events.

"I'm Mexican, and when I was a kid, it was boiled beans for breakfast, fried beans for lunch, and re-fried beans for supper."

Give Joe 200 dozen corn *tortillas,* a sack of flour, 175 pounds of cheese, four crates of lettuce, and a sack of onions, and he has the ingredients for an almost endless variety for one day's serving. He said, "Throw in 60 gallons of sauce."

After cracking open the red pepper, he scraped the inside of the thin, nearly dry skin and extracted a bit of pulp.

"That is the only part of the pepper that should be used," he said. "The stem is bitter. The seeds are bitter. The skin is bitter. Because the housewife uses chili powder—the whole chili ground—her food often fails."

It is no accomplishment to make the hottest chili in town, said Joe. The goal of every Mexican food restaurant is a sauce that will please those customers who want their sauce as hot as sulfuric acid, and those who want it as mild as milk.

Joe could charm the cockatoos with his stories about the health values of his preparations: full of vitamins and protiens. Extra hot chili will sober a drunk, perk up an appetite, improve the complexion. Some customers are sold on Mexican food as a hangover cure. Joe said he belived that chili is especially good for making men men.

DENDORA FLATS — Hospitality was a major crop, along with cattle and cotton, but Bud Bates wished people would quit stealing his mountain.

They would drive out Sundays. They would pry at his mountain with crowbars. They would break it with hammers. They would even blast it with dynamite. Then they would haul it away in their sedans and station wagons.

Dendora Ranch, 27 miles west of Gila Bend on the Gila River, had been under Bates' development for eight years.

The mountain that was becoming a molehill was about the size of a supermarket. It was covered with Malapai boulders, flesh-colored on the inside and weathered almost black on the outside.

On every rock were chiseled from 1 to 50 Indian petroglyphs. There were figures of men and horses, wild animals, and what appeared to be maps.

Bates said to the best of his knowledge, his mountain was being hauled away to provide city slickers with door stops and conversation starters.

Bill Hebner was sipping a bottle of pop at a roadside service station, and because he was handy, four airmen poured out their troubles.

"It's payday," one groaned. "But we've got the blues. We've got money, but we need some dates. Man, you can't get dates without wheels."

"Boys," said Bill, "There's my car out front. It's insured and full of gas. Bring it back the way you take it. Spread the word."

The word spread. Fast. Over the next few months more than 50 airmen from Williams Air Force Base used Hebner's car on nights and weekends. The rules were simple: First come, first served. The airmen had to have a driving license, and they had to promise Hebner they wouldn't drink and drive. They were expected to return the car with the same amount of fuel they began with.

Not only did the airmen strictly obey the rules, they never so much as scratched the car.

Ed McIntyre, who belonged to no church, stepped out into his back yard and looked for the nearest steeple.

"That one will do," he said, pointing.

Within a few days, the Glendale Pentacostal Holiness Church received a new Baldwin organ, compliments of Mr. and Mrs. Ed McIntyre.

It was one of many impulsive acts of philanthropy of the McIntyres, who retired from a Montana homestead and moved to Glendale.

"Mother and I just felt like giving an organ to a church", said he.

In the interest of scientific research, Miss Louise Bast sent seven of her fifth graders to Kenilworth auditorium.

The question was, "How boy-like are our boys." The clinical inquiry was akin to an old-fashioned police shakedown. The seven were asked to give their names and empty their pockets.

"Douglas Carr," said the first boy. He said he was 10, the son of Mr. and Mrs. Douglas A. Carr, 845 N. Fourth Ave., "but I'm no junior."

He produced two pieces of paper. One was a PTA notice. The other, as he expressed it, contained "rules we are not supposed to do." On any other day, he apologized, he would carry a supply of baseball cards and a pocket knife.

The next boy stepped forward and said, "Elias, no, make it E. J. Williams." The son of Mr. and Mrs. E. J. Williams Sr. brought forth a single nose tissue. His 11th birthday had just passed, and it reminded him: "Saturdays I usually carry my knife."

Mike Kempson, 10, son of Mr. and Mrs. James Kempson of 729 W. Lynwood, carried a plastic coin purse (empty), a rubber band, and a chunk of unchewed bubble gum. He, too, complained that he was caught short on an off day. Generally, he said proudly, he packs a wallet.

Carrot-top Mic Williams, 11, then announced his parents as Mr. and Mrs. John R. Williams, 545 W. Lewis.

"His father's the mayor," said one of the boys.

"That doesn't make me anything special," said Mic, throwing down two pieces of paper. One was a copy of a magazine ad: "Life Saver Cutter Snake Bite Kit, $2." The other was a folded, home-made puzzle. "$64 Question," it read on the outside. Partly opened, it asked, "Are you a nut?" Fully unfolded, it answered, "YES."

Paul Markow, 10, son of Mr. and Mrs. Bob Markow of 1832 N. Seventh Ave., obviously was unhappy. He swelled up his chest inside a T shirt on which was printed "BROOKLYN DODGERS" and let fall on the table a nickel.

"I wish I had some warning," he said.

Financially, Joe Gardner, 10, son of Mr. and Mrs. L. O. Gardner of 1632 N. 11th Ave., was twice as rich as any of his chums. He had a dime.

He also had a piece of bubble gum and, for some reason he could not give, two wrappers from gum he had long since chewed.

All the while, Terry Grady, 11, was beside himself. He hurried through his little speech about being the son of Mr. and Mrs. E. L. Grady of 129 W. Palm Lane, and then stated slowly:

"A jack. Found it on the playground. Be sure to say that because I don't want people saying I play jacks.

"Three pencils. Two wooden. One mechanical.

"A big paper clip. Plans for a beehive I'm making. A puzzle from a Shredded Wheat box. A little pipe on a chain. Animal stamps you get from the wildlife service. Traded them from a guy.

"Ice cream wrapper. I don't know why I have that. Not good for anything. Knife. Handkerchief. Two bike keys. Let's see, 10 marbles. And five cents."

The firehouse party in honor of Phoenix Fire Marshal Ladis B. (Deak) Graves, 40 years to the day after he joined the department, broke up unexpectedly.

A bell clanged, and everybody had to go fight a fire.

ON THE SITGREAVES BURN—The names alone could have been enough to draw tourists to the tall country between Willow and Chevelon creeks.

There was Water Draw Spring, Duran Tree, Breed Springs, Barts Crossing, Five Mile Lake, and Long Draw. It seemed proper that on the afternoon of June 13, 1956 an Irishman named O. B. (Mick) McGuire was on duty in a fire tower named Dutch Joe.

Four miles south was Dudley Lake, a *cienega* bordering the graded forest road between Winslow and Promontory Point on the Mogollon Rim.

At 2:45 p.m. McGuire completed scanning of the timber to the north of Dutch Joe. He rubbed his eyes, and then turned his glasses to the south. He said he will never forget what he saw.

"All day the logging trucks had been traveling the road," he said. "As dry as it was, they kicked up big clouds. The dust would come up, then fall back, then come up again.

"This thing didn't fall back, and when I realized it wasn't dust, it like to scared me to death."

He told Hank, his wife, "Hank, one minute all was quiet, and the next minute the whole damn forest was blowing up in my face."

Mrs. McGuire that afternoon was operating the forest service communications center at Chevelon Ranger Station, some four miles northeast of Dutch Joe. She spread the alarm. Some idea of the activity which followed could be gathered from the Chevelon log books. The station logged its business from March 1 to June 13 in less than one, inch-thick book. In the week of the fire, the station used four books as Ranger Don Jirsa led the fight.

Some 20,000 acres of ponderosa pine fed a $3 millon bonfire. Another $250,000 was spent in fighting it. Watershed damage was beyond estimate.

From his 100-foot-high seat in Dutch Joe, Mick McGuire watched the flames blacken a stretch 12 miles long, from the high country aspen to the foothill cedars.

Fred Payne overheard a story in a downtown Phoenix restaurant.

Seems a woman who lived near 13th Street and Palm Lane owned a boxer dog. She agreed to care for a pekingese, while the owners were on vacation.

The boxer didn't cotton to the peke, and the woman had to put the boxer on the patio in order to keep peace at feeding time. The boxer briefly gnawed over this development, and disappeared.

They found him three days later in a tavern at 13th Street and McDowell.

"He wandered in a few days ago," said the barkeeper, "and has been sitting quietly ever since."

You can tell it's hot in the Valley of the Sun when people appear to be smiling.

As they drive or walk the shimmering pavements, the corners of their eyes are crinkled, the skin is pouched over the cheekbones, and the mouths are poised as if to eat jelly bread. The expression is not a smile. It is a baked-on flinch.

Deceptively smiling, I opened the front door.

"In here, dear," she shouted from a back room. I went

there and said, "Hot one today," and noticed that she is prettier when she slightly frowns.

"It is all in your mind," she replied. "Look at me. I'm not complaining. Think of cool things."

"You mean like air conditioning, and ice cream? And watermelon? And tinkling drinks?"

She said, "That's the idea, but let your imagination go."

I tried. "Like say I'm captain of a ship icebound in the Arctic Sea. My jaw is jutting into the piercing north wind, my hands are frozen to the stanchion, my feet are two stones on the ice-clad desk, and my breath is a churning cloud as I say to the first mate, 'Mister, be good enough to have the steward fetch me a col' bo'l' beer.' "

She begged me to continue.

"Or say I'm driving sled out of Fairbanks. I have lost my sealskin parka wrestling with a polar bear. Bare-chested, I must deliver my load of ice cream to Nome, where a blizzard has buried the creamery."

Go on, she insisted.

"It is warm work thinking up these fool things," I argued.

"Stay with it," she ordered.

"Very well. I am hired as a well digger for an expedition to Little America. Before this I was employed during winter months as a polisher of brass monkeys in a Siberian, open-air pawn shop."

Change the subject, she suggested.

"I am a movie actor. In my latest cool jazz picture my leading lady is Subzero Mercury, who portrays a frigid woman. The big scene is when she gives me a frosty stare. A chill runs down my spine. My blood turns to icewater. I break out in a cold sweat. I get cold feet."

Much better.

"How about this? I am an archaeologist, chiseling away the permafrost which covers the site of Eric the Red's colony in Greenland. My pick strikes a stone. My eager, blue hands brush away the frozen earth, revealing runes, which translate: 'Norsemen True Use Olof's Frostbite Salve. Only Two Walrus Tusks. Leading Druggists.' "

She wondered if I didn't feel cooler, and I said that I didn't.

She splashed cold water on her shoulders. She pouted, "It's all in your mind."

"How long have you been sitting in that tub?" I asked.

"I lost track of time. I've been thinking about cool things. But you are hopeless. Now hand me my towel and get out of here."

"Tell them," said the woman, "they can't take my duck."

The Honorable Jack Williams, mayor of the City of Phoenix, spent a quarter-hour explaining that a city ordinance prohibits the keeping of ducks — even pet ducks — near domiciles.

It had been only six months since Williams took office, but already he had collected a lifetime of anecdotes.

"All the time," said the mayor, "we're asked to provide letters of greeting for use by various organizations holding meetings in town. You know, for speeches, magazines, for programs. Sometimes it's difficult to prepare the proper greeting.

"At the request of one group, I wrote a greeting—the finest restaurants in the world here, resorts, dancing, a winter playground, a city offering every sort of entertainment.

"Just in time I learned it was a religious organization meeting in Phoenix for a retreat of sober meditation."

Persons in other countries had sent job applications; hotels had invited him to spend vacations overseas at his expense. He had met visiting dignitaries, shaken hands with the latest beauty queens, and listened to hard luck stories.

One woman demanded that he exterminate two white rats abandoned by boys in a crack of her house. He side-stepped a gift of a roast of beef, by agreeing to donate it to the Salvation Army. He flatly declined a promotional stunt that would have had him giving a bride away in a local wedding chapel.

Williams said that he was trying his best to be helpful, no matter how unreasonable the requests might seem. Reminded that a man sometimes is judged by the enemies he makes, Williams responded, "There are no small enemies."

A Phoenix radio figure since 1929, "and always something of a preacher," Williams said he believed he came to the mayoralty equipped with some tact in dealing with public problems. But the trees, he said, sometimes hid the forest.

"The basic problem with this job," he said, "is you never have enough time to think. Of course, that happens to most of us, but it isn't as dramatically evident as over here.

"We're supposed to deal in policies, which are produced, in theory at least, by weighing, analyzing, and studying problems. You no sooner get started on weighing, analyzing, and studying, than some good citizen phones up with a pet duck that is threatened by the humane department, or white rats which aren't and you must drop everything for long, involved telephone talks that take hours of precious time."

Demands of the office have little regard for the clock, he said. For the first time in months, Williams spent three evenings in a row at home.

"On the third night," said Williams, "a neighbor came over and asked if I was ill."

Success doesn't seem to diminish the pride of a man for the way he first worked for pay.

"How did you earn your first dollar?" was put to some well-known Arizonans.

Governor McFarland chopped cotton in Oklahoma.

John Long, Phoenix homebuilder, in 1929 earned his first buck selling newspapers in front of the Old First National Bank building. He was 9 years old. He saved $100, bought a cow, and after the crash of that year, sold her for $35.

Wilson B. Wood, director of internal revenue for Arizona, sold pomegranates, 10 cents a dozen, to students of Phoenix

Indian School. Wood, then 8, got the fruit from his father's grove, west of the school.

Dr. Richard A. Harvill, president of University of Arizona, after gaining experience on his father's farm, went to work for his uncle who lived nearby. That was near Jackson, Miss., when he was 12, and the wage was $1 a day.

Jim Patrick, executive vice president of the Valley National Bank, went partners with his sister. When he was 6, they answered a magazine ad, and became agents in Hope, Ind., for a needle and thimble manufacturer. Patrick demonstrated needles; his sister, thimbles. Patrick took work later as a bellows operator in a carriage shop, and thereafter could not stand the sight of an accordion.

Justice Arthur LaPrade of the Arizona Supreme court earned his first dollar in a Flagstaff box factory. He cut the indented finger grips for box ends, at 30 cents an hour. Before that, he helped his father, F. T. LaPrade, Winslow blacksmith.

Royal Lescher, senior partner in the Lescher and Mahoney architectural firm, washed lemons in a California packing shed. The rate was 75 cents for a 10-hour day.

A. J. Bayless in 1917 could be found sacking potatoes in his parents' store at Second and Washington streets. Said the man who came to head his own large grocery chain:

"My first regular job was in another grocery, on the southeast corner of First and Washington Streets. I was 12, and got $15 a week, taking care of the produce department. I hate to say it, but after two years, my employers reduced my salary to $14 per week. But that is the truth, and that is why I quit."

Ray W. Wilson, Phoenix city manager, said his first dollar was slow in growing. When he was 9 he contracted to take the family cow to pasture every day from his home in Mercer County, Mo. The pay was 30 cents a month.

Pete Holmes, senior member of Holmes and Son Construction Co., delivered newspapers in what became downtown Phoenix. His route of 300 papers was bounded by Van Buren, McDowell, Central and Sixth Avenue.

William C. (Dub) Money, Phoenix new car dealer, when 11, picked cotton in Greenville, Texas.

Chapter Three

The conversation turned to whether Arizona has a language of its own.

"I ain't no cow bunny, but I been out of Texas long enough to use my right name," said Vivien Keatley of 312½ W. Lynwood, Phoenix.

"And I been around here long enough to listen to cow-men spoutin' words eight to the pound. I'm a desert rat on account of out here we got room enough to toss a rope without gettin' it caught on a fence post — a fine condition we appear to be aimin' to correct.

"I've rode somethin' wilder'n a wheelchair, even if I ain't no bangtail buster. And I've seen many an Arizona Nightingale or desert canary (pronounced boor-oh).

"I've bellied up to a bar aimin' to get my share of conversation fluid or coffin varnish — sometimes to gather a talkin' load, sometimes endin' up booze blind. I've done my share of complainin' about cut straw and molasses (sorry food), or canned cow in belly wash (weak coffee). I carry the makin's and smoke like a house afar.

"The faro bank dealer in Las Vegas sure buffaloed my husband. Sent him runnin' with a busted cinch. I still figure the dealer was in cahoots with the man with a forked tail, but my husband was chuckleheaded as a prairie dog to take up with that saddle-blanket gambler.

"As for my looks, I'm a lot bigger'n a bar of soap. I'm built high above the corns; I can't tell when my feet are cold; and if I fell down I'd be halfway home. But I ain't buzzard bait yet — that is I'm not ready to sack my saddle.

"I've slept in a Tucson bed, usin' my back for a mattress, and my belly for a cover, and when the year's first 100-degree weather arrives, I admit the ice has broken in the Santa Cruz.

"Now I don't want you to think I can't drive nails in a snow bank, or teach a settin' hen to cluck. But I can see through a bobwar fence with no cheaters. I never owned even a chickenshed outfit, but I can still curl the tail of a kidney-pad rider, or comb his hair if I have to.

"Maybe I ain't got no more business saying these things than a cow on the front porch, but I felt the urge. Maybe because my husband dropped his rope on me 21 years ago today."

Marion W. Trowbridge, who began his own criminology laboratory after he retired as police chief of Mesa, told a story about the time his police force nearly put itself out of commission.

Acting on a tip from an ex-convict, Trowbridge quietly rounded up a squad of his best officers to stake out an automobile agency that was to be robbed by burglars.

Trowbridge placed his men. Some were stationed in a funeral parlor, others in an irrigation ditch. They were armed with riot and tommy guns. Night passed. No burglars.

At dawn an officer limped from his hiding place in the ditch.

"Some fool turned on the water," said the policeman. "Stomping around trying to keep the tommy gun dry, I stepped on a nail."

Another officer fessed up. He said that the night before he had tossed his service pistol on his bed while he changed clothes, and his 5-year-old daughter triggered a round through a brand-new mattress and carpet.

The chief returned to the station to learn that another of his men had broken his arm in a scuffle with a one-armed criminal.

Sitting in a chair at the station was another policeman. He had put on his handcuffs hours before, and he couldn't get them off.

"Boys," said Trowbridge. "I wasn't going to say anything. But last night, after dismissing you with a 30-minute talk on safety, I loaded my riot gun, unthinkingly pulled the trigger, and pushed a load of buckshot through the ceiling at home."

GOD'S COUNTRY — On rainsoaked Highway 60 the cars sped past Carrizo trading post, sounding like a series of Alka-Seltzer commercials.

The sonorous rush of civilization faded in the hundred yard walk to Charlie Foster's wagon-tent camp, tucked behind brush in a red clay pasture. Water drops slipped off leaves and ticked onto the gluey earth. A bird voiced a thin squeak just below the limit of human perception.

From the camp thicket floated the low, sing-song laugh of an ancient Apache, happy with his world, his family and himself. But as I approached, two Indian girls bounded off their wagon tongue seat and ducked into the tent. The laughing stopped.

"Are you Charlie Foster?"

He was a little over 5 feet tall, slightly stooped, much

bow-legged. His crinkled brown face nodded, only enough for polite communication, not enough for conviction.

"I'm from a newspaper in Phoenix. I'd like to write a story about you."

Charlie Foster's face waxed quizzical, but he waved a silencing hand at the children who were vollying Apache translations.

"Martin Pintz, the sheriff's deputy in Phoenix, sent me."

"Martin Pintz!" Charlie Foster smiled, and his face became deeply lined. "Is he dead?"

"Oh, no. Martin is healthy. He said that for many years you were a reservation policeman, and that you could relate many interesting experiences."

"Um," he said. "Martin good man. Tell him we camp here two three days. We went to the dance at Cibecue. On the way home the rain washed out four five bridges. My son has gone ahead to see if the road is fixed."

"Martin said you were the best Indian policeman he ever knew."

"Rain about gone now. Maybe we get home soon."

A squat, round woman behind Charlie grinned; the baby boy she balanced Apache-fashion on her back frowned.

"Martin said that you used to play football at Carlisle Indian School. That you played against some of the Ivy League schools."

"How is Martin?" asked Charlie Foster. "I haven't seen him in long time. Not since he worked with us on the reservation."

"Martin is fine. Maybe he has put on weight, but he is in good health. He looks as if he has been eating well."

"That's good," responded the old Apache. "These are my grandchildren. They are the children of my son, who has gone to see if the bridges are fixed. This is my wife."

The squaw beamed and hitched her little-boy burden.

"Martin said that despite your small size, you played on the first team at Carlisle. What position did you play?"

Charlie Foster looked thoughtfully at the tent, and said:

"Usually we camp by creek. But it is too wet there now. Tell Martin that we will be home soon."

"Martin told me that your coach was Pop Warner — one of the most famous coaches of all time. Do you remember him?"

"Pop Warner," mused Charlie Foster. "Is he dead?"

"Yes, I'm afraid he is."

"That's too bad," said Charlie Foster.

GOD'S COUNTRY—Roy Sauve's outdoor stories, which he serves American-planwise to guests at his Pinecrest Lodge near Pinetop, multiply and improve with age.

For a long time Roy enjoyed the near-perfect life. He taught school in Scottsdale in the winter, and graded timber for Southwest Lumber Mills in cool McNary during the summer.

Now his life was perfect. He had his lodge, and he was working full time as foreman for Southwest. Abiding in the White Mountains had given him time to polish his stories, the best of which went:

"We were miles from camp, and the camp was miles from nowhere.

"We had been boondocking for hours, and brother, we were thirsty enough to suck the sap out of the trees. You know, a man can't work up a stronger thirst than when he's deer-hunting in high country.

"I don't know how he could do it with such a dry mouth, but suddenly I heard my buddy scream:

" 'Roy!'

"Well, from the sound of it, I thought he had stepped on a snake, or at least had fallen down and broke his leg. I ran over to where he was leaning against a tree. He shouted, in that same tone:

" 'Roy, look!'

"I looked down to where he was pointing. At the base of the tree was an unopened, cold can of Schlitz."

"Guy in here from Oak Creek Canyon," said a Payson gas station operator. "Said it was so crowded up there he couldn't find a clear place to cast a hook.

"Pretty soon another customer came in. Burned up. He said he tried to find a fishing spot near Payson, and couldn't swing a line without hooking a human. He said he was going to Oak Creek.

"Who'm I to stop them? Hell, I'm selling gas."

BENSON—Rodeo was never quite the same after Arizona's one-legged cowboy called it quits.

Pete Haverty would rope a steer, slide from his saddle, and hop down his lariat to make the tie. Enough times to turn back pity he took top money from his two-legged competitors.

"I thought I was going to go on roping until I was 75," said Pete, then 63. "The heart attack wasn't much. Heck, you get over those in a hurry. It was the stroke that laid me up. The doctors told me to slow down, but it was the Old Man Up Above who made it stick."

Even sitting on the porch of his ranch home on the outskirts of Benson, Pete gave that impression of hairline balance and compact power that hobbled a handicap. They were as characteristic of him as his sky-blue eyes and cumulus-cloud brows.

About that lost leg? Pete said he had heard so many versions, he didn't know which one to believe. He said, "Some of those stories are so good, it seems a shame to say I lost it jumping on a bed."

The accident happened in Texas, when Pete was 4. A doctor diagnosed Pete's broken foot as snake bite, and fed him strychnine. Four months later the whole left leg had to be amputated. A long convalescence left Pete stunted in growth, but he was an active boy. He demolished, on the average, a crutch a week.

While his parents were homesteading in the Huachucas, Pete helped round up wild horses. Once he and his father drove 200 head to the Midwest. Pete, then 8, didn't sleep in a bed for four months.

By the time Pete finally got his growth at 20, he was a familiar figure in Arizona rodeos.

Pete tried all the events, at one time or another, including the now-outlawed single steer tying. He was so popular, rodeo promoters sometimes offered to handicap his times and shave his entry fees. Pete refused them all, insisting that when the day came when he couldn't compete as an equal, he'd quit.

"I think I won enough to get back my entry money," Pete said. "The fun I had was my profit."

Rodeoing was always a sideline for Pete. He was a rancher, a range deputy for Cochise County, a state livestock inspector, and a peerless trainer of horses. Once a man complained about a freshly broken horse that Pete had sold him.

"I walk up to that horse and he acts like he's never seen a man before," the new owner said.

Pete thought it out, and suggested that the man hop around the horse on one leg.

"He thinks you're built wrong to be human," Pete mused.

Pete suffered his heart attack while riding atop the Rincons in 1953, and since had cut his work to overseeing some leased pastures and selling insurance policies. Pete was proud of his son, Del, world's champion roper in 1951, and consistently among the leaders.

(Pete Haverty died in 1959.)

ROGERS LAKE—The sun blazed low and yellow as Ranger Harvey Palmer stopped his pickup on a point with a commanding view of the dry lake 10 miles west and a little south of Flagstaff.

In winters and wetter summers Rogers Lake was correctly named, but now from the cover of the forest we scanned a thousand-acre basin of bronze browse. Baldface cattle and saddle horses were strung out from the road to the east, to where the lake pinched out below the setting sun.

Everywhere, there were deer. Close by, twin fawns frisked around a doe. Beyond, a bluish, barren doe froze cross-legged to stare at the truck. Far to the south a darker color and wisps of antlers identified a cluster of dots as bucks.

"If I was painting a picture," said Harvey with emotion. "I wouldn't change a single thing, except maybe make the grass green."

The ranger was one of a score of men who were assembled that day near Rogers Lake to help in Arizona's semi-annual elk survey. For 13 days the survey had moved along the Mogollon Rim from the New Mexico line to Flagstaff. Trends of elk population were noticed primarily, but other game was counted, too.

"Start at the sun," said Harvey, raising his glasses. We slowly panned through 20 degrees of the compass, and Harvey asked: "How many to that first bunch of cows?"

"Ninety-two deer."

"I count 94. We'll call it 93."

Almost in the center of the feeding herds, we agreed, were 38 antelope, and by the time we swept the remainder of the lake, we had counted and classified 207 deer to sex and age.

That night we did not see any elk.

Death can be a small, strange noise in the middle of a sunny, windless day.

Patricio A. Valenzuela was born in 1921 in the Yaqui Indian village of Guadalupe, south of Tempe, and became a man at the beginning of World War II. He was a soldier for 3 years 2 months 13 days.

With the 361st Infantry Regiment, he helped bark the shin of Italy, through the Po Valley, Rome-Arno, and the North Apennines. His valor and pain on the 15th day of July in 1944 won Pat Valenzuela, heavy machine gunner, the Purple Heart and the Bronze Star. He won an oak leaf cluster for his Bronze Star.

When Pat Valenzuela came home from the war, he sought a quiet, peaceful living. His latest in a series of laboring jobs was as a crewman on a Salt River Valley Water Users weed-killing rig. He liked the work, and it paid enough for the support of his wife, Cruz, and their three little daughters.

On Sept. 28, 1956, Valenzuela and the other two members of the crew were eating their lunches on a canal bank not far from Guadalupe.

Valenzuela picked a shady spot under a large cottonwood tree and closed his eyes for a catnap. For fall, the day was warm. There was not enough breeze to turn a leaf.

From high in the tree, the men heard a queer creaking noise.

"What was that?" asked one.

"Birds probably," said the foreman.

"It is ghosts," Valenzuela joked in Spanish, and went back to his dozing.

After a while the foreman looked at his watch and announced, "It is 25 after. We still have five minutes."

And at that moment, a sharp snap drew the foreman's eyes to the treetop. He said he must have seen the limb, 2 feet in diameter at its base, immediately after it broke off, for he had a chance to jump back, and shout a warning to Valenzuela.

They said that Valenzuela, in the second that he had yet to live, rolled over and was to his hands and knees before the falling limb killed him instantly. If he had rolled the other way, he would have escaped unhurt.

Ulla G. Little was waiting for a night with a full, yellow moon.

"I'll see her," he said. "I know how she'll look, gleaming like a jewel. I'll pick the right night, and I'll stare at her until I can't look anymore."

Little, of 1025 E. Pierce, had been blind for 30 years. Now, through the marvelous skills of a Phoenix eye surgeon, Little was regaining his vision. Slowly dissolving was the black curtain that frustrated Little's youthful dream of becoming a surgeon himself.

There was no pattern to Little's delight, just the overpowering joy of seeing—anything. Miles of gleaming automobiles: "How many colors, how they flash in the sun." Phoenix, last seen as a low, desert town not quite reaching Roosevelt—now a proud metropolis sprawling from mountain to mountain. The very practical satisfaction of knowing what he will have for supper when he opened a can. The emotion-charged moment he perceived the silhouette of a daughter he reared, and never before saw.

But for his desire to become a doctor, Little might have made an eagle-visioned Midwest farmer. He was born on a Kansas farm in 1886. It was his father's wish that he be a farmer. The promise of a steady paycheck that he could save for his education drew him to the railroads.

Little was 21, in line for an engineer's job, and about ready to pick a medical school when a drunken switchman caused a wreck in the Cincinnati yards. Little was thrown through a cab window.

"I lost my left eye," he said. "I guess the other went out of sympathy for it."

He still had fair vision when he married in 1916. He could see well to the sides when he brought his growing family to Phoenix in 1923. But in 1926, before two of his eight children were born, his right eye, too, became dim. The world became a red light that faded ever darker.

"Those were tough times, and Beulah, my wife, was a saint," said Little. "We managed. We made out, because of her." His wife died in 1949.

"I gave up hope of seeing. I went to doctors, and they said there wasn't a chance, and I didn't have the money anyhow."

He was resigned to blindness until encouragement and help came from friends in the Indoor Sports Club and at the Phoenix Center for the Blind. Through them, Little qualified for state rehabilitation, and he was given the services of the doctor of his choice.

Three weeks before, the surgeon had removed a cataract

and restored the cornea in Little's right eye. Every day after the bandages were removed, Little could see better. His vision was expected to approach normal.

The two things he wanted to see most:

"That little moon. And an auburn-haired lady. The two prettiest things in the world."

Not long ago a hulking young man confronted John C. McPhee.

"May I help you?" asked McPhee.

"No." said the young man. "I wanted to get a good look at the man who killed Santa Claus."

For going onto 30 years people had been reminding McPhee of that black day when women shrieked, children wept, and strong men stood mute.

McPhee was editor of the Mesa Journal-Tribune in 1930. Interest in a pre-Christmas parade was lagging, and he applied his fruitful imagination to the problem. McPhee's plan deserved some of the superlatives that Hollywood later would tag to fiction. He arranged to have a barnstormer parachute from an airplane at the edge of town. Dressed in a Santa suit, the chutist would then ride in a car at the front of the parade.

"The town was filling with the largest crowd in its history when I learned that my daredevil was so full of Christmas cheer he couldn't jump," recalled McPhee.

McPhee hurried to a clothing store and grabbed a window dummy which was dressed as Santa Claus. He went to the airport, with the dummy, and a new plan. The pilot was told to push out the dummy over a field near Mesa. McPhee supposed he could reach the dummy in time to swap clothing, and he, McPhee, would lead the parade.

Mesa's response to the Santa stunt surpassed even McPhee's wildest hopes.

The streets were filled with excited celebrants and shoppers. Children climbed atop buildings, scurried up telephone poles, begged to be held aloft by parents. A fever of anticipation gripped the crowd as the airplane circled Mesa once, twice, three times.

Santa appeared at the door of the airplane. He fell free. Down. Down. Down.

Down.

The parachute did not open.

When McPhee returned to Mesa the streets were empty except for a few stunned merchants, transfixed in the doorways of their deserted stores. From homes came the wails of many children. The brave parade wound through downtown Mesa, and there were more marchers than watchers. So great was the shock, a pregnant woman began her labor, and to McPhee's eternal relief, mother and babe were saved.

McPhee left town for three days. But three decades could not wipe out the memory of the death of Santa Claus.

Love dogs. Hate dogs. You had to sympathize with Mrs. L. A. Ison, of 108 N. Hunt Dr. West, Mesa.

Her blond part-cocker disappeared. After a decent interval, Mrs. Ison gave him up as lost. She acquired two pekingese dogs. A year later the cocker returned, fat, sleek, and obviously well-cared-for.

"Whoever had him," said Mrs. Ison. "can have him back."

Well, now, an Englishman in the wild and wooly west?

"Yes, and don't try to take me snipe hunting. I've been in Arizona before and I'm no tenderfoot, you see."

How was that, pray?

"Exigency of war. England was no place to be flying around in training planes, don't you know. In 1944, when I was 19, I was sent to Falcon Field at Phoenix."

You are Harvey Boswell, your wife is a gracious and lovely lady named Shiela, and you have two children, Kevin, and Karen. Is that correct?

"They all came along later, and there is a bit more to the war. I take some share of credit for cessation of hostilities on the continent and in the Pacific. I had no sooner completed my training than the Germans surrendered, and as I was being processed for the other side of the world, Japan threw in. Both out of fright of me, I suspect."

Then you returned home to England and went to college.

"I took my degree and wife at the University of Durham—spelled like Bull Durham—and cast about for a job. The housing problem was frightful, and you couldn't buy a home in England unless you had a solid position. You might say I became a schoolteacher in order to qualify as a home owner."

There is good humor in your manner, I notice.

"Thank you, and perhaps you can tell me why Americans consider Englishmen to be poor wits. Now here's one. What you'd call a hobo or bum had a parrot. He taught his pet all the songs he knew, and took it to a pub, and bet that the parrot could sing any song named. The bets were laid, and the publican, wanting to make it sporting, asked the parrot to sing an easy one, 'Home, Sweet Home.' The parrot was quiet as a dickey bird, he was, and of course, the tattered old hobo lost all of his money.

"Stop giggling, man. I haven't come to the end yet. Later the hobo was on a bridge. He remonstrated with the parrot. 'You bad bird, I'm shoving a couple of bricks into your cage, and it's into the river with you.' At that, the parrot spoke: 'Don't be a fool, man. Think of the odds you get tomorrow night.' "

Ha. Ha. Why are you in Arizona this time. Ha. Harvey?

"It's because of Kevin. In the past few winters he's been in bed as much as out of it, you see. Doctors there seemed to have no cure. My Phoenix friend, Bob Griggs, wrote that if any place in the world was helpful for those with asthma, Arizona was it."

So you corresponded with Judson School.

"Yes, and believe me, it's not an easy decision to come 6,000 miles, to leave parents and friends. The wife (Englishmen always say, 'the wife') and I talked it over late many an evening. We decided Kevin couldn't cough his way to manhood, thinking the world was full of pills and all that. He's much better here.

"Here is a bit. The institution in which I taught in England, equivalent to the public high school here, was built as an Augustinian Monastery in 1240. During the reign of Henry VIII it passed into the hands of noble families who held it until wartime taxes made it impossible for private owners to keep up large estates. In England I taught at a school where priceless paintings hung on ancient stone walls, and now I teach at—well, it is called a western ranch school, I believe. Both are excellent schools, but the contrast is so striking, you see."

And do you enjoy living in Arizona once again?

"Good show! Another Englishman is at Judson, and we are training a soccer team. We've laid out our pitch and goals, but frankly, we've had trouble finding opponents."

TOM MIX MONUMENT—A statue of a horse, saddled but riderless, trailing its reins, was put at the place where my boyhood hero died.

Tom Mix could not sing, and he could not play the guitar. He never in public rolled his eyes sensually, and he had no talent for swiveling his hips like a man with a chunk of ice in his jeans. But hero he was. He will live as long as the memories of millions of boys, now men.

He was born in Mix Run, Pa., in 1880, and he died at Tom Mix Wash, 18 miles south of Florence, Ariz., Oct. 12, 1940. In those 60 years he succeeded at enough careers for a half-dozen lesser men.

As a soldier, he saw action in the Philippines, where he opened his mouth and took a Spanish bullet which emerged from his neck. In the Boxer Rebellion in China, he won a medal and citation. A shell fragment almost scalped him while he was fighting with the British in the Boer War.

His cowboy role was honestly come by. It was his trade in most of the Western states. He became foreman for a huge Oklahoma spread, and won national riding and roping contests in Canon City, Colo., and Prescott. Always, he did things by bunches. He was a Texas Ranger, deputy U.S. marshal in Oklahoma, Montana, Arizona and New Mexico, and was sheriff of counties in three states. He was wounded twice while wearing the badge.

His prowess at rodeos caught the eye of a Hollywood agent who offered him $100 a week. Tom Mix gulped. The agent said $150. And the man who was to make the horse opera the nation's premiere form of entertainment, accepted.

His standard portrayal was of a hard-fisted cowboy with a fast gun and the biggest hat west of Nantucket Light Ship. On screen, women to Tom Mix were creatures only for rescue, not love. In all of his pictures he never smoked, and he never took a drink.

I remember him best as a radio performer (in person and impersonated, which I long thought were synonymous). Until I was almost grown, I believed that if I ate enough Ralston cereal, I would become his double, complete with faithful horse, Tony. Never was there or has there been a better man than Tom Mix at dispatching a villain with a single smite. But most heroic of all, in my eyes, was his refusal to be seen picking a guitar in places no real cowboy would pack a musical instrument.

"I'll quit motion pictures before I'll learn to play a mandolin," he once said. "And none of my fans will ever hear me desecrating the atmosphere of a theater by yodeling."

The last 10 years of his life Tom Mix spent in Wild West shows. On the day he died he was traveling alone, from Tucson to Phoenix, as advance man for an old cow waddy buddy, Ken Maynard.

No one witnessed his death. Apparently his glistening green Rolls Royce speedster went out of control in a bridge detour, and overturned. The men who found him said a flying suitcase broke Tom Mix's neck. They also remembered that Tom Mix had passed them down the road, stopped for gas, then passed them again. They said that the second time he went by "he sounded a siren."

Chapter Four

Not roots. Or adobe. Or clay. Or sod. Or stone. Yet the materials for George Ellis's house were dug from the earth—from the most unlikely treasure of building materials ever uncovered in the Valley of the Sun.

Ellis's place isn't unique. A trail of the material can be traced from downtown Phoenix northeast to the Verde River, from modest city porches, through luxurious resort bars, along pasture fences.

Pictures in Phoenix's Hotel Westward Ho were framed in it. Fifteen barns were made of it. Yavapai Apaches out Fort McDowell way built countless wagons from it. Troughs made of it watered generations of horses, and the stuff was used in doors of some of Phoenix's finest homes. Impossible to prove—but a good bet: Fire consumed the material in camps, stoves, and hearths continuously for 20 years.

The stuff was redwood—heart redwood—without a knot

in it, from the scandal-ridden pipeline that refused to stay buried.

The pipeline was built by the City of Phoenix in the '20s at a cost of $4 million. How many of those dollars were diverted to private pockets has never been fully revealed, but a couple of city administrations crumbled under charges of bribery and graft. One man was jailed, and others left town.

If the finances were improper, the engineering was abominable. For 32 miles the pipeline, 42 inches in diameter, snaked out across the desert, laid on grade, sometimes above and sometimes below the ground. It soon began to buckle and leak. When wily Indians wanted water, they tapped the aqueduct. Within four years after it was finished, the pipeline, as a pipeline, was useless. But in the days when everybody was a do-it-yourselfer, the pipeline was a boardfeet bonanza.

Ellis got his after most of the above-ground redwood was spirited away. Along Thomas Road in the mid-'30s the county uncovered miles of the pipeline and invited the public to take it away.

"I wouldn't do it today if it were gold," said Ellis. "First, you had to break a hole in the top, and crawl into the pipe. Some water had stayed in the pipe, and there were some places where it was half full. I pried out the top board for a quarter of a mile. After the top board was out, the other boards were pretty easy to free. They were floated down to the nearest hole to the surface. At times you were working in a tunnel through the earth, supported only by the iron hoops which had held the pipeline every eight inches. The boards were so waterlogged, it took two men to lift a two-by-six 14 feet long."

Used as siding and sheathing in the Ellis Paradise Valley home, the old redwood gave an effect of expensive modernness.

The redwood was still being mined, now and again, by the county highway department, whenever a stretch of

Thomas Road was widened. But judging from all the redwood structures between Phoenix and the Mazatzals, there couldn't be much left below the surface.

DOUGLAS—Here, in 1926, the spark that entered a slow fuse on a Pacific Ocean beach, hit the evangelistic powder keg named Aimee Semple McPherson.

Money and mystery, religion and crime, sex and suspense —the story had everything. Douglas had seen nothing like it before, and didn't believe it would again. Only a second "resurrection from the dead" by Sister McPherson could top it.

Mrs. McPherson had buried one husband and divorced another by the time she appeared in Los Angeles at the beginning of the '20s, shaking her tambourine and preaching her Four Square Gospel in a tattered little tent. Her flock quickly multiplied. By 1926 her beauty, her magnetic personality, her religious showmanship, had drawn together a congregation of 30,000. Fanatically faithful, her followers jammed her palatial Angelus Temple, tuned into her radio broadcasts, and dutifully filled collection plates and mail pouches with offerings.

Mrs. McPherson was rich, famous, and in its full meaning, worshipped when she went to Ocean Park, Calif., May 18, 1926, rented a tent, and donned a pea-green bathing suit. Her disappearance, reported by her secretary, electrified the Coast, and the nation.

"On the streetcar the conductor asked you for the news," recalled a Los Angelino. "The other passengers freely joined in with their own views at the greatest length.

"At 20-minute intervals, newsboys ran through the streets bearing fresh extras with false news, her body had been found, she had been seen in Winnipeg, the kidnapers had made their demand for ransom, she was in a Los Angeles hotel, her body had been washed out to sea."

Aimee's mother, daughter and assistants went on the air with prayerful appeals for her safe return. Her congregation held special services on the beach, and patroled the shoreline day and night. (And as a consequence, disrupted ship-to-shore bootlegging.) One man died of exposure while diving for her body. A young woman committed suicide rather than live in a world without Aimee. Others had to be restrained from casting themselves into the sea.

Angelus Temple offered $25,000 for information leading to Mrs. McPherson, alive or dead. For reasons never explained, the offer was withdrawn. Next day, a Sunday, a 12-hour memorial service eulogized Aimee. Strong men labored with the collection plates.

Then, early in the morning of the following Wednesday, June 23, 1926, an American woman stumbled into the outskirts of Agua Prieta and collapsed at the gate of a Mexican home. A Douglas taxi driver happened by as Mexican police were questioning the woman, and he volunteered to take her across the border. In Douglas, a merchant patrolman was sympathetic. He guaranteed her hospital bill.

Almost immediately, she was identified. Extras carried the news to Douglas citizens, and to the world. Aimee unchangingly told her story again and again—of kidnap on the beach, of being held hostage in a Sonora shack, of torture by knife and fire at the hands of her abductors, of escape across 26 miles of desert. Reports of that day differed on Aimee's condition.

"Her beautiful hair chopped off . . . , bedraggled, muddy, tired, shaking and quivering," one reporter wrote. But others said she was unmussed and not sunburned, and was wearing clean, fashionable, high-heeled shoes. Douglas believed Aimee, at first. But years later a writer who liked her had to admit, "No woman ever told a more preposterous story in a balder manner or oftener."

Her tale of terror, first uttered in the Douglas Hospital:

Two men and a woman, luring her with a request to heal a sick baby, kidnaped her at Ocean Park. They held her for ransom, and took her to a shack below the border south of Douglas. There, she was burned with a cigar and cut with a knife, but she heroically refused to answer questions—intimate, personal questions that would have given her abductors information they might use in a ransom note for $500,000.

Her chance for escape came. She cut her bonds on a tomato can, and climbed through a window. She walked. And walked. Fifteen miles south of Douglas, after a half-day hike, she climbed a mountain and sighted the glowing slag dumps of the great copper smelter. That light, as a beacon from one of her Four Square Gospel Lighthouses, led her to safety and friends.

Douglas, at the focus of the world's attention, celebrated Fourth of July, Thanksgiving and *Cinco de Mayo*, all at once.

Correspondents flew (by airplane, mind you, in 1926) from all directions. Posses and private search parties plunged into the desert, seeking the kidnap cabin. A police guard was put over Aimee. Mexican troops threw up a cordon along the border. Scores of prominent Douglas citizens pleaded with Aimee to speak to the town, and she graciously accepted the invitation. Five thousand came to hear.

But there were doubters among them.

"At Douglas, reporters handed out $20 bills like cigars," recalled one writer. "But always, directly ahead of them, and again directly behind them, was some emissary of the Lord with $50 bills."

The Los Angeles district attorney wondered (1) how Mrs. McPherson could be kidnaped in the middle of a day on a crowded beach, (2) why the $25,000 reward for her return had been withdrawn a few days before she came back, and (3) whether the $15,000 collected for a memorial to her would be returned to the donors.

Investigators came to Douglas. Douglas citizens were summoned to Los Angeles, to testify before grand juries. When Aimee arrived in Los Angeles she trod a carpet of roses, and announced she would sue her slanderers. She offered a $500 reward for the discovery of the kidnap shack, and the Los Angeles Examiner set up a $10,000 prize for the arrest of her alleged captors. Aimee even came back to Douglas to look for the shack herself.

Meanwhile, another story began to gain momentum: That Aimee was not kidnaped at all, but instead spent the month in an artist's colony at Carmel, Calif. Also there was a former operator of her radio station. Forcefully, but always in good humor, Mrs. McPherson denied the story.

She was unsuccessfully brought to trial on two painfully technical charges of "conspiracy to defeat justice" and "subornation to perjury." She stuck to her tale, and all the state's legislators could not force her to swear differently.

She always said the burden of proof was not hers. To her death in 1945 no one was able to prove where she spent the month, or how she got away from the beach, or how she reached Agua Prieta.

Percy Bowden, Douglas's perennial police chief, had a simple theory of her walk across the desert:

"Not in them shoes; not on them feet."

Except for a couple of pets at West Point, the army did away with its mules. George L. Chamberlain called it a "damn fool mistake."

"When a helicopter can fly through trees, and a Jeep can find its own fuel on trail, I'll admit the mule is obsolete," said the old sarge. "As long as there are foot soldiers, there will be a need for mules."

Chamberlain, 78 in 1957, lived at 385 N. Second Ave., Phoenix, in an apartment filled with mementos of 24 years, 11 months, and 8 days of service.

He was a courier during the Spanish-American War in Cuba, and he remembered when Gen. Jonathan (Skinny) Wainwright was a shavetail. Chamberlain took part in 21 expeditions against hostile Moros in the Philippines. His outfit served in France during World War I, and when the army told him he was over age for World War II, he got a job guarding California coastal installations.

"A man doesn't cost the army anything, we used to say," recalled Chamberlain. "But a good Missouri mule cost the army $150. We governed our actions accordingly."

A mule, he said, could carry a field piece section weighing 300 to 350 pounds, as fast as a man could walk, from sunup to sundown, with 10-minute rest periods each hour.

"I don't know what the loads got to be by the time a couple soldiers hung their knapsacks on the mule's back," he said. "Or grabbed the mule's tail for a boost up a hill. Our mules lost so much hair out of their tails this way they got to looking like elephants at the hind end."

Chamberlain knew mules that were good for 12 to 15 years of hard service, and he heard of mules being useful for 25 years.

"They're smart, too," he said. "Mules don't need near the attention that horses do. Mules know when, and how much, to eat and drink, and no horse in the world has got that much sense."

Chamberlain said that no matter how fast planes fly, no matter how big bombs get, no matter how mechanized the army becomes, there will always be times and places in warfare in which infantry will engage infantry. Gravel crunchers need artillery. Any place a mountain goat could go, a mule could go, said Chamberlain.

He said there was nothing slow about a crack mule-packed artillery outfit. Proudly he handed over a copy of the Annual Reports of the War Department, Volume Three, for the year ending June 30, 1904.

"I was the gunner for the Seventeenth." He pointed to a paragraph, underlined in red, describing an incident which occurred in Mindanao.

"There was an interesting contest between the Seventeenth and Eighteenth Batteries, Field Artillery, as to which could dismount a mountain gun, pack it, advance 50 yards at a gallop, and reassemble the gun, load, and fire. The contest was won by the Seventeenth Battery, Field Artillery, in the remarkable time of 45-1/5 seconds. The Eighteenth Battery was only a fraction of a second behind."

Chamberlain smiled. "Try that in your whirlybird."

Ed Shepard, balding, soft-spoken AiResearch engineer of Phoenix, had 30 years experience in electronics.

Early in World War II he was helping to perfect an accoustics torpedo, and was disappointed when he was transferred to an assignment described as "unimportant."

His task was to build a firing device to unusual and unexplained specifications. Shepard was even more disappointed when he was transferred to a remote New Mexican base.

After Hiroshima, Ed Shepard was told he put the trigger in the atomic bomb.

In a field of boulders at the top of Screwtail Hill off the Beeline Highway 45 straight-line miles northeast of Phoenix, an old man stamped his feet on the rocky ground.

"Here," he said, "is where I want to be buried."

"Why, Uncle Mack," replied one of his picnicking companions. "You wouldn't want to be out here all alone. You could have your choice of all the beautiful cemeteries in Los Angeles."

Newton Bedford Forest McCord snorted:

"I don't want no damned lawn mowers running over my grave."

That was the beginning of Mack's Rest. Before Mr. McCord got his way, Tonto National Forest, the largest in the nation, adapted its regulations to the old man's whim. The year was 1935. Irascible, generous, eccentric, charming, Mr. McCord was a retired railroader who lived alone in Los Angeles. He had come to know a few Mesa families, and over the course of many years, he was considered almost a member of those families. They took him along on outings, and he bought presents for the children.

Soon after the picnic, Mr. McCord indicated he meant what he said on Screwtail Hill. He asked a friend, the late

C. W. Lillywhite of Mesa, to petition the forest service for a burial permit. Mr. Lillywhite's letter, still a part of Tonto files, stated:

"In his 70s he is still hale and hearty, but insists that when he dies he wants his remains laid away 'in them thar hills.' "

An understanding regional forester in Albuquerque approved the request. Formal, detailed papers were issued in the name of B. F. McCord, and the old man must have been amused when he read them. The permit set aside one-eighth of an acre for a cemetery for the burial place of B. F. McCord. No fee was charged.

"The permittee will comply with the regulations of the Department of Agriculture," the permit admonished. Other sections of the permit read:

"The permittee shall take all reasonable precaution to prevent and suppress forest fires. . . ."

"This use shall be actually exercised at least 365 days each year, unless the time is extended or shortened. . . ."

"In case of change of address, permittee shall immediately notify the forest supervisor."

On Nov. 10, 1935, Mr. McCord reassured his benefactors, "I want to thank you for the permit, so graciously granted, for me to be buried in the National Forest. And I promise you that after I locate there, I will not violate any of the forest regulations that are enumerated in the permit. Thank you, 'it won't be long now.' "

It would be longer than anyone supposed. Mr. McCord set up a trust fund for his burial expenses. E. D. (Buster) Brown, then of Mesa and lately of Farmington, N.M., had the grave dug, or more accurately, blasted. The chisels of three stone cutters were ruined before the words "Mack's Rest" were carved into a granite boulder near the open grave.

Mr. McCord lived until March 26, 1946. Brown remembered that as Mr. McCord desired, only a half-dozen persons were present at his burial, and there were no services.

"Like he asked," said Brown. "We just put in some big rocks to hold him down, and said goodby."

Mack's Rest can be seen from the Beeline where it parallels Sycamore Creek and overlooks Boulder Mountain. Cattle have worn a path across the grave, but no lawn mower has broken Uncle Mack's eternal sleep.

In a rice-paddy village of Kwangtung Province, China, a schoolteacher whipped Wing Foon Ong for writing, "Nothing is impossible in this world."

In San Francisco, the wise patriarchs of Chinatown told Wing Foon Ong he "didn't have a Chinaman's chance."

On the floor of the Arizona legislature, a small man arose in mock Confucian dignity, and in a sing-song burlesque of Chinese accent, began a speech: "Wing Ong say—"

Wherever one begins the story of Wing Foon Ong, its facts are the stuff of legends. Yet the wealthy and respected Phoenix business and professional man said he would accept no personal credit for his achievements. He said, "I am what I am because the United States of America is what it is."

Ong was born without benefit of doctor or midwife in Heiping, China. His grandparents had come to California in frontier days, and Ong's father was born in this country.

"Thus," said Ong, "when my father died he had no fortune to leave me, but his was a legacy of greater value—American citizenship."

When Ong was 14, after a childhood of laboring knee-deep in rice fields, he decided to claim that birthright. He walked 150 miles to the China seacoast and was hired as cabin boy on a steamer. He arrived in San Francisco, unable to speak, read, or write English. He was dead broke. Public school refused to enroll him, and he rebelled at his first job, folding laundry at 50 cents a day.

"What do you want?" asked the old leaders of Chinatown.

"I want to go to American schools," he answered. "I want

to become a man of learning and accomplishment, and in America, this can be done if one has the will to do so."

The old men shook their heads. They doubted the sanity of the frail youth. When they said "a Chinaman's chance," they meant no chance at all.

At 15, penniless and alone, Ong came to Phoenix. In a hundred ways, he struggled furiously to survive, but now his life had new meaning and hope. In Phoenix the schools took one and all. Ong worked in groceries, in restaurants, in labor crews, in Valley homes, always refusing the full-time jobs that would have taken him out of school. The embarrassment of playing blindman's bluff with children a third his age soon turned to pride, when he jumped three grades in 10 days. He finished grammar school in three years. Two years later, he earned his high school diploma at Phoenix Union.

At 20, he gambled his life's savings: $300. A business man asked him if he would take over a bankrupt eastside grocery.

"If you win, you pay off the debts and keep the store," was the proposition.

Ong redecorated the market. He put out a new sign. He stocked specials, and hired school children to distribute thousands of handbills. He used promotion and advertising techniques 20 years ahead of their time. Creditors, holding a total of $4,500 in claims, were satisfied in 18 months.

In 1928, in the custom of China, Ong sent for the wife who was chosen for him when they were children. He first saw Rose Wong the day he married her, the very same day she stepped off a steamer in Seattle.

The next decade Ong devoted to his businesses and to his growing family, through prosperity and depression.

But in the middle 30s, Ong heard and read things he did not like. America was a failure and democracy was a lie, propagandists were saying. Ong knew better and he set out to demonstrate it.

"In this country, and in this country only, regardless of race, color, or creed, a man can get ahead if he wants too." With that belief as much of his philosophy as Christ and Confucius, Wing Ong ran for the Arizona Legislature in District 2, comprising a downtown section of Phoenix.

Few Chinese lived in the district, and fewer still were franchised to vote. Ong lost by 17 votes. He was disappointed, but he would not blame the defeat on racial prejudice.

"What right have I to make laws if I know nothing of the law?" he asked himself.

So at an age when most men are comfortably resigned to a familiar career, Ong entered the University of Arizona law school in 1940. His wife helped watch the Phoenix store, and his children learned to be quiet when their father was bent over his books. Ong completed the 7-year course in 3 years, standing third in his class. He passed the Arizona bar examination with one of the highest grades ever made, and when he hung his shingle on his grocery store, he was said to be one of eight Chinese lawyers practicing in the whole United States.

He and his family threw themselves into the war effort. They sold $1 million worth of war bonds, and when a wave of anti-Oriental feeling swept the country, Ong was a leader in drawing attention to the loyalty of Chinese-Americans. On a Fourth of July, every Chinese grocery was closed. The only explanations were American flags draped across the locked doors.

When Ong campaigned for the legislature the first time, his cards read, "A neighborhood's friend." In 1946 his slogan was changed: "Let a lawyer help make your laws." He won, and was re-elected, by whopping margins.

First man of his race elected to a state legislature, Ong was written up in newspapers from Hong Kong to New York. San Francisco's Chinatown, which once offered so little, hailed him as one of the most influential Chinese in the West. Ong took his responsibility seriously, but sometimes he could not resist expressing a subtle humor which seems to be a common gift of his people. Once, when the legislature approached a grim night-time vote, Ong produced a little black fife and blew a Chinese tune. Music, he explained to the surprised legislators, was a lifetime hobby in which he found relaxation and wisdom. The bill was quickly voted, and with no hard feelings.

His colleagues could return in kind. Ong, five feet tall, and 155 pounds holding a gong, was given an emergency appropriation of $1.98 for construction of a stool to stand on.

A Democrat, Ong was delighted when President Truman was the upset victor in 1948. He sent to Washington a parchment note, written in artful flourishes of the Orient:

"Honorable Sir:—I see by the papers that we have something in common. Of each it has been written, 'He hasn't a Chinaman's chance.' Perhaps we two Chinamen should get together and settle the affairs of the skeptics of the world."

The chance came, not long afterwards. The State Department made a motion picture of Ong's life, and sent it overseas. His story was broadcast in 28 languages.

In 1957 he could count five grandchildren, a modern restaurant at 1617 E. Thomas, a new home at 4601 N. 30th St. He had his law practice, and his music. And he had his creed, which he expressed with the freshness of the founding fathers:

"America is still the land of opportunity."

The world and Herman Haefs signed a truce.

Under its terms, Haefs was getting $70 per month pension. In return, Haefs was giving the world as little trouble as possible. He reserved only his basic freedoms—of ownership, of decision, of speech.

"I sit here in my own chair on my own porch of my own house on my own lot, and kid the case workers who try to help me," he said. "Pretty little girls with pencils and printed forms come 'round here telling me that just because a man's past 65 he shouldn't have no vinegar."

Haefs, 86, was living alone at 1821 E. Illini on the south bank of the Salt River. In a year, with little help, he built his home. He put in a lawn and threw up a fence and planted a pumpkin patch.

His years were no burden, said Haefs, but sometimes when laying floors or mowing the yard, he wished he had two legs. In 1952 he lost his left leg to infection. He said he hobbled out of the hospital while the doctors were talking about cutting off the right one, too.

"They said I had salt poison in one and sugar diabetes in the other," said Haefs. "I been thinking about that for five years and it still doesn't make any sense."

His life had been a roller-coaster of success and failure.

He was the only man with enough courage to drive the first streetcar in his native Appleton, Wis. He joined the U.S. Cavalry, and was kicked out when officers learned he was under age.

As a sapling youth he ran cows in the Payson area, and when he saw Phoenix for the first time in 1891, "a man could run around the city limits without breaking a sweat."

He drove stage coach in Idaho, joined the Klondike gold rush, worked as a bouncer in a dance hall. With a partner, he bought a steamer and traded in every corner of the Pacific until the ship went down in a Bering Sea storm.

"When I came to Phoenix the last time in '44, I was broke," Haefs said. "I started a second-hand business and that went bust. I wasn't getting anywhere."

That was when Haefs bought the lot, $10 down and $10 per month. He laid out his box-like house in generous dimensions. The screened front porch is 24 feet long. Friends helped him with the rafters and roofing, with the plumbing and wiring. Haefs partitioned two bedrooms, a living room, a kitchen, a bath.

Haefs grinned. "Man asks why you want a big house?

"And I said because I can do anything I please in my own house. I load up on groceries once a month, and fix myself three meals a day, and sometimes do some baking. Every month I lay aside $10 for some home improvements.

"I painted the whole house, and I did it my own way. I used a brush one-inch wide. It took me 30 days. I put my wheelchair on a table to reach the high places, but I got it done.

"In my own house I don't have somebody turning on the cooler in the summer, or turning on the heater after dark. I live my own way, and who knows what might happen to property values in the next 50 years?"

"Did you know that a member of the Goldwater family owns a bulldog which has a gold tooth?" someone asked.

"No," I replied smugly. "But I know Bill Merriman owns a one-eyed Harris's hawk named Silly which hunts jack rabbits by pouncing on their backs and dragging its tail on the ground."

Once in a lifetime a man with such an answer is offered such an opportunity.

HORSE THIEF BASIN—There's a rich story about how this piney place—now a vacation retreat operated by the City of Phoenix—got its name.

Long ropers would heist horses in the Salt River Valley and drive them to the easy-to-defend mountain hideaway, where the mounts would be rebranded. The horses were then sold in the Prescott area.

On the way back to Horse Thief Basin, the outlaws would steal other cayuses, fix the brands, and deliver them to Valley ranchers, who, the robbers knew, were in desperate need of horses.

Some historians have gone to outlandish lengths to discredit the tale, and I have never understood why.

We men smile as the dames go by, teasingly beautiful, sleek in satin. Exciting.

Our wives oo and ah the artful decorations and costumes. (And smile as the guys go by.)

But for all of its saddled, floated and self-propelled sex appeal, for all of its tourist allure, for all of its provincial hoo-raw and wah-hoo, the Phoenix rodeo parade remains a show for the kids.

To be 2, or 5, or 10 again, with a front-row view of that marvelous caravan!

Two thousand horses, served up in singles and scores. Silver-spangled, curried—even painted pink—frothing over engraved bits and foaming under silvered saddles. Fancy gaited, pop-eyed, hike-tailed palominos and duns and roans and bays and blacks, carrying and drawing big shots and heroes and fine ladies, and hey! There goes a rider just my age.

Enough ever-lovin' horses to last from late breakfast to nap time. Enough for a year of memories and imaginations. Enough, by heck, for a lifetime of if-I-coulds.

And bands. Down in the gutter, between knee-hugging little sisters and cap-gun-slung juniors, squatting on the black top, on hands and knees past the white line. Eye-level with the bottoms of the bass drums. There's the place to see a band. Not up high, looking over a pattern of hats and youthful faces, but down low, where you can marvel at the scissoring legs of marchers who tower above with instruments framed by the sky. Down low, at the bottom of a canyon of standing moms and dads, where you can feel on your skin the shock of drums and snarl of brass. There's the place to see a band.

And the floats. Big, belching smoke, frilly as petticoats, colored like cakes, shaped like things, bearing lucky people who get to ride (gosh, I'd like to ride) or animated figures that make me laugh. They had a great, big bird. Taller than a tree. And an old fire engine, redder than a Christmas wagon. A whole band was playing and a lady was dancing on one. And one looked just like a boot. Wait till I tell the gang.

Indian kids. Hundreds of Indian kids. Juke-box-playing-soda-pop-drinking-going-to-school Indian kids who are learning to be engineers and doctors and politicians and farmers, but just for this day, painted and feathered, laced in leather and bound in beads, hopping and weaving in the dances of their proud tribal heritages. Smeared with ashes and clay. Ferocious. Gay. Stolid. Chanting. Matching paleface custom for custom, reason for reason, belief for belief.

And the funny man in the high top hat on a bike the size of a dream. A dozen clowns, scary until you see how sad they look and act, then you giggle until you cry. Donkeys and goats. Boats and monkeys. Sheriffs and badmen. Real stage coach. Rifles and beards and flags and dogs and motor scooters and noise, noise.

As a spanking breeze toys with a blizzard of confetti, and a friendly sun is as warm as wool.

To be a kid in Phoenix, up front, and the tyke nearby shouting, "I see it! Way up there! Here it comes. Here comes the parade!"

John Rantanen came to Arizona to cure his arthritis, broke his hip in a fall, tripped on his crutches, broke the other hip, and just when things were mending, refractured both hips again.

But he had a better break in 1957.

John was in his wheelchair, hard at his leatherwork, expecting some customers, when a couple knocked at the door of his home at 1508 E. Desert Park Dr.

My name's Eisenhower," the man said. "I'm the President's brother."

Good thing he was sitting down in his wheelchair, Rantanen recalled. He invited Mr. and Mrs. Edgar Eisenhower of Tacoma, Wash., inside. They stayed 45 minutes, chatting about horses, trout fishing, arthritis, Arizona, sunshine, belt buckles, and leathercraft.

"I never suspected all of this would come out of a little notion of mine," said Rantanen later.

Some of Rantanen's leatherwork had won a state fair prize, and a Scottsdale shop was marketing some of his products. An Ike fan, Rantanen conceived the idea of giving the President a belt. Mamie Eisenhower sent Rantanen the President's waist size (36). Kenneth Begay, Navajo silversmith of Scottsdale, agreed to make the buckle.

On this very buckle Begay was working when a couple came into his shop.

"Those initials you're putting on that buckle," said the man. "Not many men have those initials."

"This is for the President," said Begay.

"I'm Edgar Eisenhower. The President's brother."

Begay explained the plan to make and give the belt, and told about Rantanen's tooling of the leather that would be used in it.

"I guess that's when they decided to visit me," said Rantanen. "Some weeks went by before they got out here, and I had sent the belt to Washington. They asked me to describe it, how it had a Colorado trout fishing stream, and otherwise was decorated in all-Arizona things. Well, we talked and talked. Mrs. Eisenhower said the next time she saw me she wanted to see me walking. Mr. Eisenhower had a great time talking horses. Before they left they ordered a belt for their son-in-law.

"They wanted to know if I had received a letter of thanks from the President. I said no. And he said, 'You will before long, I'm sure.' "

The Edgar Eisenhowers were no more than out of sight when the mailman delivered a letter:

"Mrs. Eisenhower has handed me the hand-tooled western belt that you so kindly wanted me to have. I am delighted with it and most appreciative of your thoughtfulness in creating such a unique gift for me. Please express my warm thanks, also, to Mr. Begay for the specially designed buckle."

Below it was the signature, Dwight David Eisenhower.

Chapter Five

McNARY—Railroad executives are fabulously wealthy. They wear butler suits before lunch and persecute the Little Man. They smoke fat, black cigars. They live on Long Island and work in mahogany-paneled offices staffed with grim secretaries who say, sorry, Mr. Freightrate is in conference.

Everybody knows that. Yet there was S. E. Mounes in third-hand clothes, including a checked shirt and a dusty, bent snap-brim. His wet shoes were propped on the arm of a seat. His face broke into a sympathetic grin as he discarded the 8 of spades.

"Gin," he cried. "You owe me 35 cents."

Mounes is executive vice president of the Apache Railway Company, "boss of the longest short-line railroad in Arizona!"

The Apache is a railroad of serious purpose. The logs it

can haul into McNary for Southwest Lumber Mills in six months could span the United States if laid end-to-end. (Getting them all back to McNary would take 14 years, 3 months, 2 days.)

Mounes runs the railroad with a brisk efficiency which has brought it out of years of red ink. Under his management, the Apache is a profit-making railroad, yet he speaks of The Apache as if he were a boy, and he found it under the Christmas tree.

Its common-carrier division is 72 miles long. Its extension to the Maverick logging country is 68. If The Apache used all of its diesels and log cars and box cars and cabooses, it couldn't make up one train as long as the average Santa Fe freight.

Small, The Apache, but modern. The diesels are equipped with radios and speed recorders. Mounes said he could speak directly to the engineer of any of his trains, and later he could review the story of an entire round trip.

"I think the most valuable asset of The Apache is its self-sufficiency," said Mounes. "We can't shut down while repairs are made for us in Phoenix. We fix things ourselves, right here. I've got some of the best mechanics in the country."

Pride of The Apache is its fancy caboose, made from the wheels up in the McNary yards. It has seats for eight passengers, picture windows, chartreuse drapes, limed pine paneling—even a fully automatic water closet.

"One of those ICC regulations," he explained. "Anybody wanting to come to McNary from Holbrook would rather ride the bus. Cheaper. Faster. A couple of years ago somebody told me we took in $10 in fares in one season."

It had been a hard day, on the first attempt to clear the drifted snow from the tracks to Maverick. The smashing of a plow in a stubborn snowbank had doubled, perhaps tripled, the expenses of the spring breakthrough.

But Mounes, graduate of the Illinois Central and 30 years a railroader, talked cheerfully of other things. McNary, he said, was progressing. A new housing development. Piped-in television. A planned shopping center.

"Fine place to live," he said. "in the most majestic scenic area in the country. Served by Arizona's biggest little railroad."

He threw away the queen of spades, face downward.

"What's the name of this game?" smiled the cigaret-smoking, French-cooking, open-collared, story-telling persecutor of the Little Gin Rummy Player.

Maricopa Farm Bureau women took their city cousins to spend the afternoon down on the farm.

"We hope to explain some of the farmer's problems," said Mrs. William Boyle, president of the bureau women, and wife of a milk, grain, beef and cotton grower.

Young and not-so-young, tall and short, native Phoenicians and from as far away as New Jersey, the women filed aboard the chartered bus. Fred Wackerbarth and Sam Maxcy, bureau manager, took turns at the public address system, and soon a truth became apparent:

You can take the girl out of the city, but in booming Phoenix you've got to take her a fur piece.

"Note the Park Central development on the left," said Sam Maxcy. "Central Avenue Dairy milking barn used to stand there." Later he told how Valley farmers "are being subdivided out of 30,000 acres a year."

Outskirting subdivisions leap-frog farms. Then the city housewives move out and shriek when the first cropduster buzzes the south forty. Or they sign petitions against the smells of a neighboring dairy herd.

"So where the city and the country meet, farmers often can't use the most efficient methods," said Maxcy. The city women could see that, but they didn't understand carrot-harvesting. As we rolled westward, Fred Wackerbarth, field man for the Phoenix farm labor office, offered a fact-filled commentary:

"It takes between $200 and $250 to raise an acre of lettuce.

An acre of celery might cost $750. It takes 350 tons of water to produce one ton of hay." Fields of barley, wheat, alfalfa, strawberries, sugar beets, lettuce, truck crops, whizzed by—only a few of the hundred different kinds of crops grown in the Valley. Then the bus boiled into a carrot field where a picking crew was lining up for the day's pay.

"Why, they didn't pick up all the carrots," exclaimed one of the city guests. "They are 15 cents a bunch."

The city women got off the bus and loped down the rows and filled their arms with cull carrots. They put them under the bus seats and in the luggage racks.

"Tell me why all those carrots are going to waste?" demanded one of the women. It was a bad moment for Maxcy. Scarred, twisted, broken, undersized carrots art not marketable, he said. Housewives won't buy them. Plowed under, they make the barley grow.

"Well, I just can't see giving government support to farmers who are so wasteful." Maxcy let it go. What could he do?

The bus paused at a southwest dairy where the city women were served ice cream and other refreshments. As magnificent Holsteins were being milked nearby, the hostess explained that her drinking milk is delivered to the farm in a bottle, just as in the city. Pasteurizing the farm's own milk would be more trouble than saving.

Maxcy was refreshed for the return trip. He said Maricopa County ranks fifth in the nation in value of agricultural products. And first in hospitality.

As Joe Pearce of Eagar told it—

Long ago I was a stockman for the Fort Apache Indian Reservation. The .30-30 rifle had just been placed on the market and I owned one with a silver-set stock and my name engraved on it.

Natzin, an old Apache medicine man, lived in Forest Dale near Show Low, on Carrizo Creek. Natzin saw my rifle one day and wanted to buy it. Next he offered to swap a good mule. Finally:

"I have two pretty daughters. I will trade one for gun. Initiate you into our tribe. Teach you Indian ways."

Well, I really needed a pack mule for my work, which involved looking after Indian cattle and counting in other cattle for grazing on Indian lands. So I agreed to trade for the mule. It was young and a dandy—very kind and gentle to ride and pack. I fitted her with corked shoes, and was riding her one day when I camped out down near Roberts' big spring. That night I hobbled her out. Next morning the mule was gone. I was afoot. Leaving my saddle with an Indian woman whose wikieup was nearby, I followed the tracks of my mule. They led straight back to Forest Dale.

It was about 10 miles to walk, and I went directly to Natzin's home. His two wives were petting and caressing the mule as if they were holding a family reunion. The cunning old medicine man was stretched out on a saddle blanket in the shade.

"Hello, Joe. You have come to take one of my pretty daughters?"

I told him I came to get my mule.

"No, Joe. You cannot have mule. You trade with me. I promise quick education Indian ways. This is cheap schoolin'. Mule stays here.

"Because, Joe, you know that when a white man sells gun to Indian, he goes to calaboose.

"Joe no talk. Me no talk."

Returning by way of the C. E. Cooley home and stage station, I picked up my saddle horse and went back to the Indian woman's wikieup to get my saddle. She was out front making *tortillas,* sitting with one knee bent up, spreading the dough down over her bare knee which gave them that peculiar flavor. I had supper with her and after all these years I can still taste those *tortillas.*

Then I asked her if she still had my saddle, or had somebody stolen that, too?

"The saddle is not stolen," she said. "There has not been a white man around since you left."

It may not be believed, but I heard a public speaker boast to a Chandler, Arizona convention that he was the past president of the association past presidents association.

I swallowed and yawned vigorously. I dug at my ears. Nothing happened. The man continued:

"It was my privilege, you see, to head a group of men who are former presidents of their state associations."

I fidgeted during the remainder of his talk.

"Forget it," said the Voice of Wisdom.

"Ask him," demanded the Hairy Beast of Impulse. "After the speech, when he is surrounded by well-wishers, go up and ask him. Ask him if there is an association made up of past presidents of the association of past presidents. If there is, ask him who is the present president of the association of past presidents of the past presidents association."

But I didn't. Looking back, I had to admit it was fear that kept me from it. Fear that he could prove the existence of such a group, name its chief, and give me the address of its Chicago director ($11,000 a year, plus expenses).

Think of almost any human problem or activity or interest. Somewhere, there is an association fighting or supporting it.

If we work, we can belong to one or several of hundreds of professional and business groups. If we're out of a job, we can join the Hobos of America. Wanting to drink quietly or noisily with peers, we can enter social clubs. Desiring to quit the stuff, we can join AA.

The simple owning of a car entitles one to membership in all sorts of societies. Serve a hitch with an armed service, and awaiting you at discharge is an organization tailor-fit to your temperament and tour of duty. The most casual interest in politics qualifies a person for membership in hosts of lobbies.

Just listing the societies and foundations and associations and fraternities set up for fighting disease, or boosting projects, or educating the public, would be a staggering job. Every church has its satellite societies. Every school, its organizations of parents and teachers and students. Every neighborhood, its special-interest committees. Yet all of these are a handful of sand to the beach, when compared with the great collections of people who are from Michigan, or breed cats, or play chess, or protect wildlife, or raise flowers, or drink more milk. We even save our money at the Christmas Club.

This may be the flowering of democracy.

Today, in this country, *every* boy and girl can grow up to be president.

Of something.

BUMBLE BEE—Mayor Charlie Penn pondered the wisdom of releasing a tentative fiscal report on his town.

"It's not something to be rushed into," he said. "I don't want to start a panic."

He stared thoughtfully out of the front window of the stone-and-frame building which is Bumble Bee's city hall, grocery, gas station, museum, sheriff's suboffice, tavern, welfare agency, chamber of commerce, ice cream parlor, land office and water department. He watched a cowboy named Jack astride a dark mustang chase three dwarf steers down Bumble Bee's dusty main street. Then Penn read and reread a hand-printed sign on the wall: "Free Whiskey Tomorrow."

"All right," he sighed. "I guess I might as well get it over with."

To begin with, Bumble Bee is 60 miles due north of Phoenix, west and within sight of the new Black Canyon Highway. Its history as a camping place for Indians, Spaniards, soldiers, miners, and stagehands is well recorded.

"Number of municipal gold mines remains the same—three," said Penn. "Amount of gold ore extracted in the current year—none."

Seven buildings and a vacant schoolhouse, on 230 acres

of patented land. Voters registered in the Bumble Bee precinct: 39. Population within the town limits: 10.

"Now that we have the remodeling and repainting done in the cabins," stated Penn, "you might say the population has stabilized."

Penn, a "magazine publisher in the process of retiring," and his wife, Helen, came to Arizona in 1954. Mrs. Penn was told that a dry climate might help her arthritis. After three days in Phoenix, Penn asked her, "How's your arthritis?"

"What arthritis?" answered Mrs. Penn.

Not liking Phoenix, the Penns began acquiring the town of Bumble Bee. They put up for sale their small mansion in New Jersey, and Penn began withdrawing from the operation of his publishing firm, which has headquarters in New York City, and a printing plant in Maryland.

Penn said he saw Bumble Bee as a resort town. He said he wanted to build a picnic area, and establish a model-railroad museum. (One of Penn's magazines is Railroad Model Craftsman, published more than a quarter century.)

But Penn and his wife said they would not hurry development of Bumble Bee. Penn said, with some pride, that he loses money on his store, and that at his last Christmas party at the schoolhouse, 270 persons showed up for turkey and presents.

The snuff-dippers down at Prescott station had a good laugh one day in 1919.

A large but unathletic lad stepped off the train, beat the dust from his Eastern-cut suit, and peered owlishly through thick-lens spectacles.

Tenderfoot, snickered the benchwarmers.

The youth ignored the smirks. He eagerly sized up his chosen hideaway, and he was pleased with what he saw. He was just turned 18, and he was running away—from books.

Prescott in 1919 wasn't bookish. The home and hangout of sons of pioneers and Rough Riders and rimrock cowboys, the mile-high town was still boot-tough beneath its thin veneer of gentility.

"If the folks in Naugatuck could only see me now," he thought.

In that Connecticut town he was known as a good, quiet lad who amused friends and neighbors with his experiments with the Marconi wireless. His home laboratory was a clutter of radio equipment and chemical apparatus. Eventually the strain of squinting at fine type and complicated diagrams aggravated an eye ailment. Severe headaches became almost continuous. A doctor ordered: "Read nothing for a year." Prescott, the youth decided, was far from tempting libraries.

The meeting of the youth and Ramsey Patterson must have been worthy of fiction. Patterson, two parts hardscrabble and one part vinegar, was typical of a breed of man nearly gone from Arizona. Small, wiry, close-mouthed, bewhiskered, he had spent more hours horseback than afoot. He was the first federal hunter hired in Arizona, and to this day he is remembered as the man who killed the last grizzly bear in the state. Patterson couldn't have overlooked the lad's glasses, his dude demeanor, his educated speech. Yet he could hardly turn down the youth's proposition: The boy would work without salary.

That year the hunter and his apprentice killed 16 mountain lions, a bear, and scores of coyotes and lynx cats.

They followed Patterson's nine hounds through every wrinkle of the Camp Wood area, up Turkey Creek, and through the Bradshaws. Once, when Patterson went to Prescott, the lad was left in camp with a case of beans. He ate them straight for breakfast, mashed for lunch, fried for supper.

Too, there were moments of high excitement. The biggest mountain lion was brought to bay on a boulder. The lad crept forward, "close enough to touch his tail," and began to raise his rifle.

The lion whirled. A shot rang. The big cat fell. Patterson had fired over the youth's head.

When the year was over, the lad had become a man—hard-muscled, mature, of vastly improved vision.

He went away, and did not return to Arizona for 28 years. And when he did, it was as a leader of a prominent electronics firm. He had continued his studies, pioneered in radio broadcasting and programming, taught a variety of college courses, developed the world's first FM police system, and headed the invention of the walkie-talkie battle radio.

Daniel E. Noble. Vice president of Motorola, Inc. Dan Noble. Lion hunter.

At Phoenix's Sky Harbor Airport, where Air Guard jets are based, a group of Arizonans gathered to talk about Jennies.

They had one thing in common: They all spent considerable hours in owning, crashing, repairing, flying, or just walking around on the wings of airplanes powered by an erratic 8-lunger called the OX-5.

Mrs. William Beard headed the organization of the Arizona chapter of the OX-5 Club of America.

OX-5 engines were mass-produced by Curtiss to power the Jenny trainers in the rush to send American pilots overseas in World War 1. After the war the used and surplus military engines were stuck on the fronts of a frightful assortment of civilian kites. Twenty years later students were still sprouting wings in the rickety OX-5 airplanes. The OX-5, "Model T of the Air," did for flying what Mr. Ford's flivver did for motoring.

Mrs. Beard, a good friend of Amelia (Lady Lindy) Earhart, soloed in an OX-5 International in 1929.

She recalled few "dangerous or amusing" experiences, aside from "the usual number of engine failures," but other club members tell tales to curl the crewcuts of today's hot jet pilots.

O. P. Johnson, 306 E. Verde Lane, said he was an American renegade with the Royal Flying Corps in 1917. He was given 4 hours and 10 minutes of dual instruction in an OX-5 Jenny in Canada, and went on to become a fighter ace in Europe.

Ben Hazelton, 4733 Cholla Lane, told of numerous forced landings after he learned to fly an OX-5 Travelair. One night, when the engine balked, Hazelton dropped a flare over Illinois. He landed unscratched. But, "That flare set fire to a corn field, and I had to pay for it. I don't believe the price of corn has ever been higher."

Dale Cortner, Tucson, in 1929 checked out in an OX-5 Eaglerock. Broke and hungry, he took work as a parachute stunter and wingwalker in South Carolina. He also scrambled around airborne planes on a rope ladder. He said he was fortunate he had the chance to quit after a year of dare-deviltry.

Bill Hixson, president and manager of Mercury Flying Service, in 1938 rebuilt an OX-5 International and flew it near Stockton, Calif. He said, "The airport was on a plateau. If the engine failed on takeoff, we'd just glide down to the river bottom. But a partner was brought in, and he hit a power line. As far as I know, the airplane is still in the river bottom."

Mrs. Ruth Reinhold, 333 E. Catalina, began piloting OX-5 craft in 1933, because she "wanted flying time and cheap flying time." She became a commercial pilot.

Wilbur E. Thatcher, airplane mechanic of Mesa, first left the ground in an OX-5 Standard. He barnstormed the Midwest, carrying fairgoers, parachuting, and as late as 1935, was training students in an OX-5 Waco.

Joe Wischler, Scottsdale, also a mechanic, learned in an OX-5 Eagle, and he remembered why the old V-8 cougher was so popular:

A new one could be had for as little as $35.

Harry Mehrtens went fishing, on a section of Tonto Creek trodden by thousands of flatlanders.

Luckily he found a quiet, vacant pool and made one cast in the direction of an Old Granddaddy trout whose shadow could be seen under a fallen log.

At that moment an elderly gent strolled by. His cocker spaniel gleefully leaped into the pool, then foundered in the rapids. Harry, who went to the dog's rescue, later complained:

"It's bad when an old man scares away your big fish. It's worse when his dog splashes into your pool. But when you go to pull out the drowning dog, and the dog bites you . . ."

"You can spend this belt buckle and still keep your pants up," said Gordon R. Chambers.

He displayed a nifty Western model which holds a silver dollar. It also epitomized the great variety of products of a Phoenix company which has had a phenomenal growth.

Chambers didn't exactly start in Phoenix with nothing. He had $65 and a high school diploma. He became the head of a company producing 3,000 belts a day, and distributing them to outlets in every state west of Big Muddy.

Chambers graduated from the high school in Freelandville, Ind., one night in 1926. The next morning he boarded a train for Phoenix.

"My grandfather had founded the town, but my father always told us to get out as soon as we had our diplomas. He said Freelandville wasn't going anywhere."

Mostly in search of a warm, dry climate, Chambers headed for Arizona. While attending Phoenix College, where he was student body president, he worked at a gas station. Later he cut short his studies at the University of Arizona to become a salesman. At the close of World War II, he quit his good-paying job, "and began looking for a business that would be typically Western."

A small shop producing rings and buckles seemed to be

the answer. He managed the shop, in a loft above an alley off Central Avenue, and took to the road as a salesman.

"I'd buy your buckles if you had belts to go with them," said a customer. The seed was planted.

Chambers mortgaged his home to buy his first belt-making machine. He locked himself in the loft until he learned to make belts. And big department stores in Phoenix and Tucson promised to buy what they could. One night in those early years Chambers and his wife, Veleska, were sitting in the yard at home after a busy, trying day. Chambers thoughtfully juggled the key to his business in his pitching hand.

"Shall I throw it as far as I can?" he asked. The house was hocked, the car was sold, and their personal savings were exhausted.

"No," she said. "Let's hold on a few more days."

In 1954 Chambers Belt Company moved into its modern plant at 2618 E. Washington. Growing sales predicated a doubling of plant size, and at times more than 50 were on the payroll.

"When I had nothing," said Chambers, "I believed in free enterprise. I still do. An opportunity is all anyone should ask for."

On an otherwise sane evening in June, 1957, Ted Cook announced in Show Low that he could devour a 4½-pound, medium-done, choice, sirloin steak within 60 minutes.

"I don't know what got into me," he groaned later. "I never did anything like it before."

Even if he was of a mind to, Cook had little chance to withdraw his bold boast. Before he could tuck in his napkin, a 72-ounce slab of beef was sizzling over charcoal, and other diners had laid side bets ranging from $5 to $20.

The main issue, however, remained between Cook and the Malapai Inn.

The restaurant-giftshop-cocktail lounge on the east end of Show Low had opened the month before, under the ownership of Mr. and Mrs. M. L. Encke. The Enckes also had a steak house in Mesa, where the steak-eating contest was a tradition. Terms were simple. If a customer could eat the steak in an hour, he didn't have to pay for it. But if he couldn't, he had to pay $12. In the years since the offer was made, the Enckes had met five challengers. Four failed. Then a quiet, middle-aged rancher from Casa Grande mildly insisted he was quite an eater. He was. He not only ate the steak—he put away a baked potato and a green salad, and gnawed the gristle and sopped the dish.

But, too, the Enckes had seen good men quit. A New Mexico eating champion made a special trip to joust with the Encke steak. He headed back to Socorro, leaving a pound and a half of meat, and a $10 bill and two ones.

Cook was an unknown quantity, even to himself.

He came to Phoenix from Chicago in 1955, when he was 28, was unmarried, and had a job in a store fixture company. He was lean of body, and had strong, even teeth.

A steak of competition size was six inches thick before cooking, which took 40 minutes. By the time it was ready, other diners had edged closer to witness the test, and to protect their wagers.

Cook began cockily. He soon settled to a methodical pace. Occasionally he rose and walked about the restaurant. He said he needed a rest.

Four times he sent the steak back to the broiler. At the end of the hour, when it was apparent Cook would lose, the Enckes graciously waived the time limit. After another half hour Cook admitted defeat. To settle side bets, the Enckes weighed the remaining steak. Fifteen ounces.

"I'm not overstuffed," stated Cook. "My jaws are tired."

He sportingly complimented the tenderness of the steak —there was simply too much of it, and "I always chew my food thoroughly." The bill was settled with no ill feeling. In fact, Cook returned the next morning and ordered a hearty breakfast.

It was hot—hot enough for mirages.

On Van Buren the hot afternoon June sunlight bounced painfully from the stream of gaudy cars, and a few of them broke from the pack to sprint northward on Sixth Avenue. Go, civilization. Hot or cold. Go.

"H. A. Jones. Blacksmith". The sign in front of Number 309 bore a quaint, old fashioned hand, pointing a finger down a narrow alley.

Twenty paces. The noise of traffic faded. Twenty paces more. A big door, open, darkly inviting, and from the cavern behind it came the measured ringing of steel on steel. Bink bink bink.

"Hello, youngster!"

His voice was as rich and loud as a bull's. His shoulders, rounded. His forearms, still square with muscle. His right hand held a sledge. His left hand, forefinger flattened to the shape of a spoon, gripped a hexagonal shaft. The point of the shaft, resting on the anvil, was cherry red.

"Be with you in a minute. Can't stop in the middle of a heat."

He resumed his pounding, drawing the facets of the shaft down to a perfect, six-sided point. Into the fire. Onto the anvil. Beginning the strokes of the hammer high above his head.

The glow of the point died in a flash of steam. He scraped the point with a stone.

"Know what I'm doing, lad?" he shouted. "I'm watching the color. The color is the temper! The temper is the color!"

Then suddenly the shop was filled with the stink of scorched oil.

He grinned, scrutinizing the finished point—a drill for a jackhammer—hard enough to break concrete.

"You have come to see me, boy. Oh, the boys who have sat and watched me work. The boys who came to see a real man work! Eighty years, I am. Fifty-six behind an anvil, and 56 years of steel and iron. A man who could lift 400 pounds, and half of it carrying a heat.

"They don't work like that anymore, boy. (And neither do I. Neither do I.)

"The horses used to be lined up for a block. 'Jonesey—hey! Jonesey, shoe my mare and mind the lameness in her off hind foot.' Fit the shoe to the foot, son, that was Jonesey's way. The young men were going to dances, and playing ball, and Jonesey was upstairs, late at night, studying the way God made the hoof of a horse. And the way men made steel from iron and carbon and blood and sweat.

"Ho, boy, those were the days! You made it from a bar of iron, and when it broke, you apologized and mended it free of charge. You made it last forever. I could do more with a forge and a hammer than they can do with a welding torch.

"But that day's gone, my boy. Must you go, too? May we clasp hands again!"

The gray head bowed. The hammer rose, fell.

Whatza mitzvah? Sam Block drew a deep breath. Explaining a Yiddish religious term to a transplanted Virginia gentile takes some doing.

"A mitzvah is a good deed. It is doing kindness to others without asking for any benefit for yourself. Going to a man's funeral can be a mitzvah. Or lending money without interest." Then, with some urging, Block told the story of the Jewish Free Loan Association. It was an answer for entrenched anti-Semites. Yet in the six years the association was in business, members kept mention of their deeds from the press. To seek praise might ruin the mitzvah.

Block and 13 others started the association.

"We all knew people who couldn't carry their financial burdens," he said. "They were good people, and maybe needed a little help over a rough spot until their luck changed."

Donations of the charter members amounted to about $1,000. From the beginning, loans were made to troubled persons, regardless of religion or race. A man broke a leg, was hospitalized for two months. He fell behind in his house payments. A mortgage company threatened to repossess. With money from the free loan association, the man kept his house until he got back on his feet.

A child was stricken by polio. Her mother was injured in an accident. The father could not pay the medical bills. He got through with an association loan.

A business man faced foreclosure. He kept the sheriff away with an association loan. A father or four, left homeless by mortgage foreclosure, borrowed $250 to buy a homesite, paid off the debt, and three others like it in building a new house.

A jobless, penniless, middle-aged man borrowed $250 and established a business worth $10,000. Another, who had been living on welfare doles, parlayed his association loan to solvency.

In no case did the association charge interest.

The association grew to a membership of 200, and to a lending potential of $10,000.

The work meant that every Sunday association officers must meet to make loans and take payments at the Phoenix Jewish Community Center. Block said the association needed no help, other than information leading to persons in financial trouble.

Thatza mitzvah.

not hospitalized for two months. He fell behind in his payments. A mortgage company threatened to repossess. With money from the free loan association, the man kept his house until he got back on his feet.

A child was stricken by polio. Her mother was injured in an accident. The father could not pay the medical bills. [illegible] got through with an association loan.

A business was facing foreclosure. He kept the sheriff away with an association loan. A father of nine, left homeless by mortgage foreclosure, borrowed $250 to buy a homesite, paid off the debt, and three years later is building a new house.

A jobless, penniless, middle-aged man borrowed $250 and established a business worth $10,000. Another, who had been living on welfare doles, parlayed his association loan to success.

In no case did the association charge interest.

The association grew to a membership of 200, and has a lending potential of $11,000.

The work meant that every Sunday association officers must meet to make loans and take payments at the Phoenix Jewish Community Center. Black said the association needed no help other than information leading to persons in financial trouble.

That is mitzvah.

Chapter Six

WILLIAMS AIR FORCE BASE—There I was. At 10,000 feet. Cruising at 350 knots. Clutching my brown paper sack. Needing to scratch an itch covered by four layers of web belts. The air conditioner was blowing little snowballs into the cockpit, but I was a Thanksgiving gobbler in aluminum foil. Sweat trickled from under the helmet. It cascaded off my brow, stained my flying suit, ran down my legs. I was close to throwing up.

What, asked the Voice of Wisdom, are you doing up here? You could be in a cool parlor somewhere interviewing a talking dog.

I was aware that my outlook was unromantic. People go up in jets all the time. Ladies, even. They tell about their exhilarating experiences in the wild blue yonder. But they don't strum my mandolin. I have always loved the ground and the feel of it under both size 10s. A lot of people are the same way. We fly, but we know that every airplane we board is going to crash. The engine is going to stop, and the parachute ripcord is going to part at the grommet. Go on. Laugh. We ground-lubbers may be in the majority, even in the air age.

The pilot must have sensed my fear as we walked to the T-33 two-seat jet trainer. His name was Capt. Ingvar Jacobsen. Naturally everybody called him Jake.

"Never been up in a jet before? Never flown much at all?" asked Jake.

"No, sir," and adding hastily, "So I'll be happy if you keep her straight and level."

"If that's what you want, that it will be," said Jake. He kept his promise, mostly.

Just a few minutes after floating off the Willy strip, we crossed the Salt River bottom. Jake sharply banked the airplane. I automatically groped for something—anything—to hang onto. I was held by four big straps to the seat and wanted more. It's strange. Very quickly the mind can reason with itself. It can begin to look and relax and enjoy. It can become brave and adventuresome. But the body of a ground-lubber is slow to learn. It clings and reacts to its stilted concepts of down, and up.

We flashed to Payson in 15 minutes, circled Punkin Center, toured Roosevelt Dam, and sailed around Four Peaks with the wings banked nearly vertically.

"Like to fly it?" asked Jake, over the intercom.

Gingerly I nudged the stick to the left. The T-33 tilted. I guess for 10 minutes Jake let me think I was flying the airplane. Then, misunderstanding his instruction, I released my grip. The T-33 flew itself.

When Jake suggested mild acrobatics, the mind wanted to say yes. The body, on consultation with the stomach, ordered no. Jake did a big apple and landed.

I had a fresh appreciation of jet aircraft, and of the officers and men who care for them, and fly them. I figured they were intelligent gentlemen.

But as an unreconstructed gravel-cruncher, I judged that the pilots are a wee bit crazy for doing what they do, every day.

Minnehaha Flats was once a pretty place.

At 5,000 feet, some 30 miles south of Prescott, Minnehaha Flats was thickly forested. Summer sunlight was filtered through mature pine and black walnut and oak. The air was cool and sweet. Minnehaha Creek rose from springs lined with watercress and grass.

All that was pretty in Minnehaha Flats exploded in a single day in 1955. Its beauty billowed to 20,000 feet, and darkened the sky as far away as Albuquerque, N.M.

Two years did not heal the scar.

Once-proud pines became black spikes, and the deciduous trees were stripped to charred, surrealistic shapes. The earth turned an almost uniform gray. There was the blue of the sky and the green of sprouting brush. Nearly everything else was done over grotesquely in black and gray. The brown-white hides of the bald-faced cattle ranging there were stained with black ash. The cattle would gather in scarce spots of shade to escape the sun which beat down upon a desolate land.

The one colorful object remaining in Minnehaha Flats was the home of Frank C. Lapham. Freshly-painted white with red trim, it stood out like a uniformed attendant in a madhouse.

Frank remembered the day the world caught fire. He said he would never forget.

"I looked to the south and saw what I thought were clouds. I turned to go into the house, and the truth struck me. It was fire. They came by pretty soon and told me I had better gather up what I wanted to save. I couldn't carry much. I just left the rest in the house."

Frank came back after the fire had passed through Minnehaha Flats. He came back and found his neighber, and fellow gold prospector, burned to death. Houses that had stood for 80 years were gone. Frank's was the only building left.

Peach trees whose limbs nearly touched a wall of Frank's home were destroyed. Fire took down a pine tree which grew three feet from the rear. A picket fence was consumed. Pine knots in the gable ends melted. But flames touched only the back door of the house, deeply charring the wood, then flickered out. Frank couldn't explain it; it just happened that way.

Prescott National Forest men called it their worst fire in 25 years. Seven hundred firefighters couldn't douse it, and 20,000 acres were burned.

Frank said he was a gold prospector, not a forester. He couldn't forecast the long-term effects of the fire. He did know that now every rain brought flash floods into the Minnehaha washes. Silt and muck filled a 400-foot-deep mine shaft that had been worked for generations. Grass seemed to have difficulty in sticking to the leached hillsides, or in the sand-choked flats. Rain puddles that used to stand for weeks were now quickly sucked up by hot winds.

By the looks of it, beauty had fled Minnehaha Flats for a long, long time.

Ammon Hennacy, 64, who for many years was known as Phoenix's One-Man Revolution, returned to town one day in July, 1957.

He visited friends briefly and quietly, and departed. The sighs of official relief in the offices of the Phoenix police, the Bureau of Internal Revenue, and Federal Bureau of Investigation, in total force, could have spawned a tropical storm.

Hennacy used to picket the post office building at income tax pay-up time.

"Seventy-five per cent of your income tax goes for war and the bomb," his signs read. "I have refused to pay income taxes for the past seven years."

Hennacy was in a position of strength. He worked in the

Valley only as a farm laborer, and taxes were not deducted from his pay. He would file a tax form, as required by law, and append a note explaining why he refused to pay taxes. He always managed to be broke when taxes were due.

A few times the police ran him in for questioning. After delivering lectures on the freedom of speech, Hennacy was back with his signs. Once revenue agents seized his signs as partial payment of taxes. Hennacy printed more signs.

Hennacy's visit to Phoenix in 1957 was not for the purpose of picketing. He was sight-seeing en route to his home in New York City's Bowery, after picketing the Atomic Energy Commission in Las Vegas and going on a hunger strike.

The AEC took pity on him and gave him a chair. One day an unexpected shift in wind delayed the firing of an atomic device at Yucca Flats. As the firing officer, a colonel, passed Hennacy's picketing post, he bellowed:

"That's one you stopped, Hennacy!"

Associate editor and street salesman for the Catholic Worker, Hennacy could look back on a life of conflict. At one time or another, he had been against everything.

Of Quaker parents, reared a Baptist, Hennacy heard Billy Sunday preach in 1909. Immediately, Hennacy became an atheist. He met a Socialist who was also a vegetarian. Hennacy became secretary of the Socialist Party in his home town of Lisbon, Ohio. He also became a vegetarian.

"I was against the killing of animals and for the killing of capitalists," he said. "I went to the University of Wisconsin and took military drills in order to learn how to kill capitalists. Then World War I came along, and it was the wrong war for me."

He spent two years in a federal prison in Georgia for refusing to answer the draft in World War I. While there he led a hunger strike and was confined to solitary for eight months.

"I was allowed to read only the Bible," he recalled. "If they had given me a cook book, I guess I would have become a chef. I became a Christian. When I came out, I loved the warden."

Hennacy said he carried a Communist card for a couple of years. But he quit, he said, and now had nothing to do with Communists.

"I am a Catholic. I am a pacifist. I am a Christian Anarchist. In Russia the enemies of the free worker are the bureaucrats and the Communists. In the United States, the enemies of the free workers are the bureaucrats and the capitalists. I don't believe in any government at all, and I am against violence of all kinds."

A Phoenix heckler drew the most revealing remark from Hennacy.

"Do you think you can change the world?" taunted the passer-by.

"No," answered Hennacy. "And damned if it can change me."

L. B. (Bar) Turley, facing one of his life's big decisions, found the solution in a 10-gallon hat.

When Bar Turley was 65 years old he owned, with his son, Jay, two famous old cattle ranches in east-central Arizona. Jay was busy teaching and studying at Brigham Young University at Provo, Utah, and also operating a farm there. The burden of ramrodding two vast rangelands became too much for Bar Turley. If not a time for retirement, he thought, it certainly was a time for slowing down. He had been a hard-working rancher for 45 years. Maybe he ought to sell the land.

Phoenix city-slickers heard about Bar Turley's intentions. They drove up to Turley's home in Snowflake and tempted him with ever-increasing bids. The offers were properly high. The ranches were in excellent condition.

One, the J-Bar, was in the cedars northwest of Snowflake. Here, the Turleys raised registered cattle. They had developed water supplies, burned out brush, and seeded with a prospering blend of grasses. The other, the Sundown, was a guest and commercial ranch near Tripine. Part of this land was homesteaded by Bar Turley's pioneer father.

The bids by the real estate men became ridiculous. Bar Turley put them off while he sought a way that would set right with his heart. Who had a better right to the land, he asked himself, than his neighbors? Those friends with whom he had camped at roundup? Those who had shared hay in hard times?

On June 19, 1957, at 5 p.m., a meeting was called to order in the parlor of the Turley home. Sixteen neighboring ranchers, some of the Turley Mormon faith, and some not, were there. Turley explained that he and his son had decided on what they thought were fair prices for the ranches. Their prices were thousands of dollars less than what outsiders had offered. Any neighbor wanting to buy the ranches, said Turley, was to write his name on a card.

The cards were collected. A cowboy hat was passed up to Turley, who put in the cards and gave the hat a shake. Bar Turley held the hat above his head and his wife drew the first name.

Lorenzo Decker was the winner. He got first chance at buying the J-Bar's 14 square miles and 100 head of registered stock for $56,000. Next, the Sundown's 7½ square miles, 125 head of cattle, and 80-head forest grazing permit was put up for sale for $61,000. Mrs. Jay Turley drew Virgil Flake's name first. Almy Bigler and Drew Shumway were alternates.

That's exactly the way it happened. Even those neighbors who lost in the drawing were pleased they were given an even chance. They stayed to celebrate the exchange of 21½ sections of land for $117,000, with punch and cookies served by Mrs. Bar Turley.

Jack Nelson collected two gallon mayonnaise jars of the little unwinding bands from the tops of cigaret packs.

Nelson was playing a long stand at a Phoenix supper club and one day he and other Valley entertainers put together a show for crippled children. Nelson came away with a desire to do something for the unfortunate.

"A gimmick," said Jack. "That's all we need."

"Well, I heard of a gimmick," volunteered one of his friends. "I heard that if you save a pound of cigaret bands, the American Tobacco Co. will donate an iron lung or a wheelchair to the hospital of your choice."

How such rumors are started is anybody's guess. They seem to live in the air, like yeast. One that keeps popping up has Reynolds Tobacco searching for a smoker who can blow three concentric smoke rings. Whoever can do this will get a free camel, or something.

Anyway, Jack wrote to the American Tobacco Co. Sorry, was the reply, there was no basis for the story.

By the time Jack learned this he had collected several thousand of the unwinding bands. He was going to throw them away, but another friend suggested, "I understand the blind people use those things in their handicraft work. They weave things out of them. They make flowers. They make whole paintings from them."

So Jack Nelson enlisted a legion of unwinding band savers. Six other Phoenix night spots put out jars where the bands could be dropped. Jack received envelopes, stuffed with unwinding bands, from Chicago, from a South Pacific island, from Portland, Ore., from Detroit, and from many towns in Arizona.

Folks stopped by where Nelson was playing to give him bundles of the strips. The jars became so full Nelson could hardly close the lids.

And then the dream evaporated. There was no use for the bands. The blind did not need them. No one would trade an iron lung. They would not buy a guide dog.

There was only one thing for Nelson to do. He played the blues. . . .

WHITERIVER—People would tell Silas O. (Si) Davis that lightning never strikes the same place twice.

"Yeah," he would say. "But I wasn't standing in the same place."

Davis was the target of two thunderbolts, and the experiences caused his attitude toward lightning to shift like a fickle wind.

"Until I was hit the first time," he said. "I never was afraid of it. After that I was really scared. Then the second one hit. I haven't been afraid of lightning since. I figure that surely lightning won't strike the same man three times."

Davis was hit the first time when he was a fire control officer in a tower in the Fort Apache Indian Reservation in 1937. Three years later he was telephoning from the agency office at Whiteriver. Both times Davis was knocked down.

(Davis died, of natural causes, in 1958.)

PINETOP—Kenny McClaren, 15, lived with his red-headed uncle between Pinetop and Lakeside in the White Mountains.

In Big Lake, Kenny swore, he caught a grand-dad of a trout that was equipped with its own hook, line and sinker.

From the physical evidence, Kenny deduced: The trout was hooked once by another fisherman. The leader broke in the fight. The fish swallowed the hook, but couldn't swallow the sinker. Eventually the hook was discharged from the trout's disposal plant. So there it was—a sinker hanging from its mouth and a hook hanging from its anus.

Kenny said he didn't exactly catch the fish. It caught him, by hooking its hook through a grommet in Kenny's tackle.

"Tasted just like any other fish," said Kenny.

WHITERIVER—Twice, the Rev. Arthur A. Guenther had his car stolen while he was holding services at one of his churches.

As pastor for Lutheran churches in Whiteriver, McNary and Maverick, he was associate to his father, the Rev. E. E. Guenther, pioneer missionary to the Apaches.

After the first theft, the car was returned with new tires.

Two days after the car was stolen the second time, it was brought back thoroughly overhauled.

Guenther said it was a struggle for him to preach in favor of the Seventh Commandment.

EAGAR—On a half a dozen counts, Milo Wiltbank of Eagar qualifies as an unusual poet.

He says it's hard work for him to write his own name. A cowboy by training and a highway department truck driver by trade, he puts down his verse in penciled longhand, and generally he composes a poem backwards. About his schooling, he wrote:

Years went by, I progress made,
Promoted me to the second grade.
And then it happened, the thing I'd feared,
The pencil sharpener caught in my beard.

Wiltbank's family came to the White Mountains in 1879. His father, W. E. (Pacer) Wiltbank, at 82, still ran 150 head of cattle without help. Because of early ranch work, Milo's formal education stopped in the first high school year. But as a boy Milo was an insatiable reader. He carried Shakespeare in his saddle bags on roundups and cattle drives.

"I've been writing poetry since I was a boy," he said. "But I've been saving the poems only for the last 10 years. I take a lot of kidding, and I tell my friends it's just a mild form of insanity."

In truth, his friends think the writings of Milo Wiltbank are the sanest utterances of this day:

My wife says, "Honey, while you're restin'
Do those dishes in the sink.
Now be sure to wear an apron,
Use the one that's trimmed in pink."

So while wifey was a-restin'
In her soft and easy chair,
I went in to clean the kitchen —
Found two aprons hanging there.

I don't 'low no darn woman
To tell me what to do.
Left the pink one in the closet —
Washed the dishes in the blue.

Wiltbank and his wife live in a house he built with his own hands. They have five children and nine grandchildren. Wiltbank is a councilman in the Eagar Ward of the Mormon Church. Understandably, much of his poetry reflects his love of hard work, family, and God. Yet he has humor:

A maiden knelt beside her bed,
In humble supplication bowed her head.
Prayed not in envy, hate or greed,
Nor asked for things she didn't need.

Said, "Lord, you've been to me so kind,
I wonder if you'd really mind
If I forgot your kindness of the past,
And of you another favor asked?

I want nothing for myself today;
It's for my folks that I would pray.
For my ma and poor old pa
O, send them, please, a son-in-law."

Milo Wiltbank wrote a poem about his neighbor, Trapper Bill, who decided to raise a skunk for a pet.

Then says I to Trapper Bill,
"I think your notion's swell,
But tell me, please, what will you do
About that awful smell?"

Do you think this worried him?
Well, not a doggone bit,
"This baby skunk," said Trapper Bill,
"Will soon get used to it."

He wrote one about Mandy, a working girl, whose husband sat at home.

I makes the livin', I does
But I does it with a smile,
For after all, it's Rastus that
Makes livin' worth the while.

Milo, a vice president of the Navajo County Historical Society, was active in other organizations. He wrote four lines that came to be quoted throughout the White Mountains by club leaders.

You have to respect a fellow
That comes out and says he won't,
But what do you think of a fellow
That says he will, then don't?

But Milo Wiltbank often places himself in danger of falling on his own sword of sharp wit:

If my neighbor would but live his life now,
The way that I could tell him how;
But if he forgot and lived like me,
What a hell of a world this world would be.

Having been a cowboy when the White Mountains country was wilderness, Milo took a dour view of some newcomers.

Cows were watering at an old windmill.
A dude stopped his car atop of a hill,
He turned to his partner and calmly said,

"Well, if this isn't something to knock me dead,
The West's gone modern, man, oh, man,
Cooling their cattle with an electric fan."

It would be an injustice to make Wiltbank out a joking runester, a man of no depth and breadth. One night the cowboy-truck driver lifted his gaze to the heavens.

Now I wonder, way out there, out there afar,
Way out beyond the fartherest star,
Beyond the reach of eye and puny mind,
Out there beyond, what would one find?
Would you find a world, a planet, or a place?
Or would you find just distance and empty space?
Oh, dare I wonder now, ah, puny mind,
Beyond the emptiness, and wonder what I'd find:
Beyond the rim of distance there afar,
Perhaps the glimmer of but yet another star.

Summer bachelors and some are not.

I anticipate a few hoots from those men who read this—those men who are eating a hot breakfast—those men whose wives are idly chattering—those men in freshly ironed shirts. Hoot away! But believe me, a woman is the timing gear of a man's motor.

I gaily put them on an airplane, those two blondes of mine. They were to spend seven weeks with the distaff grandparents in Wisconsin. I would join them later. They were crying when we parted, but I was smiling, smugly.

Free.

I'd do the chores at home, to be sure. (Anybody can do housework.) But I'd operate within my own schedule—not that of a headstrong woman, or that of a self-important 2-year-old.

I'd watch the ball games and the fights and the westerns, then turn off the Big Eye. I'd read a pile of old-new books. I'd catch up on the mail. I'd finally get those shelves built in the storage room. And maybe I'd spend a few nights out with the boys.

Things went along fairly well for 10 days. I am young and willowy and blessed with great reserve. Then I ran out of shirts. I looked out the front door and with horror realized I couldn't get through the lawn with a scythe. In the refrigerator was one can of beer, 12 gamy peaches, and a four-pound chuck roast, frozen.

One morning I came to work unshaven. That night, standing lathered before a dingy mirror, I discovered I was out of razor blades. "Why the deuce didn't you get some blades?" I almost shouted—to whom?

I began to make lists. Pay bills. Water flowers. Get grub. Write Jack. Sweep floors. Wash drawers. As I would do one of the things, I would scratch the topic from my lists. I mislaid the lists, before all of the things were done. The unfinished duties? Forever lost, transferred from mind to misplaced paper.

I think some of the lists were balled and thrown down amid the litter of newspapers and orange peels and dirty socks in the den.

And what of the projects that, at last, I had time for? Well, right off, let me inform the TV people that it is no fun to watch it alone. Mickey Mantle hits one over the wall. "Wow!" you yell, and feel queasy for 15 minutes. People—sane people—aren't supposed to talk to themselves.

The books. I couldn't concentrate without a child at my elbow, saying softly, "Da. Da. Da. Da. Da. Da." I didn't write letters, either. Nothing to write about. Every time I thought I'd fetch some lumber and build something, I'd ponder the mess I'd make. The mess that wouldn't be cleaned up, that would spread.

The boys. They were all married. To headstrong wives. The fathers of self-centered children.

I know all of this is heresy to the Cult of Maledom. Men

can shift for themselves, I told myself that morning at breakfast of slab cheese, corn crisps, and lemon pop.

Sorry feed for the ego of man.

Ross Cole's tavern at 3137 W. Glendale naturally was called Ross's Tavern, and the name of his dog, Ginger, understandably was shortened to Gin.

Gin would do tricks. She would play pool (not very well, having trouble keeping one paw on the floor) and she would sit motionless for hours on a bar stool wearing Ross Cole's eye glasses. She was a great favorite with the customers.

Gin's most impressive trick was carrying the receipts of the tavern to a nearby branch of the Bank of Douglas. In years of money-running, she never lost a dime, and no hijacker dared to interfere with the duty of a half boxer, half basenji.

"Dependable," said Cole. "She doesn't drink."

Mrs. M. B. (Ben) Neuenkirch never did think much of the idea, but Ben was a man of iron will.

"How can we go wrong," he argued, "for $125?"

The Neuenkirchs at the time lived in Waterloo, Iowa. He was a plumber's helper who always had steady work. The regular employment was the main reason the Neuenkirchs put off the thing they wanted most to do: come to Arizona. Then Neuenkirch was laid off.

They visited Arizona, found Ben a job, and returned to settle their affairs in Iowa. They sold many belongings, but some of the things they felt they had to keep. There were Mrs. Neuenkirch's new sewing machine, and their room air conditioner, and all of the personal treasures that a man and his wife and their small son can accumulate.

"Getting all that stuff to Arizona, I knew, was going to be a big expense, if I couldn't think of something," said Ben.

He bought a 1939 LaSalle. It was black as soot. The space between the back of the front (and only) seat and the rear door was 10 feet long and 4 feet wide. The man who sold him the car assured him it had never been driven faster than 15 mph, and had never been far out of Waterloo.

Ben, a handy sort, removed all the velvet finery. He stripped the exterior of 197 pounds of brass, which he sold for $35. He tightened a radiator hose, and replaced the starter.

The Neuenkirchs set out for Arizona. Ben had packed 2,000 pounds of belongings into the LaSalle. Beside him in the front seat proudly rode 7-year-old David.

Mrs. Neuenkirch refused to drive, or even ride in, the LaSalle. She followed, in the Neuenkirch Chevrolet, and drawing a small sleeping trailer which also was loaded with possessions.

"We didn't have a bit of trouble," said Ben. "That old LaSalle seemed to come alive for the first time since it was built. I'd clip along at 50 or 55."

After they arrived, Ben admitted he would never quite live down the experience. The Neuenkirchs weren't the first family to move to Arizona from Iowa, but they were the first to transport their wealth in a 1939 LaSalle hearse.

Judge J. W. Aker came to town, his coffee-colored goatee and mustache precisely clipped, his city hat stuck on the back of his head, his white-stemmed square pipe clinched jauntily in his teeth.

He hooked his wooden foot over the rail of a Tempe tavern. He shot a white, polka-dotted cuff through the sleeve of his pinstriped brown suit. He took a swallow of beer.

"Gentlemen," he announced, "I have the largest cabin in Arizona. At one time I had 21½ Akers under one roof. I consider myself only half an Aker, since I lost a hand and a foot."

Justice of the peace, educator, soldier, newspaperman, miner, rancher, farmer, political power of Eastern Arizona —Judge Aker has been them all. He brought to the autumn of his life a treasury of stories, enriched by a fast-disappearing, roll-it-around-your-mouth kind of Western demeanor.

A Virginian, he fought the Spaniards in Cuba, went to college, lost two limbs in a Pennsylvania mine accident, and fled westward when friends and relatives tried to make him a charity case.

He had lived in Greenlee County, principally in Duncan, since 1905. He built his home there in 1911. He was first school superintendent of that county, and served as J.P. of the Duncan district off and on for 20 years. When he was 76, he could count seven boys, two daughters, 21 grandchildren, two greatgrandchildren and 10,000 yarns.

"I wasn't always known as The Judge," said The Judge. "When I was superintendent of schools I was called The Professor. Once I took a high school class for an outing in the mountains. Naturally, I packed a quart of whiskey for treatment of snake bite.

"Well, after a week it looked like I never would get bit. One day I was fishing—had my attention on a tangled leader, and a kid shouted:

" 'Look out, Professor! You're about to step on a snake!'

"Sure enough, there was a big diamondback a-layin' on a rock. I put my wooden foot on top of it, so that about six inches of the head end of the rattler was free. The snake turned and struck my wooden ankle again and again.

"I said, 'Hurry up, you kids, run to camp and get a rope and that bottle of whiskey.'

"When they got gack I had killed the snake with my fishing pole. The kids tied the rope in a tourniquet around my pants, and they handed me the bottle. I took all that I dared to take. The kids didn't catch on until they had me back to camp and tried to dress the wounds."

Judge Aker was on the territorial committee which helped draft Arizona's school law. He sent all his children, who would go, to college. In 1939 one boy, Gov, was captain of the Arizona State College, Flagstaff football team, and J.W., Jr., was captain of the team of Arizona State at Tempe. When the schools played, the Judge maintained impartiality by changing sides of the field at half time.

The Judge retired in 1945. He built a summer home at Hannagan Meadows where he and his wife entertained friends, and as many Akers as could crowd under the roof.

It happened, said Francis Donnell, in the little town of Camp Verde, tucked in a pocket of the Mingus Range. Camp Verde had dozed for years in the high and dry sunshine—the home of a few Verde farmers and ranchers, beer stop for hunters and fisherman, and supply point for Yavapai Indians.

Then Camp Verde blinked to wakefulness. Tourists traveling the straight-shoot Black Canyon Highway between Phoenix and Arizona's north country began to discover Camp Verde.

Coit Wingfield was the deputy sheriff. He wasn't overworked. He knew all of the residents, and he kept a professional eye on strangers. He made his regular rounds. Camp Verde remained law-abiding, and Wingfield drowned the slower days in gallons of coffee, an hour and a cup at a time.

Wingfield could be quick, and severe, when duty demanded. But generally he was quiet and kindly—of the type of old Arizona sheriff who could solve more crimes by whittling and thinking than by pistol-whipping.

In all his years Wingfield never affected flamboyant dress. He preferred practical, dark, riding britches, a plain tailored shirt, walking boots, and in season, a straw hat. He speared a tiny gold star to his shirt front and carried a pistol in a black holster.

So dressed, Wingfield entered a Camp Verde cafe, and slid onto a stool at an end of the counter. The place was jammed with chattering tourists and townsmen. The waitress fetched his coffee without being asked.

At a table, Wingfield noticed, was a group of tourists. Probably on their first Arizona visit. One was a girl, and what a girl she was. A palomino, in her late teens, and her complexion that of a Cornville peach. Her big blue eyes darted everywhere—to an Indian strolling by, to the Western fixtures, to Wingfield.

"Oh, I have never seen a real cowboy sheriff in all my life!" she blurted. She rose, with a glittering smile for Wingfield. As she walked toward him, the cafe fell silent.

"Ah," she sighed. "They are so much nicer than the movie kind.

"Please. Won't you stand so I can see you?"

Wingfield was startled only for a moment. With a gallant flourish, he stood, still clutching his coffee cup in a smoked-ham hand. He towered, broad-shouldered and weather-beaten, above the slim, fair girl. A smile tugged at his own blue eyes.

"Wait till I tell my family in Sweden that I have at last seen a real western cowboy sheriff!"

For perhaps half a minute, there were only two people in that small, small-town cafe, and then the spell was broken. The girl blushed to her temples. Coit Wingfield's ears burned red, and his neck turned a richer brown, and his cheeks glowed.

"Turn off the lights," some wag shouted, and everybody laughed.

Coit Wingfield turned to attend to the best cup of coffee of his life. The girl left the restaurant, to continue her trip back to Sweden, and she probably never heard that her cowboy sheriff died within a year.

In case you didn't notice, newspapermen get vacations, too, same as working people.

First I flew to Detroit. At Albuquerque an angular, horny-handed old New Mexican boarded the airplane and took a seat next to mine. Together we admired the lush grass lands below.

"New Mexico must have had some good rains," I said brilliantly.

"Yas," he answered. "The roads got so muddy here last

month the ranchers couldn't get to town to pick up their drouth checks."

Chicago's Midway Airport is the most depressing terminal I have ever seen. They say it is the busiest airfield in the world, averaging a takeoff every 30 seconds. I had to believe it.

For several hours you have been dozing in the blue western sky, 2,000 feet above a 1,000-mile-long cloudbank, dreaming the lazy dreams of a simple-minded country boy, and then you plunge through the murk to Midway.

Then and there, all the romance of flying rubs off on the intense, shoving crowds, on the grease-gummed runways, on the walls of the dingy, dowdy corridors through which passengers hurtle to make connections to other cities. You ask directions of a stewardess who does not know, and from a porter who does not care. Because you are lucky, you find your airplane and, after a sweltering 30-minute wait on the ground, the airplane leaps into traffic. Again you are in the air, but flying will never be the same, again.

It is surprising how little Easterners and even Midwesterners know about Arizona.

One Iowa editor had the notion that Arizona bordered on Texas, and that Phoenix was sort of a watering place between Houston and Los Angeles.

I set him straight. I told him that Arizona is north of New Mexico, and that there is not a single drop of water to be had south of Grand Canyon, which, incidentally, is in Colorado. Furthermore, I said, Phoenix is not the principal city of Arizona; the biggest city is Tortilla Flat. Arizona is all sand, I continued. Endlessly rolling dunes of rippling sand. There are about 3,000 white settlers in the territory, counting cavalry troops at the Indian outposts.

A wise look crossed the Iowan's face. "You're pulling my leg," he said. "The Indians have been peaceful for years."

A fisherman in choppy water with two cane poles over

a school of ravenous crappie is busier than a one-legged man in a kicking contest. I flipped five fat beauties into the bottom of the boat before I paused for a breath.

"What happened to the fish?" I asked.

"Threw 'em back," said my uncle-in-law, George Christoph. He is brother to my wife's mother, Mrs. Albert J. Lenz of Menasha, Wis.

"Well, in Arizona we don't throw 'em back. People drive hundreds of miles to go crappie fishing. If they catch some, they eat 'em, or mount 'em." I was kind of sore.

"Yeah," smiled George. "But this is Wisconsin, and we wouldn't paddle a foot for a boatload."

You have heard of men who have it made. They might be wealthy, and own a town car and a country car. They change their clothes three times a day, and are seen in all the night spots. Maybe they have a town woman and a country woman.

Uncle George has all that beat nine ways. He lives in Neenah, Wis., a paper mill city which is about as big as Mesa, Ariz. Neenah is surrounded by waters which abound in game fish. And George owns a town boat and a country boat.

George is not rich. He is a general science teacher and dean of boys at the high school. He has been teaching for more than 30 years, but he is still dark-haired and built like a Green Bay blocking back. He teaches swimming summers.

He keeps his town boat at a dock in the city park. It is a 12-footer with a 7½-horsepower motor. When George wants to go fishing, he needs to take only bait, usually worms that he grows in his back yard. He drives a few blocks to the dock, lifts three interlocking plywood lids from the boat, and buzzes out into the Fox River and this country's biggest lake—Winnebago.

Weekends George drives out to nearby Lake Poygan, where he has a cabin and under it his country boat. This boat is bigger. George built it of one-inch strips of Wisconsin white pine over hardwood ribs. At the stern is a 25-horse Johnson.

Again, for fishing, all George needs is bait. Poles, seats, slickers and extra gas are kept in the boat. He can be on the water almost before the echo of the car door's slam dies.

Wisconsin has several kinds of bass, walleye, northern pike, muskie, trout, sunfish, roach, perch, bullhead, cisco, catfish, paddlefish, herring, and myriads of rough fish. George has caught most of them and thrown most back. By law, the muskie has to be 30 inches long to be retained.

A couple of winters ago George towed his 6-by-6 open-bottom shanty onto Lake Poygan's ice and stopped all the cracks with snow. He sawed a hole in the ice, and waited, holding a harpoon attached to 100 feet of stout clothesline.

Pretty soon George opened the shanty door and flopped an 80-pound sturgeon onto the ice.

"It wasn't very big," said George. But he confessed he did not throw that one back.

Chapter Seven

BUCKEYE—You could hear the roar of his engine, they say, three miles away.

And when he skidded around the corner, chickens climbed fences, and stallions in the stud barns snorted, and the Mexican irrigators wiped their eyes with their red handkerchiefs. William B. Long was standing stiffly on the porch steps, pulling at his handlebar mustache, when the car shuddered to a stop.

"A room for the night?" asked the driver, expertly flipping up his goggles.

"Our pleasure," said Mr. Long. That night, while Barney Oldfield, the most famous racing driver in the world, slept upstairs, all the Long children took turns sitting in the racer parked out front.

In September, 1957, the old Long home was torn down.

The cedar shakes and pine timbers were sold to second-hand dealers, and the crude baked bricks were given away by the truck load. Heaps of plaster and foundation were hauled to the dump. At the site of what once was the finest home and hotel in Buckeye, was built a modern one-story rambling ranch house.

William Long homesteaded 160 acres southwest of Buckeye, and was nearly wiped out in the great flood of '91. In 1900 he brought his wife, the former Nellie Hurley, back to the ruined land. They built the house two stories, 17 rooms, with a bay window looking out onto a wide porch with pillars. They filled it with their children and guests. Buffalo Bill would stop in frequently, and Bucky O'Neill practically was of the family. Anybody who was anybody prior to statehood wrote his name in the Long registry.

Two of William Long's sons still remained on the land. Marshall has a home north of the old hotel site, and the house over the old foundation is Bob's. Marshall, a freckled bachelor nicknamed Junior, collected relics: horsecollars, pot-bellied stoves, pitchforks, grinding wheels. Probably more than anybody else, he hated to see the homestead destroyed. It was the biggest relic on the place.

But as he said, "The foundation was giving way, and if it wasn't torn down, it would have fallen down."

"Have you ever wondered what happens when a person is suddenly rendered speechless," Fred Olson of Douglas asked, by writing on paper.

"A recent blow on the brain from within (a stroke) produced that malady for me, causing a series of cans and can'ts, as follows:

"Can't—yell at dogs or children, argue with wife, win arguments, sing, tell stories, make speeches, try out a good line on girls, or yodel.

"Can—ignore arguments, win every fight with my wife,

turn down requests for speechmaking, act like I don't hear so good, and throw small stones at dogs.

"So far I rather favor the cans."

A couple of sharp operators led "The Meanest Horse in the West" into Willcox one day in 1912. They sold rides outside a saloon, down by the depot. They offered $25 to any man who could stay in the saddle.

The horse threw all takers. Then somebody whistled up John deGraffenried. John got a leg over, and they turned the horse loose, and it sunfished around a telegraph guy-wire, but John stuck like honey. He won his prize.

Next day the sideshow opened for business 30 miles south, in Pearce. The operators again made their offer, this time to a knot of miners.

"Twenty-five dollars to any man who can ride this horse," they said.

"I can ride that horse," said deGraffenried, stepping from behind a tree. He did, too—up onto the boardwalk and through the window of a barbershop.

That $50 was the first money deGraffenried made in Arizona. Horses are still his business. He and his longtime admirer and companion, his wife, Ethel, live on the flats east of Mesa in a little desert ranch house which also is the office for the Superstition Mountain Pack Outfit.

They keep iron-lunged mules and mountain ponies. DeGraffenried takes dudes into the Superstitions. At the appointed time, he rescues them. He gets a lot of Lost Dutchman Gold Mine trade.

John doesn't ask questions. He packs 'em in; he packs 'em out. He said he truly likes his customers, especially tenderfeet who are willing to learn. He shows his friendship by telling stories: of his days as a Texas Ranger; of the time he sat on a boxcar in Douglas and watched a Mexican war; of the grand hour when he, as a rodeo roper, was presented to royalty in England in 1924; of his great uncle, the man who killed John Wesley Hardin; of the yarns he used to supply to a good friend, Will Rogers.

Furthermore, John deGraffenried believes in his work.

"There is gold up there. There may be no Lost Dutchman Mine, but there is a treasure of gold up there to be found. I hope I'm not the one to find it. Probably ruin my pack business."

George S. Curtis habitually rocks and thinks on the porch of the home he has owned at 25 W. Holly since 1931.

He is in his mid-80s. Some things amuse him. Some things make him sore. Phoenix Towers, apartment house dominating the northern Phoenix skyline, amuses him. Insults directed toward Doc Holliday and Wyatt Earp make him sore.

Curtis was one of the last visitors to Doc Holliday's deathbed.

"I had spent some time in Tombstone, and other places in Arizona," said he. "I was in the coal business in Colorado Springs when a friend said I ought to go out and visit with Holliday, who was dying of consumption. I went several times. He was a perfect gentleman. There wasn't a more polite man ever lived. We talked about old times, but he never mentioned the killings."

Curtis saw Wyatt Earp once in Phoenix. It was in the '20s, in front of the old federal building. Earp was waiting in a car, and a friend led Curtis to the car for a look at the famed frontier marshal.

"Earp was friendly and quiet—that's all I know firsthand, but what I'm getting at is this: I've heard enough to know that a lot of people shooting off their mouths today don't know what they are talking about.

"They are taking turns making nasty remarks about these two men. I'm no judge of their character, but I'll say that nobody would have the guts to insult them if they were alive today."

Curtis thinks modern presentations of frontier times are distorted.

"The lawless West! Now that amuses me," said Curtis. "It's true that a few men were killed, and they were generally the men that society didn't miss. Women and children could walk the streets unmolested. You could leave your door unlocked. It wasn't anything like what happens on the streets of Phoenix now."

Few men used holsters. They stuck guns in their belts and pockets, and more than likely, left the hardware home. Bar scenes in television westerns especially amuse Curtis.

"All those women in pretty dresses. Why, you hardly ever saw a woman within 300 feet of a saloon, and those you saw wore Mother Hubbards."

Curtis doesn't remember the Indians being as ferocious as they are made out these days. Twenty years before statehood Curtis was riding alone when he met six braves who were hunting illegally off the Fort Apache Reservation.

"I went along with them. I was afraid not to. All day long we conversed in grunts and sign language, and by night I was sure I wasn't going to get away alive. We were sitting on a stump around a fire, and one of them turns to me and says, 'Why don't you relax? We are all graduates of Carlisle Indian School.'"

A schoolteacher had a flat tire on Tempe bridge.

His language, as he pulled into a little roadside park and went to work, was private and peppery. A highway patrolman stopped and silently watched the toiling teacher.

"Well, what the hell do you want?" snapped the teacher.

"Nothin' much," said the patrolman. "I just want to see a man change a flat front tire by jacking up the rear end."

Mrs. Alice Prosser of Prescott owned a cat that would sit and watch television.

Then the cat took to climbing onto the top of the set and

hanging down, watching the programs upside down. Finally the cat learned to turn off the set and stalk into a bedroom.

CHARLESTON—If you are very, very lucky you shiver awake before daylight and arrive on the banks of the San Pedro River as the sun is softening the edge of an early November frost.

You are luckier yet if you have a woman who will go along with your pointless adventure.

Gnarled cottonwoods grudgingly release their yellow confetti to the fitful gusts, and the San Pedro chuckles over the sand bars and gravel beds, meandering northward through the hardy streambed brush.

Old Charleston. There was a town too tough for Tombstone.

According to Historian Joseph Miller, the Tombstone Law and Order League rode out of Tombstone one day to subdue the gay, wicked fortress of the outlaws. John Ringo stood alone at the Charleston end of the bridge that spanned the San Pedro.

"Come on," Ringo addressed the 50 armed men. "I'm a-waitin'." The Law and Order League rode home.

And now, somewhere across this wrong-way river, in the mesquite thickets on a 40-foot bluff are the ruins of the town that had 13 saloons, no jail, one church, an ever-changing number of brothels, two hotels, a store and shops, and a dance hall.

"How do I get across?" she whines.

And you, fortunate male, say: "I will carry you. Seventy-seven years ago you could have made $100 an hour in Charleston—just by dancing."

The San Pedro chills you to the knees. On the Charleston side your woman laughs as you dry your feet with a handkerchief. Then you search along the bluff, find a cow path, and climb.

"There it is," you say, in a reverent tone that must make the Charleston specters howl and roll in the sandy, curving main street. The 15 adobe shells are of a kind—some smaller and larger—but all rectangular, with gaping door and window openings, and floors filled by fallen roofs. Fifty-year-old trees burst through walls, and here and there are nests of weathered lumber where wooden shacks collapsed.

Charleston, 11 miles west of Tombstone, was a milltown. Here the silver ore was concentrated, and troopers and miners and dozens of men named Bill Smith played and plotted. Even boys packed guns, and Professor Witherspoon enforced one of Charleston's few rules—students at his school were required to check their sidearms. An Eastern writer, after a short visit, fictionalized Charleston as "Red Dog" and Tombstone as "Wolfville."

"It's creepy," says your woman. So you lead her down the main street that has seen none prettier, and pack her through the clear water to the car.

Directions would do you no good. Every man ought to find Charleston in his own way.

Juan slumped, head in hands, in a chair on the porch of his ranch house.

On this mile-high plateau, misery was seeded in the soil. One minute a hot gale would be sucking the red sand from between the bunchgrass clumps, and the next, sheets of rainwater would be crumpling into the *arroyos*.

Expecting misfortune, Juan had staked his homestead and turned loose his scraggly breeders a few miles east of Holbrook. He handbuilt his modest home. In the summers he hauled water and fought predators. In the winters he hauled feed and broke the frozen spittle from the muzzles of his cows. And for all of that, Juan had never known trouble such as this. Because of his son's carelessness with a six-shooter, his daughter now lay dying.

The wound in her foot would not heal. The closest surgeon was in Phoenix. Her fever rose, and on this black day in 1905, Juan tried to close his ears to the ravings of a delirious 9-year-old. He prayed.

"Buenos dias!" So intent were Juan's supplications he hadn't heard the cowboy approach.

"No good," said Juan. "My daughter she is seek."

The cowboy looked at the girl. He knew that whatever could be done must be done quickly. He switched his horse into Holbrook and looked up Bill Cross.

Cross was the town barber and unlicensed undertaker. He probably knew more about human anatomy than anyone else in the rough railroad town. Conrad (Doc) Hess, the druggist, agreed to help. The two men prepared for their mission of mercy. From Hess's stock they took a bottle of chloroform, a needle, tape, cotton, and silk thread. At a Chinaman's cafe they borrowed a bone saw and a sharp knife. They rode to the ranch.

"Que pasa?" demanded Juan.

"The leg must be removed," said Cross.

Juan looked at the grim pair of townsmen. He studied his mumbling daughter.

"Adelante," said Juan.

Cross and Hess severed the leg above the knee. They stayed with the girl through her most perilous hours, and saw her take her first nourishment.

The next time they met the girl, she was at a dance, wearing a cork leg, matching steps with a handsome vaquero.

And today, Ben R. Hunt, Navajo County supervisor, who tells this story, can lead you to the *muchacha*-who-almost-died. Hunt, nephew of the late Bill Cross, will introduce you to her, to her children, and to her grandchildren.

Ben Vance, who works for the state, said he wouldn't trade places with the governor. It isn't the pay; it's the variety.

He was hired as circulating librarian in the spring of 1957, and thereafter he drove his blue-and-white bookmobiles thousands of miles, from Short Creek to Portal, from Window Rock to Somerton.

"At Camp Verde I met an old prospector who didn't want any books, but was happy to take a few apples," said Vance. "At Pearce, I met an old storekeeper who didn't want any books, but was happy to share his bologna and cheese."

They were exceptions. Most of the people Ben met wanted books. They snapped up his offerings hungrily, greedily. Hundreds of miles from big cities, and served at best by small, poorly-financed libraries, these people too often had to go without. With federal help, Arizona's state library set up an extension service at 1619 W. Washington. New books. Staff of nine. Trucks and a station wagon. And Ben.

"I have held babies while their mothers browsed through the stacks," Ben said. "I have waited on some people who were so weak I had to lift them up the stairs.

"At Cascabel, a little girl rode horseback to meet the bookmobile.

"An Indian girl at Peach Springs, married young, the mother of a papoose, checked out a book called, 'How to Get a High School Education at Home.'

"At Rock Springs a giant, greasy mechanic asked for a book of poems. In a single day at Parker, I checked out 579 books."

Ben said he didn't know who was benefitting the most—Arizona or Ben Vance. "I'm learning how much this state is changing, believe me. Last week on the Navajo reservation I saw an Indian man walking behind his squaw."

Almost, I thought, like the old days.

Dr. Aubrey Roe socked the cruel-looking, curved needle into the ragged wound in the 2-year-old baby girl's jaw. The baby screamed. Her eyes were submerged in puddles of tears.

I held down her feet and right arm. The nurse anchored the baby's left arm and passed equipment to Doc Roe. Doc and I have done these things before. We are pros.

When he was an intern at Memorial Hospital I was paddling after the sirens on the police beat. We met professionally often. Late one night a drunk victim of a Buckeye Road knife fight was brought in. It was close to deadline.

"What's the story?" I drawled, in what was supposed to be Gene Fowlerish nonchalance. Doc Roe didn't look up from his crocheting on the patient's throat. "Shut up and help," he ordered. I sat on the man's thrashing legs and watched the doc's neat needlework and wondered what excuse I was going to give my boss for missing a near-murder story. Later Doc Roe and I sat in the cafeteria and we talked about his days in Canada. We had two cups of coffee apiece, and he bought.

But now, there was a difference. The wound wasn't so large, and neither was the patient. She was my daughter.

Doc hooked the needle, deftly formed the special knot, and snugged down the second suture.

"What's the story?" he said lazily.

Shut up and sew, I thought, and said: "Chain-link fence. Climbed to the top and slipped."

The girl tried to get up from the operating table. Her face was of that alarming beet-color I hadn't seen since colic. "Mama!" she wailed.

"Daddy's here, doll," said I.

"Mama!"

"Mama is outside holding down her cookies." She was, too—with both hands.

"How is everything with you these days?" asked Doc.

"Oh, fine. Fine," I lied.

"Hear any new jokes?" He drew up the last stitch.

"None that I could tell in front of the nurse."

My mouth was dry and my arms ached from holding just so much, not too much. My Maw did something akin to this for me once. The debts we owe our parents we pay our children.

Doc stuck on a bandage and handed the snuffling kid a sucker.

"Thank you." She remembered. Then, licking her candy,

she proudly displayed her operation to 20 people in the waiting room.

There are savers in this world, and there are throwers-away.

The savers are the oppressed. I know. I'm a saver. Fifty-one card decks. Merit badge affidavits. Extra aluminum brackets for a radio installed in a car sold long ago. Wide neckties. Corks. Bolts. Scraps of wire.

Mrs. Lee Berls, of 221 Kachina Lane, Scottsdale, is a saver.

She went to a white elephant sale and paid five cents for an old whiskey bottle. It was blown to the shape of a log cabin in 1860, and once contained the squeezin's of one E.G. Booz.

Mrs. Berl kept that bottle 10 years. Berl, who is something of a thrower-away, one day was reading a national magazine article having to do with old bottles.

"Darling!" he exclaimed. "All is forgiven. Bring out that bottle and kiss it. It says here bottles like that are worth up to $160."

Mrs. Berl's voice was bitter-sweet:

"When we moved, I threw it away."

Some day we may hear from some tyke fishing for panfish in the lagoon of Phoenix's Encanto Park.

Wham! The monster will strike.

There will be a great tug on the line. The pole will droop, and the surface of the city's lazy duck pond will erupt, as if someone were tossing in a string of cannon balls.

The monster is a monster bass. It has no name. It is called The Bass.

In late 1956 Tommy Orr, of Phoenix, was fishing on Lake Carl Pleasant. He caught The Bass, which weighed six pounds. Most any other fisherman would have taken his prize home and slapped it across his wife's face, and shouted: "See, I told you and I told you and I told you!"

But Orr carefully released the living fish into his water-filled ice chest, and hurried down to Pinney & Robinson Sporting Goods in Downtown Phoenix. This pioneer Arizona outdoors shop traditionally has displayed game fish in a large aquarium. Orr knew that the shop was in need of a lunker largemouth bass.

Thousands of sportsmen enviously ogled The Bass.

Bill Pinney, store manager, would wait for a knotting of anglers at the tank, and then he would stroll over and dunk his hand. The Bass would lunge for a digit. Sometimes Pinney would hold his hand a foot or so above the tank. The Bass would leap clear out of the water.

In November, 1957, Pinney & Robinson gave up its downtown location, principally because of a shortage of customer parking space. The company moved to a shopping center, Park Central, where there was a shortage of space for displaying fish. The Bass had to go.

Bill Pinney fed the fish 12 salamanders two days in succession. One night he dumped The Bass in the lagoon.

That poor kid.

FARAWAY RANCH—We talked, and the twilight slowly faded until we were sitting in the dark.

"Forgive me," said Mrs. Lillian Riggs after a while. "I have been thoughtless." Mrs. Riggs is blind, and for a woman who has lived so many years, minutes hurry by like swallows.

She was in her 70s, blind, and going deaf. Yet she was still riding and ramrodding ranges totaling more than 10 square miles of grass. Her parents were the Ericksons, both Swedes. Her father, Neil, came west as a cavalryman. He wanted revenge for his father, killed by Indians, but when Neil Erickson's enlistment was up, the Apaches didn't have a better white friend.

When he took a wife, together they picked a glade up a Chiricahua canyon 35 miles southwest of Willcox. Here they raised their cluster of sturdy buildings and reared their flock of adventuresome children. As the years passed, the ranges fell to the management of Lillian, and her husband, Edward M. Riggs.

They fought disease, drouth and governments. They carved the first trails into nearby Wonderland of Rocks, and it was mainly their doing that this magnificent work of eruption-and-erosion was set aside as Chiricahua National Monument.

Mrs. Riggs wasn't sure, but she believed her blindness had its beginning with a riding accident in 1932. In 10 years she was blind. Mr. Riggs died in 1950. Mrs. Riggs carried on.

She managed the Faraway, headquarters of the far-flung ranges. Cottages there were rented to tourists who took their meals at the main house. The summer range was out in the valley northeast of Pearce.

"I ride—almost every day," she said. "I'd ride oftener if I felt I was strong enough. I depend on other eyes. I rely on the judgment of my brother, Ben. But in any business, only one person can make the decisions, and I make the decisions."

Once she asked her banker: "Am I a fool for doing this?"

The banker said, "Financially, you're doing fine. And it gives you something to think about."

It gives the world something to think about.

One million empty bellies. Filled.

Farm workers. Winos. Deserted kids. Prostitutes. Penniless travelers. Criminals. Out-of-luck hometowners. Abandoned wives. Mexicans and Negroes and Jews and Anglos and Orientals. God's poor. From 300 to 1,500 every day for five years.

A plate of mulligan and a slice of bread, and a doughnut or an apple, and the repeated assurance: "Come back for more; eat till you're full."

This is Phoenix's St. Vincent de Paul Charity Dining Room. It has a Grade A health card, and no cash register. No religious sales pitch. No lectures. No promises demanded. The only requirement is an appetite, and the highest price is a simple thanks.

Fifty or more of the Valley's leading citizens showed up Dec. 15, 1957 at the dining hall, at 115 S. Ninth Ave., to commemorate the millionth meal. A broken - nosed cook looked up from his stewpot.

"This is the highest class bunch of bums we ever had," he said. He surveyed the collection of county supervisors, former mayors, power company veeps, businessmen, and leaders of the Catholic churches.

". . . But it goes to prove," added the cook. "We let anybody in here."

The dining hall is Phoenix's last wall at the brink of starvation.

Vincentians of the Arizona parishes support the hall. Food is collected from food growers and distributors—people of all faiths. Most of the work at the hall is done by men taken from the chow lines. Only small salaries are paid to the manager and his wife. For many, the meal at the dining hall has been a turning point:

—A doctor from another state, on the bottle, sobered on the stew and sent back to his home and practice.

—A family of seven, broke, sick, hungry, and 500 miles from their destination, given meals and medicine and sacks of sandwiches.

—A train traveler, robbed of all his money, given food and a loan, which he repaid with interest.

—A man bent on suicide, given food and shelter, and now happily returned to a fulltime job.

"We know undeserving take advantage of us," said a Vincentian spokesman. "We give no thought to that. We only pray that one person might have been helped."

To the memory of the dining hall's inspiring first manager, John Bedway, a plaque and a statue were dedicated. He died in 1956, perhaps the most beloved man south of Washington Street. The millionth meal was served by his successors, Mr. and Mrs. William Wirries, who were made in Mr. Bedway's mold. Despite what is said of the second million, they didn't seem a bit worried.

The address of Frank and Poko Petek was 7551 N. 13th St., but that was no help at all.

They told friends to come north on 12th Street to Belmont, then east three tenths of a mile, then south through a small, deep sand wash and on down through the chaparral.

You knew their place by the big gold gong out front. The gong was made from an old Coke sign, and it was supposed to be whanged.

Frank, muscular, bearded, was covered with colored cement. Poko, slim, dark, was touched with oil paints.

The artists came to Arizona to remake their lives. He was from Chicago; she from Alaska. They met and married in Tucson and went on a camping and wine-drinking trip to Old Mexico. They stayed until their money ran out.

After the giddy honeymoon Frank enrolled at a Phoenix art school. Poko taught herself. In 1950 they bought three desert lots on a high slope north of the city. Days, they hauled in soulful rocks and weathered wood. Nights, they sat close and talked and dreamed of the house they would build.

Then their rent downtown increased again, and the Peteks moved out to their chunk of desert before the house was built.

First they made a shed, with a stone floor and a tin roof. They painted and hung their gigantic doorbell. Frank made an outside bathtub in the ground, and screened it with evergreens. He put an old Chevrolet gas tank in an insulated box, painted it black and covered it with glass. When the sun shone, their water was scalding hot.

Their house rose slowly, a stone at a time. One floor was made of gravel, and one wall was to be of glass. The masonry walls were made a foot thick, and each stone was selected as a friend.

The Peteks did not own a television set. They said they

would never own one. And no telephone. Their plumbing was outside and flushless. The shed and unfinished house were drafty.

Since they moved to the desert they hadn't had a single day's sickness, not so much as a cold. At night, a lizard would come to a shaft of moonlight and catch insects at the foot of Poko's bed. There were so many scorpions, the Peteks stopped killing them.

Frank, a sculptor, chiseled and carved in metal, wood, stone, and freshly-poured concrete. He drew ideas from nature, and freshness from the very old. Poko compressed her being, like a toothpaste tube, and it tumbled from her brush.

In recent years success overtook them, but when I visited them they were working 16-hour days, and in their spare time they were prowling the desert in search of building materials. They did not have many things other people had, and they said that may have been the principal cause of their happiness.

Chapter Eight

DOUGLAS—"We'll go to Douglas," I told my companion.

"We'll stop at the Gadsden Hotel Bar and order beer. I'll not pay for it. You'll not pay for it. The bartender will not pay for it. Nobody in the bar will pay for it. In fact, nobody in Douglas will pay for it.

"Yet it will be paid for, and we will get some change back."

My pal just shook his head when it worked out as promised. We went into the place and Smitty was on duty. His name is Walter E. Smith, and he is remindful of Charles Coburn without glasses. Smitty reached up and took down an envelope from one of the row of hooks. He shook a dollar bill from the envelope.

"This was left here for you almost a year ago," said Smitty, a hurt expression crossing his pleasant features.

"Every morning I hang it up, and every night I take it down. I thought you never would get here."

In a way, Smitty was bragging. His buy-a-friend-a-drink service sets the Gadsden bar apart from all others in Arizona —maybe the world. Here's the way it works:

You are sipping a short one and you get the notion to pop for ol' Walt or ol' Jack, but they are 30 or 900 miles away. So you ask Smitty for one of his envelopes and a fat, black crayon.

Smitty will guard the enscribed envelope, you may be sure, for a week or a month or a year, until the lucky stiff shows up.

The service doesn't increase business, said Smitty, and the work is mountainous. Smitty locks the envelopes in a drawer every night, and every morning the envelopes are returned to their hooks.

"Conversation," Smitty said. "Every envelope has a story."

Most of the presents are claimed within a few days. But some have been in Smitty's care for years. Only once did Smitty violate the trust. One night Smitty and a buddy were thirsty for a free drink. An envelope more than a year old hung temptingly on a hook.

"That guy probably never will come in here, whispered Smitty. "Let's spend it."

Three days later the rightful owner hammered on the bar for his envelope. Smitty hasn't dared to pilfer another.

A well-off rancher who lives near Douglas has added a wrinkle to Smitty's drink service. The rancher, when he has a fat roll of cash, puts $20 in an envelope and addresses it to himself. It is insurance against the days when the rancher's wife is keeping close books on his bad habits.

Mr. John Olney, 11, businessman of considerable reputation in his home town of Sunnyslope, expanded his business to the big city.

He got on a bus, rode to the heart of Phoenix, and stepped out into the post-Christmas, 1957, throngs.

He shyly let three prospects pass. Then, fearfully:

"Shine, mister?"

"Sure, but make it snappy."

Three minutes later Mr. John Olney returned his paste, brushes, rags, and bottles to his homemade wooden kit. His first dime felt thin and lonesome in his denim pants.

Mr. Olney had a crew cut which looked like a Kansas bird's nest. He had, by hasty count, 4,236 freckles in the space between his upper lip and forehead. On that day he wore a mostly-white T-shirt and scuffed tennis shoes.

He was small for his age. At Sunnyslope Elementary, where Mr. Onley was in the sixth grade, he did not lose any fights because the other kids knew better than to start anything.

By his own testimony, Mr. Olney was an exceptional student. The truth was, "I never get anything less than a C minus."

It was a long day, beginning chilly and foggy, and never becoming warm. Mr. Olney kept moving. The dime in his pocket found a twin. By midafternoon, Mr. Olney had earned $4.30 plus his bus fare home.

When the sun began to slant he moved into office buildings. He closed out the day with $7.26. Expansion of his business was a success.

That night, riding home on the bus, Mr. Olney sat on his shoe box and carefully folded the $5 bill over the singles, and put the 26 cents into his left pocket. Then he folded the singles over the five, and put the 26 cents into his right pocket.

Once he thrust a money-stuffed fist under the nose of another man, a perfect stranger, on the bus.

"Do you know how much is here?"

"No," said the other man.

"Seven dollars and 26 cents," said Mr. Olney.

At home, Mr. Olney went directly to his savings bank. He hesitated. He put the key back in his watch pocket. He took his mother, Mrs. Minnie Olney Shade, and stepfather, Ralph Shade, to the movies.

To many Arizonans, he was just plain Joseph. Those who make out a check to him learn his full name: Joseph Guastella. Not a dozen people west of the Mississippi knew he was Joe the Barber.

He used to slide a straight razor along the shady jowls of Humphrey Bogart, and trim the precious curls of Leslie Howard. Amelia Earhart would tell that Franklin D. Roosevelt, her childhood playmate, was irresponsible. Peter Lorre would feign terror as Joe stropped the razor. Big Bill Tilden would top the sports stories of Gene Sarazen.

And Joe the Barber would listen, smile, and go on with his work.

Frequently book and slick magazine authors would collapse in Joe's chair and talk while Joe wordlessly cut and combed. Then the writers would go back to their typewriters and write stories about what Joe had said.

That was long, long ago.

Joseph Guastella was born in New York's Lower East Side, the son of Italian immigrants. His father was a barber. Joseph started in his father's shop. Soon he had his own place.

In 1934 Frank Case of the Algonquin Hotel asked Joseph to take over the barber shop and women's salon in what was, and is today, the favorite quarters of theater folk in New York. Nearly everybody who was anybody came to Joe at least once. Joe the Barber became an institution, even after he moved to a new shop on Long Island.

Arthritis came over Joseph with the suddenness of a head cold.

His arms locked across his chest. A lot of his dark, curly hair fell out. When the disease was at its worst, Joe the Barber had to fall to all fours to climb stairs.

He saw the doctors—the vitamin salesmen—the blood purifiers—the electric machine quacks—the heat pad artists.

Finally a friend told him to go to Arizona. That he did, in 1948. He was broke. While waiting to take a barber's exam, he got a job selling refrigerators. In three months he didn't sell a single refrigerator.

As soon as he was licensed, he went to work for Korricks. In 1956 Joe the Barber, under the alias of Joseph the hair stylist, opened his own uptown Phoenix salon.

He recovered his health in Arizona, he said, "and I wouldn't go back to New York to live if they gave me the city, the hotel, and my old name back."

Tommie Jewell said he was happy because he was satisfied with what he had.

"I jes' float along and do my job and don' worry about things I cain't do nothin' about."

Leaning down from six feet three had given him a slight stoop. He had a long, handsome, medium-brown Negroid face, skin as smooth as velvet, and bright, even teeth.

Slim, as he was called around the Phoenix railroad station, laughed often. He would toss his head back and let it go. Sometimes in laughter he would whack his thigh.

He was born in Georgia in 1905, the son and grandson of field laborers. He had eight brothers and one sister. Slim knocked around the South as garageman and handyman until 1918 when he went to Milwaukee, where he thought he would get a better deal. He did, for a while. Then his wife developed a lung disease and doctors said the only hope was in a move to a dry climate. Slim took a job in 1926 cleaning coaches for the Southern Pacific in Phoenix. The move to Arizona didn't help his wife. She died within a year.

Slim stayed. Thirty-two years later he was still washing coaches for the S.P. He said he would go on cleaning cars until retirement.

"Now that sounds like I'm not getting anywhere, don't it," said Slim. "That's not the way I look at it. I've got a nice house down at 1420 S. First Ave., and a good woman, my present wife, Maude.

"I've been everywhere I wanted to go. I could have been a porter but there's too much traveling to that. The railroad has taken me all over the Southwest. They ask me to go along on the special cars and trains, and I've been as far as San Francisco on those jobs.

"When vacation time comes my wife and I show our pass and go where we please. We went back to Chicago and Milwaukee, and went back to the South. Went up to San Francisco one year.

"Every year Mr. Russell, he brings his special car down for bird shooting south of Chandler, and he asks me to go along. He says he wouldn't have nobody else touch his car except me."

Slim laughed when he thought about his being a grandfather.

"My boy, I wanted him to be a doctor. But there wasn't enough money for that. He went to the University of Arizona and taken his teacher's degree, and now he is instructing in an Indian school in Albuquerque. Now I'd say that was getting somewhere."

Slim threw back his head and laughed. He smacked his leg.

YARNELL—"I have the power," said Alissio Carraro. "It was given to me directly from up above."

He held a machete in one hand and a short-handled ax in the other. Chunky, frowning, almost belligerent, he was convincing as all get out.

"Yes, sir," I said. Carraro dropped the tools and sat on a boulder and fussed with his pipe. A tiny black puppy frolicked with his shoe strings. A bird sang. Carraro smiled, a broad grin invented, patented and monopolized in Milan, Italy.

He was 75. He came to San Francisco in 1922, and within six years had the second largest sheet metal shop in the Bay area. He hated the pressure, and in 1928 he came to Arizona and bought 277 acres between Phoenix and Tempe.

Working without plans, and drawing inspiration from each sunrise, he erected the place known as "Tovrea's Castle" east of the stockyards. The house, atop a hill, took on the lines of a wedding cake.

"I had the great dream," said Carraro. "I was going to subdivide the land and build fine homes. The money I lost! The depression came along and I sold the place in 1931, and today it is all worth millions and millions."

At about that time, he was given the power.

"I hold a string to a bob. I sprinkle water on my hand, and the plumb line begins to vibrate, and the water structure of the land for miles around is revealed to me. It is as clear as television."

As a water witch, Carraro said he won fat fees for finding wells in Arizona and Mexico. He said he found 35 wells for one company in the Maricopa-Casa Grande country in 1945.

His sensitivity for the beauty of nature and skill with natural materials brought other jobs. He was asked to put his touch to stone structures all over Arizona. A monument to his craftsmanship is the Desert View lookout atop Yarnell Hill. He supervised construction of the roadside park for the highway department.

In 1956 Carraro bought most of a little granite-covered hillock near the Shrine of St. Joseph of the Mountain.

"All my life I searched for this place," he said. "I wanted to build a grotto. People told me I couldn't build a grotto in Arizona, yet here I have built a grotto."

He cleared brush, and made paths and steps, and filled terraces. His grotto was a small cave under huge boulders. He studied the rocks on his hill until he perceived shapes of animals, and then he had a man neatly paint the names of the animals on the rocks.

Carraro lived alone in a trailer at the foot of his mountain. Nearly every day he labored, clearing more brush, setting more stones, enlarging his grotto.

"I have the power," he repeated, reaching again for his machete.

ASHFORK—The man who tries to sock the operator of the Green Door Bar here is putting his life on the line.

Chances are, a knot of ferocious old men will fall upon the antagonist with their canes, with their bar stools, with their broken beer bottles. When they are done there won't even be a face on the barroom floor.

The barkeep is a lady, Mrs. J. E. Brownd. To the gimpy, rheumy clientele which idolizes her, she is Ruth. Compared with her fanatically loyal fans, Mrs. Brownd is young. She and her husband, who died in 1957, shared the chores of the tavern from 1934. They had four children, all now grown. After her husband's death, Ruth ran the bar alone. In 1952 she married Brownd, who had a rock quarry and oil distribution business. Mrs. Brownd continued to run the bar.

The bar is in the middle of Ash Fork and it gets a sizable tourist trade. But the bulk of the business is in serving residents of the Ash Fork area. A large number of old men hang out there. Some drink. Some don't. Some like to just sit and gossip. Many of the oldtimers are employed in the flagstone quarries near Ash Fork. Mining slabs is hard work for young bucks, and numbing labor for men of middle years, and killing toil for oldsters.

"I guess that's what got me started," she said. "Knowing how hard they work."

She asked one old man why he didn't apply for old age benefits.

"Tried to once," he said. "Couldn't get it."

Mrs. Brownd drew him out. She learned as much as she could about the old gent. At her insistence, and with her help, he reapplied for a social security pension. Soon it was approved, along with a check for the years he had missed.

Since then Mrs. Brownd helped about 20 men to qualify for old age benefits.

Some of her beneficiaries couldn't tell her where or when they were born. Mrs. Brownd obtained the required affidavits and filled out the forms.

Almost every man she helped received a check representing the time he should have gotten a pension. One man got a check for nearly $2,000, and others drew as much as $400.

"I never considered what I do as anything but a hobby," said the best protected barmaid on Highway 66.

A German shell demolished the kitchen of Battery A, 340th Field Artillery Regiment, Horse Drawn.

Tin Him, cook, peeked out of his dugout and appraised the rubble.

"Victoly fo' us!" sang the Chinese from Mesa. "Jellies use $25 shell. Brow up $2 kitchen."

Hundreds of such stories were swapped when veterans of the 340th met in Nogales, for the first reunion of the gang in 40 years.

Forty-seven of them came from homes scattered through nine states. They checked into the Rancho Grande Hotel and never left it for three days. They didn't even go across the border. What, after all, could Mexico offer men whose minds are filled with memories of cooties, horse gas masks, *vin rouge*, and *petites filles?*

They told why the regiment was recruited in Arizona during World War I. The army, remembering the fabled know-how of the Rough Riders during the Spanish-American War, wanted a similar group for duty in France. Cowboys, the army figured, would make ideal handlers of the horses which would draw the French 75-millimeter artillery rifles.

Bartenders, store clerks, railroaders, miners—and Tin Him—signed up. There were few cowboys. But the Arizonans quickly learned the difference in ends of horse and rifle.

They served in France almost a year, and fought in the

bitter St. Mihiel and Meuse-Argonne campaigns. Two of the men won Distinguished Service Crosses. When the unit retuned to New York in May 1919, it was met by Gov. Tom Campbell of Arizona. Most of the men returned to Arizona. Some drifted.

One corporal, Eldridge A. (Edward) Akers, decided to keep in touch with his buddies. He had entered the 340th at Douglas, and after the war moved to Yreka, Calif. The reunion chiefly was the result of his persistent appeals.

Eighteen lived in Arizona. Others came from California, New Mexico, Colorado, Texas, Washington, Oregon, and Nebraska. George Osmas traveled all the way from Toledo, Ohio.

Activities included a reunion dinner, and memorial services for two men of the 340th—Lon Parker, Arizona border patrolman who was killed in 1928, and William Know, who died in Nogales in 1956. Lt. Col. Orville A. Cochran, National Guard operations officer of Phoenix, spoke on the battle history of the 340th. He said the regiment's battle streamers are on prominent display in the guard's military museum.

Arizona men who attended from Company A, were E. E. Ryan, Tempe; Harry Caldwell, Douglas; Otis Barkley, Phoenix; James Royer, Cottonwood; Homer C. Sheffield, Mammoth; Gus Taylor, Tucson; Sebe Musgrove, Somerton; Ralph Mair, Miami; Tee Hinton, Fort Thomas; James Maxwell, Coolidge; and Joseph H. Lee of Tucson.

From Company B were William Farrell, Fort Huachuca; C. E. Barkley, Phoenix; Lyle Sprung, Tucson; Allen C. Clark, Tucson; John Mercer, Globe; John Stall, Chandler; and Hoyt Pilcher, Phoenix.

The Wagoner store is half an hour from the highway and 60 years behind the supermarket age.

You turn right off U.S.-89 at Kirkland Junction and wind east and south for 14 miles. The road is unsurfaced, but well-maintained. Do not blink. You might miss the Wagoner store and post office.

The single story building was painted, here and there, white. Out front was an old-fashioned gasoline pump—the kind with a glass bulb at the top, and by it was a Model A Ford.

There were two doors. The one to the store was locked. The other led into the quarters of H. W. Cole, 81, proprietor, notary public, and historian.

"I do not know how old this place is," he said. "I came here 56 years ago and the place was old then." He sat in an easy chair before a blistering-hot stove.

"If you'd like to look it over, go ahead."

The store was unattended. The battens had fallen from the rear wall and sunlight shafted onto the shelves.

There was a gingerish smell to the place. Most of the shelves were bare. Several opened cartons of foodstuffs were on the floor. Some red cans of coffee sparkled on the rear wall, and on another were cans of vegetables and fruits.

Along a wall ran display cases and a counter. A hand-powered coffee mill was on the counter, and nearby were an aged cash register and bins which once held beans and flour.

From the rain-stained ceiling beams hung a mobile grocery ad, and magazines stacked on one shelf were swollen to double thickness by frequent wettings. Tin had been nailed over the roof shakes, but it leaked anyway.

The Wagoner store was built on a rise a mile above the site of the Walnut Grove Dam.

One of the first high-country dams of the West, it was made of earth and stone, in a straight line between narrow cliffs bordering the Hassayampa. The water it stored in its two-square mile lake was to be used in placer mining, and for irrigation of 500 acres downstream.

On Friday, Feb. 21, 1890, an assistant superintendent of the dam construction company feared that the rain-soaked dam would burst. He dispatched two messengers to warn residents and workers downstream. One was not believed. The other tarried at a tavern.

At 2 o'clock Saturday morning the Walnut Grove Dam collapsed. A wall of water, sometimes 100 feet high, raced down the little watercourse. More than 70 persons died. The dam was never rebuilt.

Cole came to the valley after the disaster. Today it is seldom that a customer comes into Cole's home, gains permission to enter the store, finds what he wants among the clutter, and pays Cole as he sits by his stove.

"Doesn't worry me," said Cole. "Business never was any good."

"It's as strong as a fort."

"Yes," said Delfino Contreras. "That's why we call it The Alamo."

Arms akimbo, he leaned back and gazed lovingly at the massive stone walls. They are 18 inches thick, nearly 15 feet high, are 78 feet on the long side, and 72 on the short.

"All ours," Contreras said. "Every pebble."

Contreras worked hard all his life, in the lumber mills, as a postman, in a filling station, and mostly as a jack-of-all-trades construction worker. He and his wife saved for, and built, a grocery store in downtown Flagstaff.

Illness of the eldest of their four children forced them to move to Phoenix, in 1953.

"First," said Mrs. Contreras, "let's buy a fine house."

"We can have a house and business both," her husband suggested.

He bought the business lot at 4321 N. 27th Ave., just north of the Indian Drive-In Theater. There was a small house toward the back. Contreras hired out as a stone mason, and the family saved.

Contreras began hauling in the stone in his 1946 truck. He made 65 trips up the Black Canyon Highway and to the Scottsdale area. Each time, he loaded six or seven tons of stone onto the truck, and delivered them to his lot.

The cornerstone was placed at the northwest corner. By the time the walls were finished, 440 sacks of cement were laboriously mixed to mortar by hand.

Some of the stones weighed hundreds of pounds. One fell on Contreras' right hand and mangled two fingers. He put that stone at the very bottom of the wall at the southeast corner.

"That's my way of getting even," he said, kicking the stone. "It has to carry all of the weight."

At the north end of the building was put a barber shop, a business for the two Contreras boys, David, 25, and Fernando, 23.

In the middle was a beer tavern. The southern part of the building was to be a restaurant, serving Mexican food, prepared under the supervision of Mrs. Contreras.

Mrs. Contreras was unashamedly proud of her man. Of Angle-Saxon parentage, she was born in Concho, a decaying little town in northeastern Arizona. Her dad was a cowboy. With Delfino, she had learned to speak fluent Spanish.

"I come from hard-working folks." she said. "But that man of mine outshines anybody I've ever seen."

Said the little, muscular brown man whose dream was built of 423 tons of stone:

"Without my wife's help, I am nothing. I didn't even finish school, and I can't speak good English. All I'm good for—"

He drew his hand across his forehead and flicked away some imaginary sweat.

The distance was about 30 feet. Tex Burton Bond reared back and threw the carpenter's hammer at the sow.

The hammer bounced off the sow's ruddy rump and she jumped, grunted, and ran to safety.

"I'd kill you," roared Tex. "But I'm not set up for butchering!"

This was a bad morning for Tex Bond. The night before he had been at work. When he got home his ailing wife was crying. The sow had broken its pen, upset barrels of feed, scattered debris over the back yard, and slain $50 worth of chickens.

Now Tex faced a morning of fence-mending, chicken-plucking, and hog-hating.

Tex was his given name. He was 87 years old. Love him or leave him, he could claim to be one of the busiest men in the Valley. Most men a third his age couldn't keep up with him.

A watchman by night, he ran four cattle, chicken and swine ranches, including his leased home place at 1440 E. Encinas by day. One ranch was more than 100 miles from Phoenix.

"When a man stops working, everything else stops," he said. "I am ready to run a footrace with any 19-year-old."

Tex said he was born and educated through college in San Antonio. He had been a homesteader, law officer, Indian adviser, bus line operator, and rancher. He liked most to talk about his days in show business.

"I made the best of the circuits, big and small, and Tom Mix and Will Rogers were my good friends," he said. "We weren't particular what we rode.

"One show had a standing offer of $100 to any farmer who had a horse one of us couldn't ride. Down in Austin once a farmer led a buckskin mare into town and said she couldn't be rode. We drew tickets to see which one of us would get the $5 for riding the horse.

"I won, and then lost. I was doing pretty good until the mare put her front feet through a loop of guy rope and she fell on me. I broke both legs, both arms, both shoulder blades, had an eye almost gouged out, and my nose was broken."

Tex rolled up his sleeves to show the scars. His arms were as gnarled as redwood burls. He was short, had a comfortable paunch, and he wore his belt under it like a cinch strap. His eyes were pale blue.

"I had only one tooth for 30 years. Hated to lose it, but

the doc said it ought to come out. I lost the rest of them bulldogging and riding."

He freely admitted that whiskey had been an elixer in his long life. He said he drank whiskey 50 years until a doctor told him it would kill him. He quit, suffered his first bad sickness, and dragged himself in the nick of time to a package store.

He smoked two packs of cigarets every night. But he added proudly, "After sunup, I never smoke."

Mary Kidder Rak died in January, 1958, age 77, in Douglas. Her ashes were scattered on the land she knew and loved so well, but she will be remembered as long as there are libraries to lend books, and people to read.

No other Arizona author has told his story so convincingly to so many adoring followers as did Mary Kidder Rak.

She was a timid city girl who came West for her college education. Following graduation from Stanford University, she threw herself into a career of social work in San Francisco. In 1917 she married Charles Rak.

He was a cowboy. Temporarily, he was studying forestry at the University of California, but he was a cattleman's son, and he looked with mild contempt on those unfortunates who "didn't know a cow."

For a year they took indoor jobs in Tucson—he as a forester and she as a university teacher.

In later years, they agreed their lives did not really begin until they acquired the Old Camp Rucker Ranch. Their 22,000-acre empire was the highest spread in the Chiricahua Mountains, five hours and 56 miles by truck from Douglas, through 13 gates across 10,000 chuckholes.

Charlie Rak was like the swimming kid. "I didn't learn. I always knowed."

Mary was frightened by all of the animate, and most of the inanimate, elements of the wilderness ranch. She had to learn. And as she learned, she wrote down the lore just as it came to her, in a natural, clear, and believable style.

She told of the struggle to raise cattle against the odds of pinkeye and blackfoot and wolf and drouth and deer hunters and thieves and blizzards. She described the cattle as individuals, and the OCR "Old Charlie Rak" stock were pictured with characters as complex as the few neighbors.

The Raks first lived in the rambling headquarters building of Camp Rucker. When fire destroyed it, they were forced to move into a house so small "you couldn't curse the cat without getting fur in your mouth." It was here that she wrote the immortal *A Cowman's Wife*.

This and other books earned her a spot in *Who's Who*.

"We get up at 4 o'clock, cook and eat breakfast and do the indispensable chores of milking and feeding horses and chickens. Kettles of water are heated to warm the cockles of the truck's heart. A hind wheel is jacked up; motor oil is drained and warmed on the back of the stove until the whole house reeks like an engine-room at sea. While I dress in my town-going garments, Charlie pours boiling water into the radiator and warm oil into the crankcase. Then he cranks, cranks, cranks! I dash out to sit in the car with my finger on the gas throttle, warming up the motor. Charlie lowers the hind wheel to the ground; then goes inside to warm his half-frozen hands, put on a necktie, and his best shoes. We are on our way."

And like the front door of the OCR, her books were left ajar to the hungry and tired.

Cowboys are notorious for their poor memories for names.

Bud or Partner or Pal or Stranger suffice—a hangover from the days when it was downright dangerous to know a Westerner's real handle.

Frank Allen retired from the rodeo circuit and took a job as head wrangler at Rancho de los Caballeros near Wickenburg.

"Frank," his boss told him one day, "we've got a very important guest. You remember his name. It's Colonel Armstrong."

The wrangler memorized the name. He repeated it aloud as he did his chores. "Colonel ARMstrong. Colonel ArmSTRONG. Colonel *ARMSTRONG.*"

Next day Colonel Armstrong appeared at the corrals.

"Howdy," shouted Frank, rushing up with extended hand. "I'm Colonel Armstrong."

Chapter Nine

CHAMPIE RANCH— It is not every day that a man has to soak the tail of a rattlesnake, and to this fact Francis D. Hyde attributed his cheerful nature.

"Once was enough," said Frank.

He used to be a broker with a seat on the New York Stock Exchange. In the '30s he took his biggest flier. He closed his business and came to Arizona to find and mine metal. The sledge coarsened his hands, and the weather tanned his face, but he kept his Northeastern twang. He established main diggin's about 6 miles from the Champie dude ranch.

"We had killed a rattlesnake on the morning we were visited by a doctor from the American Museum of Natural History of New York," said Frank. "He was collecting specimens.

"We showed him around the mine. He was a pleasant sort until he saw the dead rattlesnake.

" 'You fools!' he shouted. 'Why did you kill that snake?'
" 'Because we didn't want to be bitten,' we told him.
" 'Well, that is a very rare kind of black-tail rattlesnake, and I want to find its mate for the museum.' "

The second snake was cornered, and according to Frank, the doctor pinned the snake with a stubby, rotten stick.

"Hold that ore sack," commanded the doctor.

Frank reluctantly obeyed. The doctor swept the writhing reptile into the poke.

Frank said he thought that would be the end of it, "but I was the only one in the party with saddlebags. The doctor put the sacked snake into my pack, and I got up on my horse, a skittish roan mare.

"The snake buzzed, and the horse broke into full gallop.

"I couldn't stop her. She came down the canyon faster than she ever ran before, down that canyon that drops 700 feet in the course of a few miles. Thirst, I guess, finally stopped her at a little spring. It must have been a half-hour before the doctor caught up."

The naturalist was angry. "That was a terrible way to treat a rare museum specimen," he shot at Frank. Then the doctor removed the groggy snake from the saddle bags, revived it, and held its tail in the spring water.

"You know," said Frank, "those rattles became soft in the water, and no matter how fast that snake wriggled its tail, the rattles would make no noise. We brought in the snake without further trouble, by stopping to soak the snake's tail in every water hole along the way."

If anybody doubts this story, said Frank, he can prove it by showing them the water holes.

Sam Feilhart died the way he lived—scared.

The police called it suicide. Others called it murder. Delayed. But still murder.

For no apparent reason Feilhart wounded his best friend. Then he shot himself in the chest, and when that didn't get the job done, he picked up another gun and put it to his head. The friend recovered.

I first met Sam Feilhart in 1955 shortly after he came to Phoenix from New York City. He was so short he could walk under my arm. He had opened a trinket and clock shop at 326 W. Washington. He aimed at a $10 gross each day, and sometimes he closed early when he made it, and sometimes he closed late.

He had a suggestion for treatment of U.S. Communists.

"Round them up. Send them to Russia. Just three days. Then bring them all back here. Poof. No more communism in the United States."

Sam was there. When the Nazis invaded his native Poland, Sam fled eastward. The Germans killed his mother, his four sisters, and a brother. Sam was picked up by the Russians.

"We are put in railroad cow cars. So many people, so little room. January. Many kids die, and when the train stops, they are thrown out."

The trains were no longer overcrowded when they arrived in Siberia. For a year Sam felled trees and dragged them to a river. His shoes were made of old inner tubes. He was so hungry he ate grass. His weight dropped to 80 pounds. He was not mistreated because he was a Jew, he said: "We were all treated equally. French. Czech. German. Dark. Light. They treated us the same, like dogs, like stones on the ground."

His life was saved at the entry of the United States in the war. Because of Allied pressure, Poles were released from Russian prisons. Sam was sent to an Asian butter factory. He said his trunk was his bed, and his forearm was his pillow. Once he was three minutes late for work, after he ripped his leg in a fall. Only by stripping in court and showing the injury d.d he avoid another six months in prison. He stayed at the factory until his liberation at the end of the war.

He scraped and saved, hoping to go to Israel and start a

printing shop. But the equipment he sent ahead was lost at sea. He was not allowed to go to Israel without money or equipment. He came to America, to New York. Sinus attacks drove him to Phoenix.

By then, he was a grave, untrusting man. He came to believe that even visiting social workers were persecuting him.

I could almost hear again his ruptured English of the day we talked: "This is my life in Russia." He picked up a brush by a single bristle. The brush swung like a pendulum. The bristle broke.

"But I did not break," said Sam Feilhart.

He did at last, in Phoenix.

A rally at the state capitol by Arizona State students March 4, 1958 reminded oldtimers of a sensational outburst 19 years before.

On both days the school of higher learning at Tempe was seeking a change in name. Back in 1939, Arizona State Teachers College at Tempe wanted to drop "Teachers" from its handle.

A group of students, led by the captain of the football team, Wiley Aker, for several days pressed their opinions upon any legislator who would listen. When the bill came up for bitter debate, Aker and five of his chums were in the gallery.

Sen. Daniel E. Rienhardt of Gila rose and directed his remarks to the students. He said Aker and his followers were unduly pressuring the legislature. He said their lobbying was illegal. He accused Aker of being a stooge for Dr. Grady Gammage, president of the college.

Aker fumed. He went downstairs; got a drink of water. It didn't cool him. He walked into the senate chamber and in a voice that carried to the corners, he said to Senator Rienhardt:

"You're a damned liar."

Then Aker gathered up his buddies and drove to Tempe. Aker ate lunch, and when he returned to his room, Senate

Sergeant at Arms Frank (Two Gun) Gillick was waiting for him. He handed Aker a subpoena, charging him with "conduct unbecoming a gentleman on the senate floor."

Meantime, as a result of Gillick's campus inquiries, news of the subpoena had spread. A cavalcade of angry students followed Gillick's Model A Ford as it returned to the capitol with Aker.

In the senate, Aker was marched to the front and seated.

The accusations droned. (One senator was so incautious as to say, "A senator is not responsible for what he says." Later his hometown paper thundered: "Upon what meat doth this, our Caesar, feed?")

Some senators wanted to press criminal charges against Aker. Another senator, from Aker's home county and a friend of the family, asked for moderation. Would Aker apologize?

"Yes," said Aker, a trifle in awe of his starring role. "I'm sorry for the way I said it. Maybe I should have said plain prevaricator. I'm sorry I called the senator a liar.

". . . But it's true."

Aker was let go with a warning. After graduation he did well in the mining business, and became an assistant superintendent in an Eastern tungsten mine. At the time of the outburst, Dr. Gammage gave Aker a sharp lecture.

"I never encouraged or condoned the boy's actions," said Dr. Gammage. "The school lost good will, and possibly appropriations, because of the incident. Nonetheless, I've always had a warm spot in my heart for Wiley Aker."

TOLLESON—This town's first public library was so small the librarian had to leave so that a reader would have room to browse.

Between shelves there was space for a card table, and two pre-school children.

Nine years later, in 1958, the library occupied a cheerful, spacious building furnished with desks and chairs. Open six days a week, it boasted a fulltime librarian. Stacked tall on three walls were 3,500 volumes. Probably no library in the state has had such an incongruous financial beginning.

As women will, they formed a club, and as is their custom, they called it Tolleson Women's Club. The usual fund-raising feeds followed, and for a common goal—the building of a clubhouse. But money was slow in coming. Finally the women agreed they'd all be dead before they could afford a clubhouse. They voted to cash their bonds and found a library.

"At least," said one practical member, "we'd have the pleasure of spending."

Space, 8 feet by 10, was found in an old barracks-type building which had been an emergency nursery for working women during World War II. Mrs. W. A. Davis was the first librarian, succeeded five years later by Mrs. Clifford Lamar. In 1956 the city gave the library more room. The women's clubbers nagged their husbands into fixing up the place. A school principal did the cabinet work, and one of the women painted the floor. (She couldn't stand straight for two days.) Then the city gave operating funds.

"Most gratifying," said Librarian Lamar, "is the way the town has responded to our opening six afternoons a week. In four months our circulation has grown from 339 books to 1,459 books a month. This is in a town of 3,500 people."

The moderator was trying to hurry a panel discussion at an Industrial Development Workshop in Tucson.

His panel, including some of the Indian leaders of the state, resisted the speedup.

After throwing out a particularly challenging question, the moderator turned to Tom Dodge, the full-blood Navajo and superintendent, strangely enough, of the San Carlos Apache agency.

"Can you give us an answer in 30 seconds?" asked the moderator.

"To summarize," said Dodge. "Ugh."

John Cornelius and Dick Claxton never really left the army. They brought it home with them.

Many GIs of World War II, thrust into strange occupations, figured they would capitalize on their new-found talents in civilian life. Few did. Tank drivers became shoe clerks, and store keepers became insurance agents.

But Claxton and Cornelius stayed with the same old grind, dealing with the same equipment, providing the same services.

Both did wartime hitches in motor pools—stateside and in the Pacific. They learned all about recon cars and six-by-sixes and half-tracks and personnel carriers.

The war over, thousands upon thousands of these military machines were declared surplus and sold to civilians. Claxton and Cornelius predicted correctly that there would be a lasting demand for spare parts.

Their Western Truck Sales sprawls over a big lot at 3530 E. Washington. Without any apparent planning, earth shovels crowd against diminutive Jeeps, engine blocks share a corner with tank transmissions, and tractors are parked beside the hulking shells of gutted trucks.

"A lot of guys just come in here and wander around," said Cornelius. "They poke around the old military vehicles as if they were visiting old friends. We just weigh 'em coming in and going out and charge 'em so much per pound."

The partners take turns scouring the Western states for surplus military equipment. They have gone as far as Norfolk, Va., to bid in government sales.

It is on their bidding that their fortunes rise or fall. The surplus equipment business is as competitive as a pack of wolves. When a military base or other government agency has a surplus stock, the goods are offered first to other government units. What is left is offered to favored civilian organizations, such as school districts. Claxton and Cornelius and other dealers bid on the residue.

"We take the stuff as is," said Cornelius. "It's our job to get it here, and some of it we ship all the way through the Panama Canal. Then we try to get rid of it. Some of the vehicles we resell as they are. Others we rebuild. We dismantle a good many of them."

The men boast that there is not a four-wheel-drive vehicle made that they can't furnish with spare parts.

They sometimes buy multi-ton lots of assorted parts from military motor pools. All they can do is spot check the pile of iron before they buy. When such a shipment arrives on their lot, says Cornelius, "It's like Christmas morning sorting it. We've found everything from locomotive wheels to machine gun barrels."

Yet so thorough are the men in stripping and selling off spare parts to sportsmen and contractors, that they have only about 10 tons of scrap metal left over at the end of each year.

Mama Csicsely was a hug-ably round lady whose beaming face disguised an enormous sadness.

She and her husband, 62 in 1958, were working 16-hour days. When the Csicselys fled Hungary they abandoned $30,000 in cash, a doll factory, a restaurant, a contracting business—and the graves of nine sons. They were luckier, they said, than some. At least they escaped, only an hour before the Russians overran the railroad.

In February, 1958, they started a cafe in Phoenix. Their friends were worried. Mama had some old country notions.

"Here," she said, "goes the big table. The customers sit at the big table like happy family."

Business was slow, and it stayed slow.

Friends said, "Mama, Americans want small tables. They don't want to chat with strangers. They want some privacy."

Mama capitulated. She installed small tables. But it was her only concession to American restaurant technique.

She bustled about the kitchen like a hen with chicks, a dab of dough on her cheek, her forearms floured. She made all the strudels, cheesecakes, fruits, bread, soups, goulashes, cabbage rolls, rumcakes, stuffed peppers, rich pancakes, and meatballs, and prepared with her own hands the many American dishes on the menu.

Meat salesmen feared her. She opened every package while they stood before her. She would poke and sniff. If the meat was not perfect, she would throw back her head indignantly.

"Tek it bek," she would say, aflame.

The Csicselys invested their total wealth in the new business. It would either be a success, and provide them with a comfortable retirement, or it would fail and they would start all over again. They were braced for misfortune.

In happier days, they lived in Budapest, across the street from the famous Gabor girls. Mama Csicsely (pronounced Sicily) ran a doll factory and a bustling 300 customer-per-day restaurant. Paul was a contractor and master bricklayer and stonemason. Mama's mother and father were killed by a German bomb. Eight of her nine sons were conscripted and died in forced fighting for the Russians. One of Paul's sons, by a former marriage, was also killed.

Mama and Paul fled on Christmas Day, 1944. They brought out some silverware, and $15,000 stuffed in a suitcase. Language difficulties kept them in low-paying jobs in America. By the time they came to Phoenix, and were naturalized, sickness had used up their savings. Mama worked as a dressmaker. Paul, turned away by the bricklayers' union, mowed yards.

They saved $3,500. All of it went into the restaurant, in the old Palms Hotel at 620 N. Second St.

For many months some of the very best food of the world was served to few customers.

(I was pleased to learn this column increased Mama Csicsely's business. That had been about half my purpose in writing it. But in 1959 her long hours and unremitting craftsmanship brought on a heart attack. Mama had to close her kitchen, drat it.)

The little, rear hotel room smelled like a pharmacist's trash can.

Next to the rumpled bed was a metal magician's stage

stand covered with embroidered velvet and supporting a glass half filled with Coke. Lurid posters decorated the walls and dresser. In the closet was a long-tailed black coat. A framed picture of Blackstone was inscribed: "From one horsethief to another."

The Great Martinelli had just got up. He blinked against the streaming daylight, and drew a tattered red robe about his thick body. His black hair, which he usually combed straight back like a shingle, was sticking up in the comic-page symbol for surprise.

Maybe he was 60, but he looked 40. At the moment, he felt like 80. He went over to the corner sink and ran water until it steamed and melted salve which he stooped to smear on his foot. The foot was swollen and darkly discolored. He lurched to the bed like a man with a tack in his sole.

"It hurts," he said dispassionately. "It hurts."

The Great Martinelli had been in Phoenix almost a year. He came out West for health reasons, injured his foot in a fall, and as his fortunes diminished, made a five-block migration through Phoenix's hotels. He had come down to a Madison Street hotel, where he rented two rooms. He lived in one. He stored his stage paraphernalia in the other.

The Great Martinelli, formally named Peter, came from a family of magicians. His grandparents and parents and four brothers and one sister were magicians. Martinelli is an Italian name, but Peter was born in Chili. He traveled around the world too many times to count.

"I have been to all the islands," he said, "and to all the continents.

"Once my show was so big I had 20 people working for me. While crossing to London in World War I, we were torpedoed and I lost $45,000 in equipment."

In his earlier days, Martinelli was an escape artist. He allowed doubters to bind and chain and blindfold him, stuff him into a box, and nail the lid on the box. Then the box was dumped into the Atlantic. In a few minutes Martinelli would pop to the surfice.

Declining health forced him to give up his specialty. He sawed women in half and caused large, lumpy objects to disappear. All of this was documented in his scrapbook. One Florida writer could not understand how Martinelli could produce three alarm clocks, a brassiere, three vases of flowers, and miles of colored tape from his top hat.

Martinelli put on a few shows in Phoenix for clubs and banquets. But his foot swelled so badly he had difficulty in putting on a shoe. When I saw him he was whiling away most of his nights in taverns.

"I," he would say, transforming his white gloves into a bouquet of paper flowers, "am the Great Martinelli."

Some of the bar customers believed him. And some did not.

Early in 1939 three men slouched against the bar of Phoenix's Luke-Greenway Post No. 1, The American Legion.

They weren't falling-down drunk, but each could count two wings to fly on, and one for the road, and another to mud-in-your-eye. The men reached for cigarets. One struck a match and lighted the smokes.

"That's bad luck," said a legionnaire, "but I bet I outlive the both of you."

"You're on."

"Count me in."

And in such a casual way originated *Sociedad del Ultimo Hombre*, or the Last Man's Club.

Each man, believing he would outlive the others, vowed he would drink a toast to his departed comrades. John Stanewich and Guy Keeney and Larry Lutz saved the three cigaret butts and the charred match.

Other Legion members heard of the grisly pact. At their insistence the Last Man's Club was expanded to 13 members on June 20, 1939. At subsequent meetings that summer, membership was increased to 3 x 13, 39. Stainless steel membership cards, suitable for riveting to caskets, were issued. The club acquired some bizarre traditions. The first cigaret butts and match were framed under glass. The annual banquet was set on April 6, the day on which World War I began. Places were fixed for all members, living or dead. A bottle of *tequila* was purchased, so that when all but the last man is left alive, he will have a suitable toast to his fallen comrades. A skull, wearing a spiked German helmet, was placed in the club archives.

On Dec. 28, 1939, Lutz, Keeney and Stanewich went to the Arizona Corporation Commission to file papers of incorporation for the club. Another member, one of the original 13, was secretary of the commission. W. I. Stephenson assisted in the filing of papers.

"Now," said Stephenson, "some of you sonsabitches start dying."

Two and a half hours later Stephenson died of a heart attack in a Phoenix restaurant.

He was the first Last Man to go.

Maybe it was like being born again, nine feet tall.

Or perhaps it was the travel. The gawking crowds. The movie cameras. The newspaper headlines. Three hundred dogs barking in frustration and fear.

The why of it all, not even Pete McDonnold understood. He only knew he was hooked, good or bad, and that he never again would be truly happy unless he was wearing a pair of stilts, with a road inviting him to the horizon.

One day he read an ad placed by Everett Skaggs of Skaggs Manufacturing Co. It seemed the Skaggs company was making aluminum stilts for plasterers and other home construction men. Skaggs offered to pay $1,500 and expenses to any man who would walk on stilts from New York to Los Angeles, as a way of proving the safety and durability of his product.

"I can walk," said Pete, who was dealing oysters in a Southside fish house.

"How can you prove it?" asked Skaggs.

Pete bared his gaudy tattoos, and said, "I was in the infantry for 15 years."

The bargain was made and kept. Pete walked 3,250 miles in four months of 1958.

Girls blew kisses to him from Pennsylvania cornfields, and his picture appeared in the Cincinnati Post. A Missouri couple drove 100 miles to see him stalk by. He was interviewed on three television stations in Oklahoma City. Never a day passed that Pete wasn't asked to stop and chat with newsmen. One Midwest reporter, speeding to cover a highway fatality, tarried to question Pete.

"What about your other story?" asked Pete.

"That's nothing," said the reporter, "compared with you."

Never had Pete been held up to such wonder and adulation. Never had he done something which so many people thought was admirable. When he strode into downtown Los Angeles the world was his oyster, and not the other way around.

Pete came home, to 4126 E. Lincoln, his weight down to 135 pounds and his legs, iron. He acquired a string of amusement machines.

But it wasn't good. A nostalgia dominated him. He took to putting on his yellow walking clothes, his boondocker shoes, and his stilts. He began to practice—to harden his muscles for the march.

"I want to walk around the world on stilts," said Pete McDonnold.

"Whew!" said the man in the Palm Beach suit.

That was Mistake Number One.

Never say "Whew!" It is almost as dangerous as gulping ice water, or attempting to fan yourself with a magazine. In recent years some 40,000 newcomers have faced Valley of the Sun summers for the first time.

They are the ones likely to be saying "Whew!" and slugging gallons of frigid liquids or nervously flapping about with scraps of paper.

"There is nothing you can do about the heat," said an oldtimer, W. G. (Gig) Kneeland. "But you can control your state of mind.

"The rules are simple. Never look at a thermometer. Never talk about the heat. Don't believe the weather reports. Make no unnecessary movements. And remember that heat is relative."

He explained that a modern desert city is a cluster of cool cubes. Homes have coolers and offices are refrigerated.

"Let me tell you about the old days. There was no ice at first, and it remained scarce and expensive well into this century.

"Water was cooled in *ollas* made of porous clay and hung in the shade. Some of the water would seep through the sides of the pot and evaporation would keep the drinking water potable.

"Perishables were kept in what we called a desert cooler. This was a box with shelves, and covered with burlap. A pan of water was set so that it kept the burlap soaking.

"Thick adobe walls insulated some homes, and the large frame houses had big windows and high ceilings. Most people, rich and poor, slept out-of-doors. Next time you're downtown look for the older homes, of California airplane design, with a screened, second-story bedroom at the peak of the roof.

"Housewives sometimes hung wet burlap in the windward windows. Breezes blowing through the loose, wet cloth were cooled.

"After transportation improved, many Phoenix men became summer bachelors. They would send their wives to Prescott and points north. Phoenix used to be full of celebrating summer widowers, and Prescott was a city of lonesome women. Ah! the good old days.

"I'll never forget arriving by train in mid-August and asking a bartender for a cold beer.

"He said his beer was warm and wild and made you sweat.

He said that to survive here a drinking man had to develop a taste for whiskey and branch."

Gig's eyes frosted with nostalgia. He shivered.

"I hope the sun takes the chill off by August," said he.

Joe Greenberg, forgotten man of the theater, was doubly forgotten.

When he was 74 in 1948 he took his pension in Chicago and headed for Phoenix, to live in a neat bungalow at 2134 E. Harvard. He had his yellowed union cards, his quaint photographs, and his memories.

"One thing hasn't changed," he said. "Nobody ever gave a thought for the man who was operating a movie projector, until something went wrong. I imagine that is still the same."

Greenberg was a projectionist 50 years. He hand-cranked his first machine. When he quit, he was bossing the most modern of the automatic, wide-screen projectors.

The first motion pictures were shown in opera houses and town halls—even large stores. Of course, there was no sound, except for the clatter of the gears, and perhaps the hammering of the piano. For some machines, Greenberg took his power from street car lines and ran it through a barrel of water to produce the desired voltage. For other machines he manufactured bottles of oxygen and hydrogen. Because of bad light and worse lenses, the projected pictures were dim and fuzzy.

Many God-fearing citizens refused to watch movies, even at 5 cents per show. They thought it was a work of the devil. Greenberg was inclined to agree. If he didn't crank the early machines at the proper speed, a scene of a leisurely stroll could look more like a steeplechase.

Greenberg recalled a fright in Danville, Ky. The projector's booth was made of an iron furnace casing, attached to the ceiling of a second-story hall. Greenberg hitched an electrical do-dad to the ceiling of the booth, which was connected to the building's tin roof, which was affixed to metal columns.

"Juice was running wild, and customers were bouncing like billiards."

Sound for the first talkies was put on a record. The projectionist was supposed to start the projector and the record simultaneously.

He said, "Many a time the crash of the death car arrived late, right in the middle of the funeral."

The first color picture shown by Greenberg was crude. A color wheel, offering green and red, whirled in front of the projector. If the wheel and projector were synchronized, color effects were believably suggestive. If not—"I have seen green bears and red actresses and brown grass."

Greenberg said he didn't go to the movies anymore. He didn't own a television. He said electronics have taken all the fun out of the picture business.

Chapter Ten

Bob King, who works for Goldwaters, came into the office carrying a big box and wearing a cunning smile under his sandy mustache.

"This is the latest thing in toys," he said, handing over the box. "Try it out. It's yours to keep." No strings attached, he said, except please if you use the name of the store, spell it right.

The box contained an "Alpha I Ballistic Missile," and:

A launching pad.
A base pivot pin.
Motor chamber.
Nozzle plug.
Release hatch with remote control cord.
An oxidizer mixing bottle and storage tank.
Packages of dry fuel and oxidizer.
A launching manual.

That night I took it home and whistled up my good neighbor, Brad Henshaw, who would be 11 that Thursday.

"The latest thing in toys," I parroted. "It's your to keep. No strings attached, except I want to be around when you launch it the first time."

Gusty winds bedeviled our Little Canaveral. Twice we postponed the launching. Then the weather improved and we carried all the equipment into the Henshaw front yard.

The toy was said to be perfectly safe, and this was comforting. The missile had a rubber nose cone, and a kid could eat the chemicals and not be harmed.

"You shoot it off first," insisted Brad.

We secured the launching pad with the base pivot pin, and prepared a supply of oxidizer solution.

Countdown procedure became more complicated:

"Turn nozzle plug counterclockwise to unscrew nozzle and motor from missile.

"Using 60-70 degree F. water, make up dilute oxidizer solution as directed on back of dilution tank, pour into missile, and place missile on its side.

"Unsnap motor from nozzle, wet with water, and fill motor with fuel directly from fuel storage tank, holding fingers over slots in bottom of motor. (Fuel is completely harmless to skin and clothing.)

"Snap motor back onto nozzle, replace nozzle in missile, and screw securely into place by turning nozzle plug. DO NOT FORCE."

Something went wrong. I placed the missile on the pad and Brad backed away with the remote control cord.

"Six. Five. Four. Three. Two. One. Fire!" said Brad's dad.

With a hopeless "Sput," the missile rose 3 inches and toppled.

"My turn," said Brad. He deftly mixed new chemical, filled the motor and rocket, assembled the missile, and pulled the cord. The rocket soared higher than the power poles.

I tried to be big about it. But I still felt 10 years older

than I did before Bob King exposed me to the Brave New Toy of the Brave New World.

There was this guy, see, all dressed up in green tights and carrying a long bow and a quiver of arrows. He was Robin Hood.

And along came this girl who rode a white horse and swung a sword and wore a chemise of chain mail and scowled through the visor of her helmet. She was Sir Galahad.

Don't snicker, Wilbur. That's just the way it happened.

Tom Council worked at the Green Gables Restaurant. For most of seven years he was the man on the horse.

He was much man. Tall, red of hair, muscular, Tom was captain of the track team at Phoenix Union. The job of playing Sir Galahad, official gatekeeper for the restaurant, appealed to his manliness. He wore his raiments and sat his steed proudly.

After a hitch with the army, Tom enrolled at Arizona State for a major in business administration. He continued as Sir Galahad for the Gables.

Then Tom was promoted to Chief of Pageantry and Parking.

A green Robin Hood's suit went with the new task, and no longer was Tom required to ride the white horse at the front gate.

Something about his replacement bothered him.

What with all the armor and shields and iron pants, it took Tom a while to figure it out. The truth slapped him like a gauntlet. The new Sir Galahad was a girl! And a frail thing at that.

She was Donna Marie Fenwick, of 5039 E. Earll. Five feet six. One hundred pounds.

Tom stomped into the office of Owner Bob Gosnell. At stake was the masculine tradition, generally, and the ego of Tom Council, specifically.

"Now look here, sir," said Chief of Pageantry and Parking, "hiring a girl as Sir Galahad is going to give this place a bad name. I'll bet she falls off the horse."

"Simmer down, son," said Gosnell, "that girl learned to ride before she could walk. I want you to teach her the work."

"Okay," said Tom, "but I don't have to like it."

Tom sullenly instructed Donna. He ignored her expressions of thanks. He found fault in her whenever he could. He was slow with praise. Donna endured the man in silent terror. The age of chivalry, despite ever-present rituals of King Arthur's court, was dead.

One night Tom leaned on his long bow and stared at the impostor on the horse. At length, he walked to the gate.

"After work let's go to the drive-in and have a hamburger," he suggested.

Zounds! On Oct. 4, 1958 in St. Theresa's Catholic Church Sir Galahad and Robin Hood were married.

KINGMAN—A famous Mohave County 2-inch rain—2 inches between drops—began falling as Chet Brantner finished snugging bolts on the cattle scales.

He was a real-life cowboy. This meant that often he would go hatless, wear khaki trousers, and clump around in field shoes.

Chet was in his 60th year. His long, leathery face was as brown as an Indian's, and his build was a slim as it was when he helped drive 500 bulls straight through Phoenix from Squaw Peak to the railroad. He still worked full-time for the Long Mountain Ranch, a job he had held a quarter-century.

They said there weren't many cowboys like Chet around anymore. Truth is, there never were.

Chet was seriously injured in World War I and he came West for a cure. He learned the cattle business quickly. Ranchers hired him from Phoenix to Flagstaff. Chet liked everything about cowboying except the long, lonesome hours of the line cabin and bunkhouse.

In 1927 Chet bought a hand-winding Brunswick phonograph, and some records of symphonic music.

When he knew he'd be holed up in a place six months, he packed out his record machine. He filled his clapboard shelters with the finest music available.

The hours were no longer lonesome.

From books and album covers he learned the history, structure and meaning of classical music. Every payday he set aside money to increase his collection.

Once, when he was riding for the Munds Park Cattle Co. south of Flagstaff, he read that Richard Crooks was going to sing at the Metropolitan Opera House in New York. Chet pushed his horse through drifts of snow and took the train to New York to hear that one opera.

His fellow cowboys kidded him. That was jake with Chet. He kept on playing his music, and spouting his fancy-sounding musical vocabulary.

As the years passed, the record collection grew in size and value.

His original recording of "O Soave Fanciulla" from "La Boheme" by Enrico Caruso and Nellie Melba was one of only six cut. A collector offered Chet $2,500 for it. Chet was asked to sell a Geraldine Farrar recording for $1,500.

He gave away many records he considered mediocre, but he never sold one.

Ten years ago Chet "took Jesus" at a Baptist revival in Kingman. A bachelor, he began to wonder what would become of his collection of music. He sought a way to put his precious records in the hands of young people.

In 1956 the Chet Brantner Library of Recordings was dedicated at Grand Canyon College. Chet gave 5,000 records, valued then at $20,000 and afterward donated a hi-fi player.

The cowboy critic continued to collect records which he spun on his old Brunswick.

KINGMAN—Ed Edgerton was celebrating privately.

This was the day doctors told him he was going to die. One month before the medics at Fort Whipple gave him 30 days.

"I am of another breed of cat," Ed told them, demanding his clothes and pocket gear.

"Well," said Ed, "my time is up, and tomorrow I'm taking a new job over in California consulting for an oil and minerals outfit.

"I'll be hiking in the field, wearing a pack across my chest, and sleeping on the ground. I think I've got this cancer whipped."

A good many folks from Topock to Temple Bar prayed he had. In Arizona's least-populated county, world-renowned authorities are scarce.

Ed had some formal education at the University of Michigan and in California, but for the most part he was self-educated in the sciences of geology and mineralogy. He hired on as consultant in the Oatman gold mines in 1915, and held every mining job from stope to stamp mill.

He established Ed's Camp on old U.S.-66 in 1927, and it became the Northwestern Arizona mecca for rockhounds.

Ed made a dozen fortunes, and he blew them in on more prospecting and development. He shipped 29 different types of minerals from his holdings in Mohave County.

So adept did Edgerton become, he could tell you within a few miles the origin of any Mohave County rock handed him.

Students would drive up from Tucson just to hear him speak on his specialty, the rare earths. Universities and societies asked him to prepare and present papers on his favorite minerals.

Ed didn't share the perennial gold fever of Arizona old-timers.

"I've been a practical man," he said. "Gold isn't going to come back, because it always will be too expensive to get out of the ground."

Ed has more faith in his rare earths mine. He ships ore to a variety of companies for use in science and industry. His minerals are needed for cosmetics, for atomic devices, for alloy steels, for electronic components, for ceramics and plastics.

"Here is the future of Mohave County mining," he vowed. "All a man has to do is use his head and his heart. He has to think of a way to use something new, and go out and find it. It's all here. I can see a possibility in every mile of this country.

"Not all the operations will be small. This county has huge deposits of low grade copper ore, and someday there will be mining operations here as large as those in southeast Arizona."

Whether the doctors are right or wrong, Ed Edgerton will be remembered so long as there is a record of scientific discovery. He found and described an undiscovered mineral —and science officially named it Edgertonite.

(At presstime of this book, two years after doctors gave Ed Edgerton 30 days, Ed was still hiking about the Mohave country.)

A commentary on compartmentalized government was scrawled on the body of a dead cat in Phoenix.

The carcass lay in the middle of Camelback Road, just east of Grandview School.

Along came the crew which paints the white stripes on the pavement. When the men left, the glistening new center-stripe of Camelback ran straight to the cat, up, over, and down its torso, and thence onward to Glendale.

Some fastidious citizens may have been horrified by the health dangers. Sentimentalists may have mourned the passing of the cat. Taxpayers may have winced at the waste of paint. But what I couldn't wipe from my mind was an imagined conversation which must have preceded the deed:

Crewman: Boss, there is a dead cat in the road. It's right where I gotta run the new stripe. I don't know what to do.

Foreman: That's what I'm getting paid for. Decisions.

Crewman: Maybe we ought to call the trash truck.

Foreman: What? And get hung up here for an hour? Man, we've got a schedule to keep!

Crewman: Well, sir, I was thinking I'd just give the cat a little kick. You know, nudge it over a foot or so.

Foreman: Now don't get hasty. You move that cat and it's our responsibility. Our department isn't set up for the disposal of deceased stray cats.

Crewman: Gee, I never thought of that.

Foreman: Okay. We're not going to call the trash truck, and hang around here filling out forms. We're not going to move the cat. Not our job. The big question is this: Are we going to paint the stripe to the cat, break the stripe and start it again on the other side of the cat, or do we paint right over the cat, like it wasn't there at all?

Crewman: I have to admire the way you get at the core of a problem, Chief.

Foreman: Thanks. If we don't paint the cat, and some meddling motorist calls the trash truck, and then if the trash crew makes out a report and there is an investigation, somebody upstairs is going to conclude that we knew the cat was here.

Crewman: I'm beginning to see your reasoning.

Foreman: On the other hand, if we paint over the cat, we can always claim we didn't see it. In fact, the stripe will be proof that we never saw the cat. Nobody can blame us for not seeing a cat.

Crewman: Brilliant! Well, Boss, do you see any cat?

Foreman: What cat?

Crewman: (In open adulation): You've got a touch of greatness. Remember what they used to say in the service? It it moves, salute it; if it doesn't move. . . .

Foreman: Paint it.

Two days afterward, I was still trying to catch up with what I saw and heard at the Willy Air Show.

At first I felt sorry for my daughter, who would soon be 3. The jets scared the socks off her. She was leery of low-flying grasshoppers, so you can imagine her reaction to supersonic aircraft buzzing her at 50 feet.

But I was overawed, too.

A fingersnap of time ago I was building models of P-38s. In its day it was a hot, deadly fighter. Now it is just another grasshopper.

One air force captain showed the 15,000 assembled civilians how to deliver an A-bomb.

He skimmed across the air field at 600 mph, hauled back on the stick until his F-86 was flying perpendicularly. Release of the bomb was simulated at the top of the climb. The airplane heeled over and dived for the next three counties while the bomb supposedly arced onto target.

Next, four journeymen demonstrated skip-bombing. In this tactic bombs are bounced on the earth in the way a boy would skip stones on water. Four fighters. Eight bombs. Eight passes. Eight direct hits.

A few minutes later a mild-mannered gent named Bob Hoover took off his suit coat and flew away in an F-86F. He was a test pilot for North American Aviation, maker of the Sabre.

For 20 minutes, the earth was Hoover's yo-yo. He pulled the string, and the planet leaped up and almost kissed him, then fell away to walk the dog and rock the cradle.

He made the airplane rhumba. He rolled it slowly at the threshold of a stall. Once he purposely put the craft into a whip-stall and the plane fell tailfirst. Hoover let his bird slide sideways and dive for flying speed.

After he landed Hoover taxied to the reviewing stand, asked for his coat, winked at a movie star, and sat down to watch the remainder of the show.

The finale was by the Thunderbird demonstration team. Four F-100Cs flew as if they were locked together with invisible wire, through rolls, loops, and turns.

Their purpose was to exhibit the repertoire of tricks which is taught to air force fighter pilots. The Thunderbirds flew straight up in a diamond formation and blossomed in loops toward the four compass points. At the completion of these loops they flew at 700 mph toward a common point above the crowd.

When they passed over, at slightly different altitudes from 30 to 100 feet, four sound shocks slapped against our skin. My daughter dug another foxhole in my chest.

"That's my son-in-law," proudly said a lady in the crowd. "He's flying left wing man. They didn't let him drive the Chevvie until he was 17."

Look at him now.

One week Bill Vale impulsively telephoned a friend in Africa.

The month before he won $55,410.20 on a $72 bet. Three years before he played golf with the President. One day he may be playing a 20-inch trout in a White Mountains lake. The next, he may be following the ponies at Agua Caliente.

It's all the same to William R. (Bill) Vale. Win a little; lose a little.

In his mid-30s, Vale was on his way to becoming a Phoenix legend of gambling. It was whispered he operated on the brink of financial ruination, that he won and lost fortunes, that he would lay a bet on anything, that he hadn't done a day's work in 10 years.

"He made enough in one race to buy a Cadillac," said one of his friends. "Next day he was so broke he couldn't buy a tank of gasoline."

The truth didn't quite match the legend, but the truth was wild enough. When Vale was still coming up through Phoenix schools he started breeding and training greyhounds. When it was time for him to go to college, he couldn't afford to go. He was averaging $300 a week with his dogs.

Excepting wartime army service, Vale's principal occupation remained the running of greyhounds. He had 40 dogs, 18 in his racing kennel, which he would enter at Phoenix and Tucson and Denver.

"That Cadillac story is just about true," said Vale. "In

1946 I was down to $204 in Florida. I didn't bet the $200. I bet the $204. I lost.

"The biggest bet I ever made on a race was $1,500 in Portland. My biggest winner, on one race was $13,000. When my wife and I were married, I had $8,000 cash. Thirty days later I was so broke I had to borrow $300, and on my way to the Coast to pick her up I was arrested and fined $300 for a traffic violation."

Vale figured he poured millions through the mutuel machines since 1946. He said he frequently bets two or three hundred on a single race. Many nights, he said, his bets total several thousand dollars.

Mrs. Vale, pretty and blond, said riding Bill Vale's financial roller coaster didn't give her the Willies. Her job was taking care of their six children, and making a living was Bill's business.

"Bill is my security," she said. "If he loses a house today, he wins a mansion tomorrow. We've been broke, but not for long."

As for that part of the legend which pictures Vale as a loafer, he said: "I have only one helper with me in my racing kennel. That's plenty of work for me. And if anybody thinks you don't sweat over a $1,500 bet, try it."

Most fund-raising drives are as grim as a murderer's funeral.

History of sorts was made by the Valley of the Sun Kiwanis Club which raised a wad of money for charity, and had fun doing it.

A crisp $5 bill was passed out to each of the 106 members of the club. They were asked to invest the money in any way of their choice, and return the profits. It was to be a latter-day version of the "Parable of the Talents" of the Bible. St. Matthew tells of the rich man who gave money to his servants and later rewarded the industrious and punished the slothful.

Joe Porter, of the western store chain, was the champ

money-maker. He bought stamps, wrote letters to suppliers asking for donations of merchandise, and sold it through the 11 Porters' stores. Profit: $467, on a $5 investment.

William W. Clore had to confess a $28 loss, and a fast recovery:

"I invested the $5 and made $15. Then I bought some balloons and tanks of helium, but nobody wanted to buy balloons. Now I'm ahead $8, but don't ask how."

Len Huck said he bought a barber's kit, and, "I sold haircuts to the kids in my neighborhood. It wasn't a financial success, but now, when any kid in my block is lost, he is returned, immediately, to our neighborhood."

Charles H. Garland commissioned an artist to paint two pictures which he hoped to sell. "I liked the paintings so well, I bought them myself," he said.

Jerry Poole played poker, and "but for three four-card flushes, I'd have had considerably more than $8 to turn in," he reported ruefully.

The club's only minister, J. Ford Forsyth was in an uncomfortable position. It wouldn't look good for a preacher to fail to live up to a Biblical admonition. He threw a breakfast for the men of his church. After paying off his helper, Fred Cutler, the Rev. Forsyth profited by $50.

Don Zahn purchased a large supply of desk telephone directories, mailed ads to hundreds of friends, and turned in a gain of $91.90.

Stan Blythe, one of the originators of the fund drive, made $97 in a project described variously as a ".30-30 rifle raffle" and a ".30-30 raffle rifle."

Doyle Willis capitalized on the weak will power of fellow Kiwanians. He started a Fat Boys' Club in which members pledged to lose a pound a week or forfeit a $1. Willis turned in $82.

John Sheely drew the most guffaws with his story. He said he spent $5 on "suitable liquids." He determined from the club's treasurer the one who owed the most dues. Then, by plying his victim with liquids, Sheely convinced him he should pay up $67.

All talents totaled $1,500.

If your riding boots cut your insteps, fill them with black Mexican beans, said Ben Vance, driver of the state bookmobile.

Then pour water over the *frijoles*. Place a flatiron on top of each boot. Wait 12 hours.

This will ruin the boots. Expanding beans will rip the tops loose from the soles. The boots will not cut your insteps anymore.

In June, 1958, Mid Jones went from the Right Bank of Cave Creek to the Left Bank of the Seine.

Mid moved from California to Cave Creek with his parents in 1946. From the beginning, Mid was driven by one all-consuming desire: to provide a home and income for his parents.

The Joneses bought 120 desert acres bordering the creek. The older couple lived in a 10-by-12 shack. Mid slept outdoors for eight years.

Starting with 100 chicks, Mid slowly built up an egg ranch. The first hens were sheltered in surplus army tents. Mid hauled water from the creek.

"I became the champion scrounger of Cave Creek," he said. "I bought used building material for next to nothing, and kept adding lean-tos until the roofs almost touched the ground. At our peak we had 6,000 hens in seven buildings."

Building, feeding, doctoring, sorting, candling, packing and peddling took up a good deal of Mid's time. But he had a few spare hours. He set out to build a house—a huge imaginative rambler with 2,500 square feet under roof.

He didn't have a bit of professional help. He poured all the concrete floors. From sand he carried from the creek, and in a Sears, Roebuck mold he bought for $12, Mid produced 10,000 concrete building blocks.

He laid the block, stuccoed the outside of the walls, and plastered the inside. He installed the wiring and plumbing (2½ baths) and he lugged the boiling tar for the roof in five-gallon cans. By himself he set the great picture windows of the den, and he, who had never built so much as a dog house, put two fireplaces in his dream home.

"When I came to something that stumped me, I asked someone who knew," said Mid.

The place was finished in 1957. But it proved to be too much for his parents to care for. Mid built a smaller house nearby.

He sold his dream house. The Joneses began to sell off parcels to investors and city people who wanted to escape from crowded Phoenix.

With his folks secure, Mid left for a vacation in Europe.

Hairless caterpillars are all right to eat. Hairy caterpillars may be poisonous.

Also good for rounding out a desert supper are grubs, bird eggs, tortoise, lubber grasshoppers, lizards, snakes, Mexican free-tailed bats, wildcats, coyotes, and mountain lions.

The word is in "Desert Survival" published by the Maricopa-Phoenix Civil Defense Joint Council. The book contains basic information for sustaining life on the Sonoran Desert.

Conceivably, almost every Arizona resident and visitor could be stranded on the desert, with little or no food or water. Cars break down. Planes crash. Hunters and picnickers become lost.

Dehydration, explains the book, is the desert killer. A human needs about a gallon of water a day to survive temperatures of 120 degrees. If a person should try to hike in such weather, he could die in a day.

Chances are good for finding water. By following game trails, or watching for flocks of circling birds, a person might discover a spring. Some dry washes have water just below the surface.

The book also has hints for finding food, avoiding poisonous animals, starting fire, erecting shelter and determining direction. One food section lists 33 edible animals, and 18 kinds of vegetables. Some marooned souls may want to dine on hairless caterpillars and broiled bobcat.

But the cunning and nimble can set a table of acorn soup, roasted quail, a salad of miner's lettuce, water cress and *tomatillo*, green or dried mesquite beans, prickly pear fruit, and pinon nuts.

Sylvestre Herrera, Arizona's Medal of Honor soldier, tried to speak before a Phoenix civic club. A naturally shy man, Herrera stammered and then stopped in embarrassment.

A club member rose.

"Relax, son," he said. "We know you didn't win your medal by talking."

Herrera delivered his speech flawlessly.

Bob Gardiner may have hit the elusive electronics jackpot. He developed what some experts called the "world's greatest scintillation counter." And before Gardiner could put it on the market, the uranium boom fizzled out.

Then he invented a metal detector, working similarly to the old battlefied mine detectors, but more sensitively. Gardiner's device could find a penny in a sawmill. Just the tool for the weekend treasure hunter.

"Unfortunately," said Gardiner, "there weren't as many hunters as I thought."

Next Gardiner built a contraption for finding metal under water. It would operate to depths of 300 feet. There was nothing quite like it in the world.

"The trouble with it was—a man had to find a treasure before he could buy one of my treasure finders," said Gardiner. "I can't sell the thing for less than $1,800."

Gardiner thought he had a money-maker in his latest

gimmick. A light sleeper, Gardiner rested best when a steady, hard rain was falling on his roof. The noise would blot out all extraneous noises, he said, and he'd sleep like a baby.

Gardiner went to work with a soldering iron and a fistful of transistors. He brought forth Sleepatron. It was a box about the size of a table radio, and powered by four flashlight batteries.

Sleepatron would fill a bedroom with the sound of falling rain. It could be adjusted from a faint fog drizzle to a beating frog strangler. In fact, Gardiner's invention could be turned up to obliterate the noise of real rain falling.

"It worked for me," said Gardiner. "I decided to manufacture the sets."

The man behind the ideas came from pioneer Arizona stock. His grandfather owned Phoenix's first water works, and his father operated a motorcycle shop. Young Gardiner didn't become interested in electronics until he graduated from Phoenix College. He took correspondence school courses. In 1955 he founded Gardiner Electronics Co. at 2545 E. Indian School.

"So far I've been a day late and a dollar short," he said. "It's tough competing against the big companies. You can't make something by hand that is both good and cheap. But some day I'll hit."

The cargo space of the station wagon was jammed with caged sidewinders, diamondbacks, Gila monsters, scorpions, and tarantulas.

The night was dark, 60 miles east of Albuquerque.

In the front seat were Dr. Herbert L. Stahnke, director of the Poisonous Animals Research Laboratory at Arizona State University, and his wife, Lydia. They were heading for Las Vegas, N.M., where Dr. Stahnke was to speak to a National Science Foundation summer institute for high school biology teachers. The lethal creatures were props for his lecture.

"Herbert," said Lydia. "Something's bumping against

my leg. The windows are closed and I don't think it's an insect." She jokingly added, "Maybe it's a snake."

"Well, here," said her husband. "Shine the flashlight around and see what it is."

She switched on the light. A 3½-foot diamondback was coiled around her feet. It was nuzzling her ankle with its head.

Dr. Stahnke eased his foot from the throttle and allowed the car to coast to a gentle stop. He carefully opened his door, found a snake stick, and opened the door on his wife's side. She sat as still as a Buddhist statue. After a couple of failures, Dr. Stahnke snared the snake.

"Vibration must have jiggled loose the hook on the cage," said Dr. Stahnke. "How do you feel, my dear?"

"Oh, fine, fine. It seemed like an eternity, but I'm not even frightened, now that it's over. All these years you've been telling us to remain perfectly still when we're within range of a rattlesnake. It really works, doesn't it?"

"Yes," said Dr. Stahnke. "I'm proud of you."

"One cup coffee," the recipe called for.

The Chandler bride followed instructions. After the cake was baked, it tasted awful.

"I think the recipe meant a cup of coffee," suggested hubby. "Not a cup of grounds."

The old man is dead now, and he almost took his secret to his grave.

What a proud, stubborn buck he was in his prime!

His pappy had staked a square of hardscrabble in central Arizona, turned out a hundred longhorns, and taught renegade Apaches the effective range of a Spencer repeater.

The ranch work was endless. Paw was up riding at daylight, and he didn't quit until dark. Maw put in a longer day. She ran the fortress home with no help—chopped wood, hauled water, canned fruit, sewed clothing, cleaned house, slopped hogs, cooked food, and washed dishes. And if that wasn't enough, when the ranch was shy of hands, she mended fence and tended roundup fires.

For 25 years the son watched her perpetual toil.

"Someday, son," said Maw, "this ranch will be yours. Your father and I can't last forever." And soon her prophecy came true.

The orphaned youngster redoubled his own efforts. He pitted his quick mind and strong body against disease and drouth, rustler and predator, tight money and low prices. For several years he had time for little else. Fellow ranchers grew to respect his savvy, his talented fists, his skill with a 70-foot rawhide *riata.*

At length the work eased. The young man began to want for a wife.

At 30, he was handsome, tall, slim, dark. He wore his hair shoulder-length. He saw a girl in town, and the girl smiled. She was a tiny, blond thing from back East, and she melted under the stare of this Western giant.

"Marry me," he asked one day. "Come with me to my ranch, where the moon is as big as the sky, and the sky is bigger than the universe."

She did.

Naturally, chores had piled up while the young rancher was courting, and before breakfast the first morning he told his bride:

"Top hand and I have to ride out to fix a water hole. The wood's in that box, and over there's the ax. The ashes got to be cleaned out of the stove, and mind you don't break a finger on the well winch."

He rode away. When he returned, his bride, his best mare, and his buggy were gone. Neighbors said they saw all three headed for town. The man saddled a fresh horse and followed. His heart was ice. He found his bride at the railroad station.

"If you'll come back," he promised, "I'll cook meals and wash dishes and fetch water and scrub floors. You'll never have to work a day in your life."

He was good as his word. For a year she sat on the porch and rocked while her husband minded the house. One day she grabbed up the ax and said:

"I'm going to split some wood. I'm going to work, but I'm going to rest some, too."

They shared the work for 55 years. Together they took time to sit on the porch. She is there today, rocking, rocking.

Men drifted in from Roosevelt Dam on the east, and the Agua Fria River on the west, to honor a woman who had excelled in what used to be man's work.

Mrs. Nina E. Duncan, of 2437 W. San Miguel announced her retirement as editor of the Salt River Project's employe magazine. Some wondered if this was possible. She was the magazine. The magazine was Nina Duncan.

When she came to Arizona she bore a raw wound on her heart, deep enough to defeat a weaker character. She had married in 1917. Two years later her husband died in the great influenza epidemic. She brought her infant daughter from the East to Phoenix, and took what work was offered women in the days: church secretary, store clerk, telephone operator, office worker. In 1937 she was hired by the project's water service department. Petite, cheerful, and gregarious, she seemed a natural choice to edit the newspaper which employes wanted to publish at their own expense. She had no experience, but she made up for it in drive. After company hours she gathered up the news and gossip, typed stencils, and ran off the first issue of the modest monthly on a memograph machine.

A year later, 1942, the paper was named *The "Current" News*. She babied it along until 1950, when the project made her full-time editor. The magazine became a slick, 20 page, color-cover production crammed with pictures, special feature stories, and correspondent columns.

Four years in a row, 1953-1956, it was judged the best company magazine in Arizona by the Phoenix Advertising Club. Twice the magazine won Clement E. Trout awards for excellence. Mrs. Duncan won recognition in other ways —from Arizona Press Women and from Arizona Industrial Editors, who elected her president.

Project President Victor I. Corbell and General Manager R. J. McMullin were on hand for the surprise party in the cafeteria of the project headquarters.

They handed her a round trip airplane ticket to Hawaii and expenses for hotel, meals, and sight-seeing trips for 11 days there.

Money for the trip was contributed by employes from throughout the far-flung project.

"She entered into her duties and obligations with a determination and will to do her best," said Corbell. "She never turned down an opportunity to lend a hand to anyone."

Mrs. Duncan's family had grown also. Besides her daughter, Mrs. J. Clark Nicholson of 6816 N. 11th Ave., she had two granddaughters and three great-grandchildren.

There was something else.

In the grandest tradition of the Salt River Project, Mrs. Duncan planned to continue doing one home chore by herself. For years, with boots and shovel, she irrigated her own yard.

For three weeks I went out in the woods, hunting.

I went armed with my girl of almost 3-year-old caliber, and I came to feel pity for those men who hunt only with guns. The best game cannot be shot, and the most valuable trophies cannot be mounted. With a child slung over your shoulder, it is open season and no bag limit, and every new quarry is a world record.

First were storms. Daily at noon armies of squalls gathered for evening assault on the castles of Tonto Rim. Stray volleys landed near us neutrals, and I soothed her fears. And on another night when lightning stripped a pine 100 yards away, she saw me flinch and comforted me with her soft smile.

No less a marvel was Woody's place, a black hole in

a blighted oak. Almost every morning we would stop there and knock. After a while I would say, "Is he at the store shopping for grubs?" and she would shake her head, "No. He's sleeping."

We could not hunt squirrels together. They'd scamper up and across the pines and call me dirty names. But my girl one day almost touched one on the nose, and for half an hour three wild, half-grown squirrels frolicked at her feet and made her the joke of their hide-and-seek game.

Other animals we shared. She herded Jack Anderson's calves while I looked out for the apprehensive cows. Together we measured a 34-inch timber rattler skin, smelled skunks, heard coyotes, and watched birds bathe.

We fished. Three times we went to the creek with poles and line and split shot and worms and hooks and cheese. We hit the water with our poles, lost the sinkers, and ate the cheese. She could not fathom why we caught no fish.

A deep-bellied mare was ours for an hour. We climbed a fire tower and met the ranger there. In town we saw her TV favorite. "Are you Maverick?" she asked a handsome rodeo rider. "No honey," he stumbled, and recovered, "Oh, yeah, sure, I'm Maverick." She'd have ridden away with him.

Probably our finest trophies were our deer. At a cress-covered spring we saw a doe mincing in the heavy shadows. Later was the night of the buck. As we drove abreast, he leaped across the headlight beams in frozen ballet stance, landed like a leaf, and was gone. For a magic moment, we had a four-pointer for a hood ornament.

South of the cabin across a lush meadow an abandoned ranch hugs the edge of the forest. Yellow rose vines climb through the shakes of the sagging house. We prowled the caverns of the house and outbuilding, and inspected the vintage car, mower and phonograph rusting in the sun. We tasted black walnut, and they were puckery; plumbs, tart; and apples, sour. We picked a hatful for mama's pie.

On the sad, last day we went down to our sometimes

creek, and solemnly stared at a muddy pool. My child threw in a pebble and giggled when it plunked.

"Wait here," I said. I lifted a mighty moulder and heaved it. Water exploded 6 feet high.

Hunters two, we held hands and laughed.

Chapter Eleven

Mrs. Stella Carruth, who runs the Call of the Canyon Lodge on Oak Creek, had some visitors.

They were well-dressed and drove a big, expensive car. Mrs. Carruth showed them a flossy cabin with all the conveniences.

"We were hoping you had something with outdoor plumbing," the man said, and the couple left.

A man deposited 16 years of his life and soul and genius into the vaults and niches and caverns of Mystery Castle.

After his death, his wife and daughter made daily withdrawals.

Nothing in the Valley of the Sun quite compares with the six-story, 18-room castle built at the end of Seventh Street against the base of South Mountain. Modern architecture is just beginning to catch up with it. And the bitter-sweet love story behind its creation seems to grow fresher with each telling.

Boyce Luther Gulley, an angular, arty and airy Arkansan, took a beautiful wife and fathered a comely daughter in Washington. There was some in-law trouble, and Gulley was too much of an artist to succeed as a storekeeper. But when he disappeared in 1929, without a word, no friend or enemy could offer a reasonable explanation.

Many years later he wrote to his abandoned family. He said that he wanted freedom and art, and was building a castle for his queen and princess. Someday—his letters were always vague—he would invite them to join him. Gulley died in 1945. Only then did Fran, his wife, and Mary Lou, his daughter, learn the reason for Gulley's exile. It was revealed in a final note to his daughter:

"Can you ever forgive me? It wasn't art I wanted; it was you. I left home, not because I wanted freedom, but because I had tuberculosis. I couldn't stay."

Shortly after Gulley's death, Fran and Mary Lou came to Phoenix to claim their inheritance. They had little warning of the unique monument which awaited them.

It was a castle with 13 fireplaces, disc-harrow ornaments, free-form walks, a well but no water, no gas, no electricity, and no plumbing. Stutz Bearcat wire wheels were set as windows in the massive stone walls. Obsidian and quartz contrasted with polished river boulders, and everywhere the personality of the builder was reflected: A whiskey bottle whimsically set in a patio gate, an underground bar (although Gulley rarely drank), a dozen spacious patios, telephone pole beams, a cantilever staircase, and secret chambers.

Hundreds of curios—Spanish picks, tile, casts, oxidized glass—were hung and set on the walls. A Mexican jail bunk bed was a door, World War I shell cases were doorbells, and discarded rails were I-beams. Most of these materials came from nature, or from the junk yards.

Long before such things became fashionable, Gulley built an oven in a wall, made a vented hood over his range, put an island in his kitchen, and chose clinker brick for his walls and columns.

The castle became the home (open to visitors at small charge) for Fran and Mary Lou. New Year's Day 1948, according to instructions left by her father, Mary Lou opened a trapdoor. She found $1,000, and as Mary Lou reports in her book, *My Mystery Castle*, a letter:

"My love for you and Fran is carved on the foundation of the Castle."

HUMBOLDT—"Five dollars," say the tourists. "Ten. Twenty dollars. A hundred dollars."

"Nothing doing," says Mrs. William L. Selby. "I couldn't bear to sell any of these things." And when Mrs. Selby makes up her mind, no force on earth can change it. So it is that she preserves one of Arizona's finest collections of colonial and antique Americana.

In her own right, Mrs. Selby is a remarkable woman. She admits she is old enough to receive social security, but I found her sanding down a wall in her tavern. She runs Selby's Place, a roadside spot on the new Black Canyon Highway south of Humboldt.

One side of her family descends from Col. Charles Washington, brother of George. The other side comes from a niece of William Penn. Most of Mrs. Selby's collection was passed from the Penn side.

Mrs. Selby, whose maiden name was Washington, was born, reared and educated in Missouri. She came West to teach, and settled in Phoenix to marry and establish her own family in 1924.

Her prize possession is General Washington's Thanksgiving Day tablecloth. Made to special order in Belfast, it is woven of the finest flax and has scores of figures commemorating the Thanksgiving ritual. It was supposedly given to Mrs. Selby's family by Robert E. Lee's wife.

She also has the J. D. Washington family Bible, printed in 1853, and showing births and marriages from that date.

Another Washington relic is a cherry root box which was used to hold $20 gold pieces.

Her collection of early American tableware is extensive and authentic. There is a complete setting of original Rogers 1847, the second pattern produced by this now-famous silver manufacturer

Two petite items are her bitters bottle and betty lamp.

"Every lady carried her medicine in a bitters bottle in those days," said Mrs. Selby. "The betty lamp used oil from a fish called betty." The bitters bottle is dated 1679.

Mrs. Selby has nearly enough early American furniture to fill a house. Copies of chests similar to her black cherry dresser sell today for $250, and hers is a hand-made original. It has an oval mirror and grape-cluster drawer pulls. A matching set in light cherry includes a bed, Bible table, and two chairs. Dominating the rear wall of Selby's Place is a foot-pumped organ well over a century old.

"Does it play?" I asked her.

"Does it play!" exclaimed Mrs. Selby. She unlocked the cover, began pumping with one foot, and tickled off a moving rendition of "Rock of Ages." The tavern's acoustics were perfect.

"I used to play the organ in my church," she explained.

Time was, opined Tex Hall, a boy needed only a love of action to appreciate a Western movie. Nowadays a kid needs a degree in psychology.

"All the bad guys are a little bit good, and all the good guys are a little bit bad," said Tex. "This may be more true-to-life, but it's not as much fun."

Tex appeared in some 100 pictures during the days of Tim McCoy, Smiley Burnette, Tex Ritter, and Gene Autry. Occasionally Tex played the hero or honest sidekick, but mostly he was cast as a black-hat villain, complete with side-burns, shifty eyes and sneer. He foreclosed more widows' mortgages than a real-life banker.

He sold firewater to the Indians, robbed stages, wrecked

trains, cheated at cards, shot sheriffs in the back, leered at schoolmarms, and stole stock.

For these foul deeds he invariably reaped a whirlwind in the last reel. He died often, and painfully, and the nation's theaters rocked with the cheers of children who hated his guts.

"When I'd make a personal appearance, especially after a picture was shown, the kids would hiss and boo and throw whatever they had in hand."

This pleased Tex. In his Westerns, good guys won and bad guys lost. The children were getting the message.

But now (sob!) horse opera plots are thicker than Russian novels. Infiltration by the Smelly Armpit School of Drama is complete. A hero is likely to be a man with burning temptations and base lusts. And the villain usually has a psychiatric alibi. He had mean parents, or he was framed, or one day in Laredo he suffered a brain injury when he tripped on the chancel rail.

"There's too much talking, and not enough motion," said Tex. "When we made a Western in five days, we had a fight going from Monday to Friday. The more black eyes, the better the director liked it."

Just about the time the shoot-'em-ups were perverted by motivation researchers, Tex left the business. It was a good ride while it lasted.

Tex (whose real name is George and whose home state is Virginia) was a barnstorming pilot when he was asked to do his first picture. His genuine drawl, powerful features, and skill at inspiring disgust made him a perfect badman.

The war interrupted. Tex witnessed the Japanese bombing of Pearl Harbor. He enlisted and asked for combat with the 11th Airborne Division. A man of action, he saw all he wanted in the South Pacific.

In 1952 he settled with his wife and three children in Phoenix. Savings from his movie and stage careers went into the Luau, Hawaiian nightclub at 4119 E. Indian School.

Few of Tex's customers suspect that he used to be the worst rascal west of the Pecos. Children, strangely enough, adore him.

Jim Trayner's adventure may sound dull to his own "beat generation," but old-timers will probably envy him.

Trayner went cross country in a Model A Ford.

When Ford brought out the A after a long factory shut-down, showroom windows in New York were crushed by customers trying to place orders. It wasn't the best car in the world. But it was the first modern Ford, and after a quarter-century of Model T torture, Ford fans would have been satisfied with a motorized monocycle. The A Model was simple, solid, self-starting, and available in many models. If old Henry hadn't been so stubborn, the Model A would have had hydraulic brakes, too.

Millions of the cars were sold before the Model B succeeded it a few years later. Many original owners drove their sturdy A Models through the depression and the war. Then, as the junkers fell out of use, teenagers snapped up the Model A frames and bodies for hot-rod conversions.

Lately, stock Model A Fords have become scarce.

Trayner, a Phoenix College sophomore, of 2602 W. Marshall, in the summer of 1958 returned to his family's original home in Rhode Island to visit friends and relatives.

At an uncle's farm Trayner saw a pile of dust in a barn. He brushed the dust, and discovered a car—a 1931 Model A Ford.

It was a rumble-seat roadster with wire wheels and a bad case of dry rot. Trayner had intended to fly back to Phoenix, but he impulsively asked his uncle for the car.

"If you can make it go, take it," said the uncle.

Best as Trayner could learn, the car had not run in eight years. The speedometer read 70,000. This could have meant 70,000 or 270,000.

Trayner drained the oil and changed the plugs. He installed new distributor points and a new battery. He poured in some gas, turned the ignition switch, and gave the old heap a kick.

Started right off.

Encouraged, Trayner tuned the engine and fitted the Model A with wheels and tires of more modern size. He had the brakes and steering system overhauled.

The last Wednesday in August Trayner picked up his 15-year-old cousin, Richard Trayner, in Connecticut and headed for Phoenix. Their first trouble developed on the George Washington Bridge in New York. The Model A backfired and refused to run faster than 3 mph. The Trayner boys escorted a major traffic jam off the bridge, pulled over, and fixed balky distributor points. The second day out the carburetor began to leak. They made a new gasket from a sheet of newspaper. They repaired a broken fuel line with electrical tape.

Across the nation they rolled, at a steady 45. When they were almost home, a man in a sleek new car flagged them down.

"I've been passing you for days," he said, "but every day you're out in front. How do you do it?"

"Simple," said Trayner. "We don't stop at every gas station."

Ingleside School sent this mimeographed note home to mothers:

"The first meeting of the Second and Third Grade Blue Birds will be hell Monday, Oct. 6, after school at 2:30 p.m."

Chicago and organized baseball recovered from the Black Sox Scandal, but Kingman and a bunch of disorganized old-timers are still grumbling.

"They cleaned up the big leagues, but brother, what that did to ours! You couldn't tell by a scoreboard who was playing," complained one Mohave County patriarch.

Some history might help younguns to understand. The Black Sox Scandal was the darkest episode in baseball. In

1919, the favored Chicago White Sox met the Cincinnati Reds in the World Series. The Chicago team was the marvel of its day, and some writers were calling it the best ever, yet the White Sox lost, five shoddily-played games to three.

Jim Crusinberry, later a Phoenix resident (and who died in Chicago in 1960), was writing for the Chicago Tribune. He couldn't blow the stink of the series out of his newsman's nose. A year later Jim broke the story that forevermore named that White Sox team black. Eight players—five regulars, two star pitchers and a utility infielder—had conspired with gamblers to throw the 1919 series. Jim's grand jury testimony fingered the guilty, who were banned from organized baseball for life.

To this point, Kingman's interest in the scandal was impersonal. But over the next few years the little railroad town in Northwestern Arizona began to build a championship team of its own. Town baseball was well supported in those days, and nothing fanned chauvinist urges hotter than a rousing Sunday game. Kingman knocked over opposition along U.S.-66 from Williams to Needles. Never hesitant to cover their mouths with money, Kingman fans grew wealthy.

Oatman was Kingman's bitter rival. The booming gold town was populated by millionaire prospectors and prosperous miners, but feckless ballplayers. Advice was solicited from a Los Angeles sports promoter.

Next Sunday, nine strangers wearing Oatman suits appeared at the Kingman ballpark. Simultaneously, Oatman citizens circulated in the stands, placing bets.

Kingman lost 5-4.

Then, as a former Kingman third baseman, Thomas Bale, recalled, the Kingman team and backers went to Williams for a big game. The Williams players wore shadowy mustaches and cheap sunglasses.

Again Kingman lost, by one run.

Later Kingman played Needles. There was something vaguely familiar about the clean-shaven Needles team, which played with a grace and polish rarely seen along the Colorado. Kingman couldn't buy a run.

"They made plays against us that they never made in the series," said Bale.

The only way you can kill a rodeo cowboy, it's said, is to cut off his head and bury it where he can't find it.

Somehow it doesn't seem likely you'd catch many of them soldering transistors in complex guidance systems.

"That's why I didn't have much hope for my idea," said Tom Thomas. A long-time cowboy, Thomas was working at AiResearch Manufacturing Co. in Phoenix. He suggested that the men of AiResearch hold a company rodeo. He thought he might round up a dozen experienced men and fill in with reckless dudes.

"I couldn't believe it myself," said Thomas. "Fifty men —all of them with professional rodeo experience—entered the rodeo."

Buck Sossaman, one of the entrants, completed in Rodeo Cowboys Association-approved shows in southern Colorado and Arizona from 1952-1956.

Hank Dunlap, a native of Phoenix, rode everything with hair from boyhood, and as a bullrider, he appeared in dozens of Arizona town and sheriff's posse rodeos.

Clyde Marster, and his son, Joe, between them could count 40 years of rodeoing. Clyde used to win bronc and bull riding events in the Northwest. He had never finished out of the money in a wild horse race. His son competed in rodeos in Hawaii during a hitch with the navy.

Jim Palmer had a try at Arizona and Texas rodeos.

Basil W. Cox participated in some of the big drives and roundups of the Pleasant Valley country, cutting his teeth and hide on the infamous rimrock mossyhorns.

Thomas, too, was raised "in the school of cowboying that believed that if any job couldn't be done on horseback, it wasn't worth doing." He made his living breaking horses in the Dakotas, in Montana, in Wyoming for a decade, and later hired out as range detective and hunting guide. When he came to Arizona in 1954, he stayed on as wrangler at a Wickenburg dude ranch, and hand for the Cowden Livestock Co.

"I was riding from sunup to sundown up to the day before I came to work for AiResearch," said Thomas. "Now I'm punching a time clock instead of cows, and I doubt if they eat beef on the moon.

"Do you?"

Somehow or other the conversation got around to hangover cures of the Great Southwest.

"The Bull," said a gent. "On the border it's pronounced the Bool. It is made of equal parts orange pop and stale beer."

"Too complicated," said another man. "Leave out the pop."

And so the investigation was launched. We remembered a friend, Jack Yelverton of Douglas, who swore by *enchiladas con huevos* smothered in warm *tequila*. If that didn't work he slipped into sneakers and ran 4 or 5 miles, followed by a cold, needle shower.

"Moose milk," suggested a woman of the West. "A shot of bourbon in a glass of cow's milk."

We asked around. "The best hangover cure is really a preventative," said an oldtimer. "Eat a quarter pound of lard before you take your first drink."

Said another, "Soak for two hours in a tub of steaming water."

And from a career battler of barleycorn: "Drink two glasses of hot water just before you go to bed. This will fill your bladder and drive you from the bed in the middle of the night, and then you must drink two more glasses of hot water. That is the Desert Rat cure."

Many Southwesterners, of course, swear by *menudo*. It is as much an institution as it is something to eat. Traditionally Mexican hosts will put *menudo* to simmering before the guests arrive. A stew of tripe, corn, onions, red chili, oregano and coriander, *menudo* is served as a midnight snack or breakfast.

"There is the Prairie Oyster," said a Phoenician whose credentials include an Alcoholics Anonymous card. "The Prairie Oyster is a can of chilled tomatoes, a tablespoon of steak sauce, a dash of tobasco, and a raw egg. It is taken as a mass."

Something old: Grapefruit juice, tequila, a spoon of salt. Something new: The Bullshot, a shot of vodka, over the rocks, covered with beef consomme.

"The best, but kinda impractical for civilians, I discovered at Biggs Field, Texas," said a former flier. "Sufferers from the effects of *cabeza de Juarez* used to go down to the flight line and mooch a big whiff of bottled oxygen."

"Hah," exclaimed a young Arizona mother. "I have a hangover cure that never fails.

"Three kids screaming for breakfast."

"Funny thing," said Gene Luptak, heading for his degree at Arizona State University. "I used to be terrible at directions. The first day I tried to find the campus I wound up in Mesa."

Luptak started a hobby of collecting Arizona postmarks. He traveled to the most distant corners of the state, mailing himself postcards. He felt foolish mailing himself blank postcards, so he would scribble: "Dear Gene, never forget the swell time I had here. Best of luck. Gene."

He got more than 250 cancellations. In fact, he got them all.

"I still don't know where a lot of Arizona places are," said Gene. "But I finally know where I am."

GLEESON—"Yee Wee," my informant had said, "is 106 years old and quite a character."

Ah so. Exaggeration and understatement.

Yee was standing in the junk-cluttered front yard of his

ramshackle home in Gleeson, in the hills east of Tombstone. He was a bit over 5 feet tall. He was not wrinkled. His teeth were bad, he had rheumatism, and his sparse whiskers were gray. A gusty wind generated by an approaching thunderstorm tugged at his grimy hat, and pierced his checkered wool shirt. He was cold, but his smile was warm.

"Hokay!" he shouted. "Sit down. Sure. Rib rone no eschool no estore no postolifice, catchee water lainstolm, my God, yes."

He went on to explain that after Gleeson became a ghost town and the water system was shut down, a man offered to haul water for a price beyond Yee's pension budget.

So Yee collected rainwater from his rusting tin roof into a dozen storage cans.

I asked him if he was 106.

"Rib rong time my God yes cook alla time cook anyting wait minute, please."

He went into his house and brought out a cookie can. He opened it, unwrapped a package, and from an envelope, withdrew a work certificate. It attested that Yee came to America from China in 1900, and in 1938 was 53. If correct, he was 73 when I talked with him in 1958.

Why do you live in the country? Why don't you move to the city where you could have running water and electricity and a house that would keep out the wind? I wondered.

"Come on," he said. "Takee allaround. I own house thlee loom bedloom cookstove arso good house next door my God yes. Arr paid fol. No lent. Buy house next door mighty cheap. Catchee lain. Cally wood fol cookstove cook anyting Yee 55 years best cook. Lectlicity too espensive."

As he led me around his estate—two tiny lots in a dead town—the little Chinaman's eyes glowed. Savings of a lifetime of mining labor went into his house, into the investment next door, into his chicken coop, into his rickety furnishings and tools.

Couldn't I see that? It was no matter that other homes of Gleeson were melting and rotting, and that even the once-prized lots along the main street were long ago abandoned to weeds. Here Yee was free from obligation to the world, and no other human was burdened by his existence.

"Mebbe you come back again," said Yee. "Yee plobry gone. Yee neel reave, but ho! some day Yee die my God yes."

Sheets of rain folded over the shack as I drove away. I looked back and saw the old Chinese lining up his water cans under the eaves. Does he have anything of value? I thought. He has a peace of mind, my God, yes.

BISBEE—Frank Cullen Brophy, who was born here, used to say that Main Street was the place for banking business and Brewery Gulch was the place for monkey business.

Maybe so, but there is nothing apish about the Brewery Gulch Gazette. Since it was founded in 1931 the little newspaper with the worldwide circulation has slogged upstream against the trends of modern, speedball journalism.

Take the handmade name plate. The word "Brewery" leans somewhat to the left, and the word "Gulch" yaws to the right. "Gazette" is a compromise. Under the crude lettering is a cartoon of the brewery of the gulch, and below the cartoon, the newspaper's weekly reassurance:

"The sun shines on Brewery Gulch 330 days in the year, but there's moonshine every night."

Folks who don't know the Gazette well, even some who subscribe to it, believe the tabloid was founded in territorial days. F. A. (Mac) McKinney, the founder, lives to set the record right. He began the Gazette in his job printing shop March 1, 1931.

"I just wanted to keep my printers busy for a while," he said. "Job work fell off in the depression, and in a little town you don't fire two good printers and a promising apprentice. From then on the Gazette was the big thing, and the job work a side line."

All political flowers were allowed to blossom in the Gazette. Mac, a Republican, appropriated Column 1, Page 1, for his "Brewery Gulch Philosopher Say —."

In 1946 Mac hired a columnist, George Bideaux, a Democrat. Often the columns of boss and employe, running side by side, expounded opposing views. When Mac retired the first of 1957, Bideaux bought the paper, and the two writers continued to exchange ideas.

Big shots seem to like the Gazette. Conrad Hilton subscribed, along with several state governors, senators, and leaders of commerce and industry.

Bill Epler, a strapping Montanan, became the Gazette's managing editor in 1958, encouraged by his pretty wife, Betty, and fetching daughter, Nancy. Epler started out with the objectivity of an editorial referee—taking ads, selling subscriptions, writing two columns, and gathering up the copy of Stan Adler, Nelle Merwin, Robert Lenon, Vada Carlson, and other Gazette regulars writing on anything from gold prospecting to presidential campaigns.

But Epler soon caught the spirit of the scrappy Gazette, and his Mule Mountain Moonshine column became noted for its tenacity to principal. Epler got a grip on the promiscuous coyote-poisoners and he didn't let go for six months.

Adler, as much as anyone, perpetuates the Gazette's political and philosophical balance. In recalling a Brewery Gulch election campaign of long ago, Adler wrote that Bingo Johnson, a rawboned timbersetter, and Ned White, an eloquent poet, were running for justice of the peace.

White stood on an explosives box and spoke to the customers at a Gulch bar:

"Gentlemen of this revered *arroyo*, I am a candidate for the high office of justice of the peace. It is a position of responsibility and determination. Order is the primary law of civilization . . ."

At this moment Bingo Johnson rose up and smacked White full on the mush. White picked himself up and concluded his speech:

"And self-preservation is the first law of nature."

Ned White walked out of the Gulch and onto the pages of the Gazette.

STANFIELD—Hunting deer, occupation of some 80,000 Arizonans, was tame stuff indeed for William C. Dallis.

Dallis killed the largest elephant of the 1958 Africa hunting season. He did it with one shot.

The man hardly fitted the popular conception of Great White Hunter, and Dallis was not above enjoying the joke on himself: a Negro, a schoolteacher, 62 years old.

"The exploits of Teddy Roosevelt started my dream," said Dallis. "As a boy I promised myself that some day I would go to Africa and hunt the game that Teddy Roosevelt hunted. I never suspected that it would take so long in coming true."

Dallis carried the desire through college in Tennessee, and later training at Ohio State and University of Southern California. He set aside money for guns, ammunition, equipment, cameras.

In the summer of 1958 Dallis had the money and the gear. He had the choice of buying a new car, or going on the hunt. He went. He engaged a white hunter and left Arizona June 3, flying by way of New York, London, Paris, Munich, Vienna, Istanbul, and Nairobi. Soon he was trekking along the base of Mount Kilimanjaro in a safari of 12 natives, a Jeep and a 5-ton truck.

Goal of the expedition was Africa's big five—rhino, elephant, water buffalo, lion, and leopard.

Dallis got three. The elephant was tracked for two and a half days. The tusks totaled 207 pounds. Dallis's buffalo, an exceptionally large one, was killed cleanly with two shots. His leopard measured 7 feet 4 inches. Dallis also took a zebra, a wart hog, an impala, and an oryx. He was back home Aug. 1.

Licenses alone cost Dallis $500. But the compensations,

he said, were worth it. He said he might go back to fill out his limits some day.

We dug the e-l-e-c-t-r-i-c t-r-a-i-n-s out of an old trunk at grandpa's.

On C-h-r-i-s-t-m-a-s morning these t-r-a-i-n-s would be running under the t-r-e-e. If we could keep spelling the words, our child would be wonderfully surprised.

The toys were very old. One locomotive came into the family before I was born. To the credit of the Lionel people, it not only was running perfectly after more than 30 years, its headlight was original equipment.

After so many years of storage, between the disenchantment of one generation and the birth of another, the equipment needed some attention. Track was sprung, insulation on a few wires was rotted by grease, and most of the working parts were invaded by dust. So I spent an evening in the roundhouse, tinkering with O-gauge tracks, transformers, blinker lights, whistles, uncouplers, and automatic unloaders.

In three hours or so, after very little repair, and much oiling and polishing, the equipment was as good as new. Maybe better. I had a feeling the stuff was just beginning to be broken in.

Well, I mused, why can't toy makers put out long-lasting, easily-repaired playthings anymore?

Toys that a poor father can fix without benefit of a welding torch and vulcanizing kit? Toys that a kid can't pound, rip, and scrape apart in 30 seconds?

I don't know how well made are the new trains, but I have a low opinion of the plastic-and-paste in modern nurseries. I am frustrated in attempts to join together what baby hath rent asunder. Almost every week one of her crenulated, fragile do-dads finds its way to my workbench.

"Daddy fix it," she will say, with the flattering implication that her old man can do anything, and I want to put off her learning the awful truth as long as I can.

So I get out my pliers and screwdrivers and can of wire

brads. I study the problems. A piece of plastic has come unglued from a rivet, and the crimped gizmo has slipped off the arc-welded rubber axle.

My kid doesn't need a father. She needs a division of the Olin-Mathieson chemistry research department, a consultant on alloys, and a high-temperature ceramic oven.

I put the tools away and promise to fix the toy later. The toy goes on a high shelf until she forgets about it, and then into one of the growing number of boxes full of hopelessly damaged toys with which her room is furnished.

I wish she could have seen me, with the trains, tightening bolts and tending the brightwork.

Claims of modern toymakers notwithstanding, there never was an indestructible toy. But some used to be repairable.

When, how, and what to salute was never a problem in the Old Corps. You just saluted everything in uniform, including doormen and bus drivers.

Members of the Phoenix Air Reserve should have it so good.

They are civilians most of the time, living in the comfortable snap-brim and knit-tie stratas of everyday society. But when they button on their blues, they must remember another set of values—those of the military.

For example—usually Lester L. Ferguson was called captain, title of first pilot of Bonanza Airlines. At reserve functions he was lieutenant colonel.

Col. William E. Willey, commander of the state headquarters group, out of uniform was far from the wild blue yonder, as state highway engineer.

Some men changed names when they changed uniforms. Ralph Jenkins, county juvenile probation officer, became M/Sgt. Marion R. Jenkins. Al Evernden of Blake, Moffitt and Towne became Lt. Col. Charles A. Everndon. Jim Watson of Camelback High became Capt. Lyndon J. Watson Jr. "Jacque," Scottsdale hair stylist, became Maj. Jack P. Smith.

Arguments concerning public vs. private power disappeared in the common cause. Col. George Green, executive vice president of Arizona Public Service, and Col. Leslie Alexander, assistant general manager of the Salt River Project, could hardly pull rank on one another.

But some of those Old Corps dreams came true in the air reserve.

Maj. Dick Smith, during the week at his swim gym, was boss of Lt. Col. McCauley Clark. In civilian life, Capt. Charles W. Bigando was a postal clerk, talking orders from Martin Bruton, Globe postmaster, an air force reserve master sergeant.

Some men had divided loyalities.

Arizona football teams had no better booster than Sam Maxcy, executive secretary of the Maricopa Farm Bureau. But when Sam put on his silver leaves, he became liaison officer for the Air Force Academy. Maj. Ben Foote, information services officer, had to treat all news media fairly. But then, his boss wondered why he couldn't get stories exclusively for The Phoenix Gazette, for which Ben was a sportswriter.

Two guys were taking navy money by day and air force pay by night. M/Sgt. James M. Sluder Jr. was aircraft maintenance supervisor at Litchfield Naval Air Facility. M/Sgt. J. W. Stone was material planning superintendent at the same base.

Only one man seemed to slip smoothly from civvies to blues. Orme Morehead, in plain clothes, was a Phoenix detective captain, and in air force uniform he was a captain studying air force management.

LUKE AIR FORCE BASE—Capt. Walter C. McMeen thought of himself as something of a throwback to the silk-scarf, box-kite, cow-pasture age of flight.

His buddies outsped sound; Mac got his kicks in the slowest of flying machines.

McMeen was one of five helicopter pilots stationed at

Luke Air Force Base. They had three choppers—new banana-shaped H-21As with rotors fore and aft. All in all the ungainly creations looked like outsized grasshoppers. They were the ugliest aircraft since Kitty Hawk.

"They can't fly, either," said McMeen. "But they do."

McMeen, a tall, trim Breckenridge Texan, flew 100 jet fighter-bomber missions in Korea, and returned to instruct new jet pilots in Nevada. His base there was issued a helicopter for rescue purposes in 1954, and nobody knew how to fly it. Mac learned, and it was his buggy from then on.

He said, "I'm getting some of the thrills out of flying that the pioneers did. Heck, a jet goes overhead and today's kids don't even look up. But when I go over all the kids wave, and I've got time to wave back. Flying a jet is a desk job. You're sitting up there in a great big office, with push buttons and lights and switches. You punch in and out, and sometimes it's just another day's work."

We went for a ride, and it was easy to see why Mac enjoyed his work. A helicopter is a powered picture window. You sit up front inside a plastic bubble. Your view is hemispherical. It's like having a chair on a cloud.

Getting off the ground is a comical series of actions. The engine whines and sputs; the craft huffs and groans; the blades begin to churn. Before the propellers reach top speed the chopper imitates every dance step between bunny hop and samba. And the noise! It sings and whines and screams.

"When you can't hear anything else," drawled Mac, "you know it's running right." So pervasive is the noise, the copilot and pilot, sitting side by side, can exchange words only through the intercom system.

Mac leaned on the control sticks and foot pedals. The chopper rose steadily, hesitated in a pivot, then crabbed across the fields in the direction of Gila Bend. We beat along at 90 mph, now at 100 feet, then up to 300, then back to 150. Cotton pickers lowered their sacks and stared. Cattle below us milled. A goose chandelled into a thicket. A coyote zigzagged between greasewood bushes.

Returning, we approached a farmhouse east of Buckeye. A curvaceous housewife burst through her back door. She smiled. She waved. McMeen, a happily married man with three children, threw the woman a salute.

"I don't know who she is, and I never will know. But every time I fly over, she waves. We're good friends."

Such friendships cannot flower at the speed of sound.

Frank Mulkins of Glendale, did not pretend to be a poet. He just had something to say, and he sought a method. Long ago he and his brother, Forrest, of Phoenix, were carried a mile by a Mobeetie, Texas, tornado. Their house was wrecked, but the Mulkinses were protected by a feather tick and were set down unharmed.

As Frank Mulkins told it:

> Uncle Jess, our stepgranddad on our
> Mother's side was thrown out the house into
> The woodpile, and killed therein.
> And our parents' marriage license was carried
> Some 90 miles away and was found by someone
> Who knew the folks and mailed it back.
> Splinters were driven deep into the walls
> Of a rock jail.
> This tornado escapade was the cause of us
> Coming to Arizona in the early '90s.

I never had a pet rabbit, through some quirk of chance. By my mother's graying head and soiled rugs, I had everything else. Chameleons, frogs, turtles, guppies, and dogs and cats and rats and mice. A naked, freshly-hatched robin fell from its nest, and I made a bed for it in the front room and fed it milk, bread and houseflies. After that robin was turned loose, it would return to the porch every day for weeks for a handout.

There was a loyal springer spaniel that every morning

would sit mournfully by a saguaro when I boarded a school bus, and every afternoon he would be waiting there. Somebody fed that dog poison, and at the time I swore I'd shotgun the person who did it. I still might, if I ever find him.

I remember a chicken, too. Chickens are supposed to be dumb. This chicken outwitted my Old Man, and there aren't many human beings who can make that brag. Paw got 100 chicks and set up an incubator in the garage. Very quickly one chick learned to respond to a name, Cheep-Cheep, and Paw would feed it grasshoppers which he had slapped down in the yard.

Long after the other 99 chickens had gone across the stove to chicken heaven, that pet bird had the run of the place. One day mother traded pets with the lady next door, and we had baked duck, and they ate stewed chicken. The implications of this example of man-chicken-woman wisdom stirred me then, and have since.

But anyway, never a rabbit.

So we went out to a Phoenix zoo to kill some time with the camel and the ostrich and the orang-utan.

The tyke streaked past the exotic fauna toward the boxes of guinea pigs, chicks, chinchillas and rabbits. Children were allowed to handle these cuddly creatures, and our girl made such a commotion, she caught the attention of Ray DeBerge, operator of the zoo.

"Would you like one to take home with you, honey?" said Ray. I made parental faces and kicked at his shins, but Ray went on:

"You can have anything you want—a chicky, a guinea pig, or a bunny." Yeah, she said, a bunny.

We don't have a way to get him home, I muttered faintly, or any place to put him up, and we're fresh out of rabbit food.

"Turn him out in the yard," said Ray. "He'll keep the grass mowed. Or feed him table scraps and Wheaties. Aw, heck, I'll give you a box for the rabbit and a supply of pellets."

An hour later we turned the rabbit loose in the rye.

He ate. The neighbor's cat stalked him. Into the house with the bunny. But we soon learned that you cannot allow a rabbit to hop on the carpets. For every pellet you put into a rabbit, you get seven in return.

Rabbits also are great jumpers. The rabbit jumped out of the biggest boxes we could find in the neighborhood, and his droppings were to be found from the kitchen stove to the bathroom sink.

I did not remember cleaning up after the pets when I was a kid.

Somewhere, I heard the wheels of justice grinding.

Chapter Twelve

A friend said of Wilmar Goodwin (Buster) Holsinger:

"He is a girl rag-picker's Marlon Brando, he has the gait of a homemade Sherman tank, and he can do anything."

More accurately, Buster Holsinger in 32 years had a fling at nearly everything, and succeeded with most. He was far-and-away Arizona's do-it-yourself champ, and possibly the world's. He built a bomb shelter. He rode a motorcycle to Mexico City. Oh yeah, he raised an alligator in his house.

Holsinger was brought to Phoenix a month after he was born in Los Angeles. He started asking questions when he was 3, and never stopped. Yet he wasn't a standout student in grammar school or at Phoenix Union High, except in those subjects which stimulated his checkerboard curiosity.

When World War II broke out he went into the navy as a diver. Off Saipan one day in 1944 he was almost killed. He made a too-deep dive with inadequate equipment, and they hauled him up 130 feet, cold and lifeless, suffering from carbon dioxide poisoning and the bends. Somehow a medic got his heart going again.

Holsinger finished high school under the GI Bill, and took a job cleaning transformer tanks at Daley Electric Co. About that time he signed his wife, Jeannie, to the Holsinger code:

"I'll be a horrible husband," he swore. "If you want somebody safe and sane, get lost. If you want me, be prepared to give up all your constitutional rights."

"Yes, dear," she said, with a meekness uncommon in becoming brunettes.

Their first mutual madness was their house. They bought two acres at 3229 E. Osborn and hired an architect. Buster got a contractor's license and supervised construction. When the house was done, Buster painted it kelly green.

Then Buster fell in love with motorcycles. He tuned his machine to atomic explosiveness, and lost interest only when he missed hitting a burro by a few inches during his record run to Mexico City.

Perhaps in self-defense, Jeannie began breeding Persian cats, and her judgment brought forth a double grand champion sire.

Next it was orchids. Adjoining the living room Buster established a huge steam room which soon was filled with a jungle of tropical plants. Buster also raised bees and built an 8-inch telescope. On weekends he went to Guaymas for skin-diving in gear he made himself.

In the time he had left over Buster built two sprawling greenhouses where he propagated philodendron and exotic vines, for his amusement and profit.

The alligator, Buster admitted, was his most senseless project, and the bomb shelter, his most practical. The way Holsinger went about building a bomb shelter is indicative of his uninhibited imagination.

He trusted steel more than he did concrete. So he purchased a used cylindrical storage tank, cut out the ends, and split it. Then he pried it open and set the quonset-like steel arch into a hole in his back yard. Concrete formed the end walls and floor and hatch, but Holsinger's hide-away principally was a buried dome of flexible steel. It cost $150.

The bomb shelter was built to save his life, and it also saved his house.

He was raising orchids. Their beauty was short-lived.

Buster took pictures of them, first in black and white, and later in color. He wasn't satisfied with the color processing, so he bought some chemistry books and began to make his own developers. The University of Physical Science gave him an honorary degree for his discoveries, and Buster's wife, Jeannie, almost gave him the door.

His foul chemicals ruined plumbing, destroyed sinks, peeled furniture, and disintegrated tile floors. The bomb shelter became Holsinger's laboratory. Neighbors who feared a Holsinger explosion more than they did the H-bomb, breathed easier.

Holsinger wondered about alligators. He bought one. It grew. At first it was fun having an alligator in the house. The critter was useful for frightening Jeannie's friends, and Buster's pals would marvel at the way the beast could snap thick pencils between its beartrap jaws.

When the alligator grew to 3 feet in length, Holsinger no longer could control it. The critter was given the run of the orchid room. Finally, Buster knew the alligator had to go.

"I will not say what I did with it," said Holsinger. "But people at Arizona State University are still wondering how an alligator appeared one morning from the depths of the goldfish pond in front of Old Main."

Despite, or perhaps because of, his eccentricities, Holsinger was advanced to a responsible position in the accounting department of the electric company.

In recent years, Holsinger lost interest in jungle plants, and was thinking of turning his greenhouses into rearing rooms for aquatic life.

He cleared out the orchids and turned his Little New Guinea into a library to hold the medical books which he consulted for self-treatments. Only memories were the bees, the telescope, the alligator, the man-eating plants. Just one black, long-haired persian cat stalked the halls.

Buster for two years channeled his diverse drives to the study of organic chemistry at ASU.

"I think I've found my life interest," he said. "I may not make a living at it, but it will be my preoccupation."

Which isn't to say nothing interesting happened anymore at 3229 E. Osborn.

"We didn't invite any friends for New Year's Eve," said Buster, "and 26 couples dropped in."

A 78-year-old gentleman who used to have a jewelry business in Cleveland settled in the Valley, and passed out calling cards which read:

NO ADDRESS NO PHONE
Retired
John H. Holkenborg
NO BUSINESS NO MONEY

WICKENBURG—It now takes a pound of prevention to effect a 40-ton cure for galloping gold fever.

The doctor with the headache in 1958 was Carl Beillen, general chairman of Gold Rush Days in Wickenburg. Beillen was known locally as the operator of Montevista Ranch, and noted nationally for his comment:

"You can't make any money dude-ranching, but you live as well as your guests, and that's pretty good."

In 10 years the gold rush idea grew from an afternoon tourist picnic to a three-day wing-ding drawing more than 20,000 celebrants. Used to be the tenderfeet panned a few pinches of color from some nearby streambed. In 1953 a promotional genius brought the gold ore to town. Gold Rush Days went big time, and it now took 40 tons of gravel to keep the tourists busy.

Along 700 feet of placer ditches as many as 1,000 dudes grubbed and swished from dawn to midnight, and some did right well. In 1956 a woman from Chicago recovered an ounce of raw gold, worth $32. It was no trick at all to take out a few grains.

But the popularity of the gold panning was almost its undoing.

It's against the law to salt gravel with processed gold, and raw gold is scarce. And professional panners are still plentiful.

Wickenburg leaders hadn't found high grade gravel in Arizona for years. Lately they trucked in loads of the best native stuff, and improved it with raw concentrates. One year, the sweetener came all the way from the Mother Lode in California.

The search for concentrates became frantic until a bearded prospector from the Yukon walked into Wickenburg with a pound of dust in his poke.

Joe Lutch, Wickenburg jeweler, weighed the gold on his antique scales, and advised Beillen to buy the whole batch for something more than $500.

But Wickenburg had its share of oldtimers—knowledgeable retired miners and active prospectors who could find a fleck of gold in a sand dune. Their ranks were swelled during Gold Rush Days by brother prospectors from the back country of Arizona and neighboring states.

There was no denying them places at the Wickenburg placering trenches, and many of the sourdoughs made good day wages. One year, a California prospector panned three ounces.

Beillen thought it more than coincidental that the same prospector returned the next year with exactly three ounces of gold for sale. And Beillen had further cause for worry when the Yukon prospector, supplier of the 1958 gold, said: "I think I'll stick around for the show."

CHAMPIE RANCH—Tony Pocek was camping on

French Creek below the ranch. Steve Carson convinced me we should have a visit with Tony.

Well after sundown that frosty night, Steve and I set off, carrying bags of hot dinner and chocolate cake which had been prepared by Ruthie the cook. Steve would soon be 8. He led the way, pointing out obstacles with a powerful flashlight. After stumbling for 10 minutes through the arrowweed and over the mushy watercourse, we caught sight of Tony Pocek's fire.

"Come in! I'll show you around," said Tony, the way a rich man might invite honored guests into his mansion.

The camp was on an elevated sandy patch protected by the trunk and thick branches of a fallen cottonwood. Heat from Tony's small fire was reflected into the camp by a scrap of sheet iron.

Earlier in the day, Tony had built his fire in the middle of the camp. At sunset he had skimmed off the coals, stirred the sand with a stick, and made his bed of twigs and a single blanket.

Steve and I sat near the warm bed and listened to Tony's story.

Tony had a full gray beard and one suit of clothes: field shoes, bib overalls, wool shirt, surplus army jacket, and billed cap. All his belongings fit into two square metal cans which Tony would sling on shoulder straps.

As a boy he came to this country from his native Austria in 1906. He tried all sorts of work, but he enjoyed none of it until he began looking for gold in Arizona's Bradshaw Mountains 30 years ago.

"Gold is the most valuable metal," Tony said, "because through the search for gold most of the discoveries of the other minerals have been made."

And according to Tony, it is the finding, not the possession, of gold which makes his life worthwhile. When he strikes a rich pocket, said Tony, he either gives it away or uses it to finance another adventure.

Scattered over the Bradshaws, to the northwest of Champie

Ranch, Tony had set up 35 camps. Some were in abandoned cabins; others in the open; still others in mine tunnels. In each camp he kept a cache of gear and grub.

Tony talked for an hour. He told of his headquarters on Lynx Creek where he stayed in a tunnel in "darkness, silence, and solitude." He related his escape from friends who almost ruined his life with wine. He spoke of his freedom to move with the seasons, to do what he pleases.

It was past Steve's bedtime. We said our goodbys and I boosted Steve onto my shoulders—50 pounds of tired but thoughtful boy.

We were halfway back to the ranch before Steve spoke:

"I know that the President of the United States is the most important man most of the time. But once in a while couldn't Tony be the most important man in the world?"

TOURING WITH THE DONS—This was my first trip to Hopiland, to that strange and beautiful people who drive 1959 pickups and live in stone-age houses.

I became aware of some of the paradoxes which have puzzled the white man since he first met the Hopi people.

Students of the Hopi tribe may be amused by my elemental observations. The trip was fast; my knowledge small. But the Hopi marks the virgin mind like a hot iron on hide, and some things I would never forget.

A century of religious pleading and economic bribery has not pried large numbers of the proud Hopis from their stark mesas. They live in primitive dwellings. Their women fetch water from the valleys. The men go by foot to till their scraggly patches of corn scattered for miles about their mesas. This is the way of their fathers.

And their favorite delicacy is strawberry pop!

Water is their scarcest necessity. They are the cleanest reservation Indians I ever saw. Their homes are tidy, their maidens dainty, their menfolk spruce.

They toss their sewage and garbage over the edges of the cliffs.

Surly no society rears happier children. I must have seen 500 children in five villages, and never heard one cry. We were told about the ingenious Hopi disciplinary system. Mothers and fathers never correct their children. They give them love and guidance. And who, then, slaps down the little rascals when they need it? The uncles, and with an iron hand.

Yet these same well-behaved children I saw spit toward a god. At Shungopovi six underground kivas were "live"—that is, occupied by the kachinas performing religious rituals. A kachina wearing a fox skin emerged from a kiva. He ran to the other kivas where he circled and barked. When he trotted through the muddy streets of Shungopovi, the children spat—but this was just a part of the timeless ritual.

At New Oraibi a buffalo dance was in progress. The village square was lined with several hundred Hopis who had patiently watched this social ceremony for eight hours. Two little girls, about 4 years old, danced with two buffalo braves in flawless unison to the beat of a drum and the chant of a male glee club. The discipline of the singers, the dancers, and the observers was almost painful to see.

And what brought the children running to the tourist buses while their parents laughed? Bubble gum.

Hopis do not like to have their pictures taken. They think a photograph captures a piece of their soul. The leaders at Walpi are offended if a white man merely asks to take a picture. And at Old Oraibi a 100-year-old chief had a sign on the door of his store: "Pose for picture, $2."

Contradiction is everywhere. Much is explained by the division of the Hopis themselves, into progressive and conservative factions. They are a people who believe they had achieved a cultural utopia. Some Hopis have reluctantly broken with the old ways. Others are between. But you cannot walk the narrow streets of Walpi and believe that one day they'll be deserted.

My first impulse, when first I heard the name of the

Ladies Auxiliary, Central Arizona Chapter, American Society of Professional Engineers, was to go get drunk.

But Jim Stone is a friend. I heard him out.

Jim said that LACACASPE had 58 members. The gals wanted to do some good in this wicked old world, so they launched Project Earn Five.

Idea was, each member would earn some money to bolster a loan fund for engineering students at ASU.

"Come back here," begged Jim. "Listen to how these women earned their money."

Mrs. J. D. Bullock, of Scottsdale, earned $5.51 by salvaging bottles from roadsides, peddling a pint of spaghetti sauce, baby sitting, and selling one yet-unborn kitten.

Mrs. Harold Hudson, of 1222 N. Third St., charged her husband $5 for stenographic work in connection with his club duties.

Mrs. T. M. Marong, of 4802 E. Exeter, knitted TV slippers.

Mrs. Harry Doberstein, 916 W. Moreland, made and sold *tamales*, and a man's shirt.

Mrs. Robert Eveland, LACACASPE president, of 2451 E. Elm, went into the coffee cake business.

Mrs. K. K. King, 1535 W. Virginia, drove her sister members to club meetings, and charged taxi rates.

Mrs. James Warne, 4125 E. Minnezona, sold grapefruit instead of giving it away as usual.

Mrs. O. O. Farley, of 1532 W. Flower Circle, washed the family car and confiscated a liberal fee from the family budget.

Mrs. Stephen Chalmers, 4044 E. Whitton, made and sold date nut bread.

Mrs. Bert Griffin, 312 W. Glenrosa, sold hand-painted vanity jars.

Mrs. Ted Boothroyd, of 1351 W. Catalina, made stuffed toys and sold them as playthings for kids and cats.

Mrs. Leslie McDougall, of 802 N. 10th St., sold cake recipes for 10 cents each at a meeting of engineers in Tucson.

Mrs. Harry Bigglestone, of 3337 E. Flower, turned over $5 she earned as a substitute teacher.

Mrs. George Wilbur, of 116 Palmcroft, Tempe, took in sewing.

Other members cut their family's hair at $1.75 a head. Some fixed kitchen plumbing and electrical appliances. Two women (not identified by Jim Stone) won their $5 bills playing poker.

"And now," said Jim Stone, "Let me tell you about the plans for National Engineers Week of the Central Arizona Chapter, American Society of Professional Engineers. Hey! Come back here! Friend!"

His voice grew weaker and weaker, and in about an hour, I could not hear him at all.

A hundred million Americans can describe this television scene by heart.

The camera zooms into frontier Arizona, into a rustic but spacious home of the struggling family.

Mature ornamental trees overhang a long veranda in a way to delight the picture editor of Ladies' Home McTogetherness magazine. The camera dollies through the wide front door. There is Mother, preparing the evening meal for her man and flock.

Dominating the main room is a wide fireplace where great black pots suspend simmering feasts over a snapping fire. Artistically hung and placed about the room are heirlooms and about 15 blocky, hand-hewn pieces of furniture. Doors lead offstage to bedrooms. All in all, the cabin is so big and comfortable, you wouldn't be surprised to find an indoor water closet concealed behind the elk head and bookshelves.

Well, I couldn't help comparing Hollywood's notions with something I saw.

We went to Columbia, an old gold camp on Humbug Creek northwest of Phoenix at the foot of the Bradshaws. Columbia is not many airline miles west of the Black Canyon

Highway, but the country is so broken you have to go nearly to Wickenburg, double back through Castle Hot Springs region, and shake a year's life off a good pickup truck in the last five miles. Fortunately, the claims at Columbia were held by a resident prospector who would just as soon shoot a vandal as a sidewinder.

A few hundred feet up creek from the prospector's home stood a stone cabin. It may have been the most nearly complete, abandoned, relic, family dwelling in the state. Other cabins are older, but weather and idiots have damaged them. Still other pioneer houses have become portions of modern homes.

But I had never seen, from Dos Cabezas to La Paz, anything to equal the Columbia cabin as an unblemished example of the kind of shelter settlers used before the Indians were whipped.

The cabin made a room 10 by 14 feet. The walls were put up without mortar. Small stones more or less filled the chinks between the larger ones. The one door was about 5½ feet high, and there were no windows. Four gunports, from waist to eye high, guarded the sides. Obtuse gables of stone anchored a crooked juniper ridgepole, and the rafters and beams of small cedar logs supported a roof of thatched arrowweed.

The fireplace, at the rear wall, was 18 inches square. Still hanging from the rafters were whittled wood hooks for storing food and equipment. The floor was dirt, and it always was.

That is where they lived—our pioneers.

(After this story was published, George Stewart of 3700 N. Central, identified himself as an Arizona native son. "That was my grandmother's home," he said. "She raised her family in that one little room, and in a tent outside.")

"P.S. I found the parts in the bottom of the box."

Those words end a famous American business letter. It was written by a complaining customer, and it has been printed in a variety of forms for a half a century in business magazines across the nation.

"That letter is often misquoted," said Ruth A. Mosher of Avondale. "The original was written to my father, whose place of business was La Junta Hardware Co., La Junta, Colo., in 1907.

"The writer was a German living in Tempas, Colo. He had ordered a cistern bucket pump. These were used to bring soft water to the kitchen, from a cistern under the house.

"Pumps were packed and shipped from the factory in long, narrow boxes, and on the lid was bolted a frame to hold the handle.

"I was keeping books when the letter of complaint arrived. Daddy called me to read it. We had a good laugh, and Daddy pasted it under the glass of a large showcase. Soon it was picked up and printed by Iron Age magazine, and it has been circulating these last 51 years.

"The letter really said, 'P.S. Found the damn handle in the box.' "

Jack L. Willems tells a story about one of the world's champion drinkers.

This man was a wealthy general contractor in California. He habitually downed at least 10 shots of whiskey before breakfast. He went to church one day, fortified by 13 martinis, and stood up in the middle of the service and heckled the preacher.

But all in all he was a refined lush. Somehow he kept his business, and maintained a luxurious home for his wife and three daughters. He wouldn't drink at home. He wanted his liquor served over a bar. He liked the excitement.

He would walk into one of his many favorite saloons, and his chums would cheer. The drinks usually were on him. His capacity was enormous. From hair-of-the-dog to night-cap, he would drink 50 or 60 shots of whiskey. Between gulps of Old Hammerhead, he would chew up and swallow 10 cigars a day.

One day in 1949 he reformed. His health was declining. He was thinking of deserting his family. He lost his business. On this day, he was driving a truck. He prayed. He felt a surge of strength. Without missing a gear, he took the pledge.

He didn't swallow another drink, or smoke another cigar.

After he dried out, the man took correspondence courses in theology. Before long he was making $600 a month with his own truck line. He spent some of his spare hours helping at a mission for alcoholics and other derelicts.

In 1954, the International Union of Gospel Missions asked the man to found a mission in Phoenix.

The man quit his job. He moved his family to Phoenix. He rented an old church at 501 E. Jefferson. He and his wife scrubbed every corner, and spread 27 gallons of paint. Phoenix Lighthouse Rescue Mission opened its doors in May, 1955, with the support of many Valley churches.

Soon the mission was serving 4,000 meals a month. A dormitory was outfitted upstairs for 22 men. Sample drugs were donated, and three doctors gave their services when needed. Churchwomen collected and cleaned old clothing for the mission.

The man in Willem's story became an expert in rehabilitating drunks. He could reach beyond the alcoholic haze and bring forth the courage that lies dormant in many sots. The man, from personal experience, had earned a passkey to the private hells of alcoholism.

Willems said he knew all the facts of the story to be true. The man of the story is he.

"This is Elliott Nugent," said the voice in the telephone. "Elliott. Two Ls and two Ts."

Yes, sir, Mr. Nugent.

"I am a playwright, author, producer, director. New York City. Staying at the Outpost. Do you ever do stories about people visiting here?"

Once in a while, Mr. Nugent.

"Well, I've got a story. If you don't want it, I'm going to put it into the hands of people who don't like Arizona. Look me up in *Who's Who*. That'll give you the background."

(Sure enough, such a name was listed on Page 2,067 of the 1958-59 edition. He has had a hand in some Broadway plays—"Voice of the Turtle," "The Male Animal," "Seven Year Itch.")

Go on, Mr. Nugent. What is your story?

"This town ought to do something with its streets and signs. A guy has a couple of drinks or lights a cigaret and he could drive right into a canal. Some of the streets dead-end at canals. Did you know that?"

Yes, sir.

"Another thing. This place is so fouled up a stranger can't find his way around.

"The other night I left the Koko and tried to find my way back to the Outpost. I drove part way into several canals. You find a place marked 58th Street and you can't find 60th Street. I finally found the Valley Ho. Know where that is?"

I do.

"I went inside and asked a bellboy if the place was a hotel, and he said it was, and I asked him for directions to the Outpost, and he told me how to get there.

"I must have spent four hours getting from that night club to my room. This is a terrible place. No consideration for strangers who come out here for a little relaxation."

And what do you want me to do, Mr. Nugent?

"Write a story about it. Don't you want the story? I'm not kidding. I know people in some states who don't like Arizona and they'd be happy to get the story. Don't you think I won't give them the story, too.

"I called your Chamber of Commerce, and a man down there is going to call me back. They know what I can do with such a story."

So do I, Mr. Nugent.

"You don't like the story? Well, I don't like you. Goodbye."

Goodbye, Mr. Nugent. Goodbye.

An idea of grace and imagination had admirable results at Arizona Children's Hospital.

The bell rang in the mind of a Phoenix official of Mountain States Telephone and Telegraph Co. He read a story in a medical magazine. An old telephone switchboard had been installed in a children's ward of an Eastern hospital. The kids were having fun, and also teaching their tired and injured muscles new manipulations.

So the official spread the word to his friends to look for an old switchboard. It took a while, but an ideal piece of equipment was turned back by a Phoenix business. It was an old-fashioned, cord-plug-and-key switchboard, with lights and hand-crank bell-ringer.

It wouldn't do to steal the switchboard, and throw the enventories out of balance. A memo was sent up the chain of command. The memo went all the way to a vice president in Denver, and big shots added their initials all along the line.

In February, 1959, William Butler, a telephone installer, took the switchboard to Arizona Children's Hospital. On his own time he had overhauled the relic and fixed it so the children could not shock themselves. He connected three telephones to the exchange. Mrs. Roberta Hall, a dial instructor for the company, went to the hospital to teach the children how to use the board.

Pauline Trister, elementary and music teacher at the hospital, said that she never saw anything so catch the fancy of the children.

Nobody in the Valley of the Sun was better prepared for running to the hills on Grudgement Day than Frank Gilpin of Mesa.

"And when they tell me an H-bomb is coming my way, I'll not move a foot," he said.

Civil defense officials probably wouldn't like Frank's attitude. That was all right with Frank. He didn't like theirs. Ever since the superbombs were invented, the official preachment of survival was headlong flight.

You were supposed to lay in a permanent store of chuck. Keep your car gassed. Buy a water can. When the balloon went up, you were instructed to toss your grub, medicine, water, blankets, and assorted kin into the family car, and strike out for the designated evacuation route.

"Not me," said Frank. "I'm staying put."

Frank could go in style, if of a mind to.

A few years before, he had retired. He had been a specialist in machinery nearly all his productive life. He could fix anything, and his talents took him to construction jobs in foreign countries.

He and his wife desired to explore Arizona after he quit work. Frank bought a 1954 Studebaker truck with a big six-cylinder engine and four-speed transmission. Frank's son extended the spread of the wheels so that they could carry fatter tires. The truck rarely got stuck, no matter what kind of country it was in.

The cargo bed of the truck was made to hold a compact camping outfit: Innerspring mattress, 30-gallon water tank, compartments where Frank kept enough gear and food for a month's stay. Here and there were attached other luxuries and neccessities—a spare gas can, tools, folding chairs, and an extra glove compartment for Mrs. Gilpin's notions and sundries.

"I've thought it through," said Frank. "There's going to be the biggest traffic jam in history. Most of the people are going to forget their manners and lessons. Soon these Arizona hills will be crawling with desperate, hungry people who will take any means to stay alive and provide for their loved ones.

"I'm staying out of that. We'll run the bathtub full of

water, live off our staples, and protect our home from looters.

"If the bomb gets us—well, it's been a good life. We've tried to live lives of decent human beings, and I have no intentions of ending mine like an animal."

Gus Fotopulos, owner of La Casa Chiquita Cafe, believed he held title to an outsize and unique momento of early Arizona.

Fotopulos had the deed to one of Wyatt Earp's mining claims in Tombstone. Fotopulos knew that he would have to press his contentions against the builders of a grocery and motel on the property, and he had a formidable brief of yellowed documents and certified photostats. He didn't know what he would do. He was like a kid with a grip on a rug where an adult was standing. Fotopulos didn't know whether to yank or run.

"I'll go on paying taxes," he said, with a Grecian shrug. "It may amount to something some day."

The 17-acre trapezoidal claim was named the First North Extension of the Mountain Maid. Wyatt, Virgil, and James Earp, and Robert J. Winders patented the claim Oct. 21, 1881, five days before the famous O.K. Corral fight. Although within the charter boundaries of the original Tombstone townsite, the claim was not built up in 1881. Despite the claim's proximity to the rich Tough Nut and Contention claims, the Mountain Maid Extension apparently never bore much of a mine.

In modern times, however, the claim was crossed by U.S.-80, and by the Southern Pacific. Friends told Fotopulos he ought to put up drawgates and charge tolls.

If of legal worth, Fotopulos' claim had a simple history. It was granted to Wyatt Earp, et al, directly by and from the United States. It was never sold, until 1945, when Cochise County auctioned it off for unpaid taxes. Steve Elmer Tima paid $20, and was given a deed by the board chairman and clerk of Cochise County. Tima's purchase was not contested by any former owner or their heirs. Fotopulos bought the claim from Tima in 1952, for cash and a car, and Tima gave Fotopulos a quit-claim deed. Taxes, varying from $10.22 to $20.87, were paid each year. Fotopulos kept the receipts. He figured he invested some $2,000 in buying and holding the land.

The famous lawman's claim made Fotopulos an Earp fan. An artist friend put murals of Western scenes on the walls of the cafe at 1021 N. Seventh St., Phoenix, and a portrait of Earp looks down on the plates of Greek *tacos.*

Teetotalers and other practical people in this evil old world may not understand my affection for Fred Elfstrom, or why I'll miss him so much.

It was a raw night in mid-January when I came off Tonto Creek with two stones for feet, a sprinkle of snow down my neck, and hands nearly frozen from cleaning trout.

"Cup of coffee," I said. I was shivering like a jack hammerer.

Fred was alone at Kohl's Ranch fishing lodge. Wordlessly he slipped a horny hand inside his denim jacket and withdrew a pint of Old Slowdeath.

I never did get the coffee. We sat by the fire and Fred talked of his cowboying days in Idaho, and how he came to manage a fishing lodge, and a dozen other things I couldn't remember the next day, let alone now. Other memories are sharper. He'd let us in on the best fishing holes, or dig worms for us, or lend a buck saw, and no man was more proper than was Fred the day he brought us the news of a death in the family.

But it was Fred's rugged appearance and air of freedom that a friend would remember best.

First thing you noticed was the hat, sort of gray, greasy and slept-in. Generally there was a checkered shirt over his thick shoulders, and a tidy paunch straining at his Levi's. All this was held aloft on a pair of saddle-bent legs that were rooted in boots so scuffed they looked like suede.

His hands had become as rough as bark, and when he had been on the job a while, he acquired a perfume of kerosene, sweat, paint, beer, pine pitch, trout slime, pump grease and tobacco. He must have shaved some time, but always two days before anybody saw him in public.

Not that Fred was downright sloppy. The women thought him a desirable partner in a schottische or a fox trot, and he could be as courtly as a dandy.

On those occasions when he was fortifying himself against an attack of pit vipers, Fred would become talkative, with his friends. He was about six sheets the time he told us about his unfailing method of luring lunker trout into his creel. He said he would find a nest of baby mice. He'd put them into his pocket and ride a horse down creek to where the water pooled against a cliff, all overhung with timber and grapevines.

Fred would hook one of the wee mice through a pinch of skin at the shoulder. As Fred told it, the mouse would paddle around until Old Fighter was tempted to his doom.

Ironically, Fred met his end in a similar way.

In 1956 a refugee widow from East Germany named Lottie Caspar came to the fishing lodge to help run the kitchen and clean the cabins. She clucked and nagged. He shaved and shined. He even bought a repair kit for the brakes of his old Buick, a chore he had put off for years. He took to drinking soda pop.

Fred and Lottie were married, and soon they moved to Idaho. The woods would never be the same.

It took white man 100 years to build a decent water hole on the 40-mile desert.

Drivers for the old Butterfield line used to say that when God made Arizona he tied off the umbilical cord between Gila Bend and the Pima Villages. Across more than 40 miles of monotonous dunes and alkali flats, there wasn't a single oasis.

Only in recent years had civilization much marked the

Forty Mile Desert. Modern sodbusters leveled land and drilled wells and planted crops. Overnight, Maricopa took the step from razor-brawling cotton camp to law-abiding farm community.

Still, there wasn't a place where a human could get wet to the skin. A swimming pool—that's what the Forty Mile Desert needed, then and now.

Dick Broderick of Maricopa was pretty proud of the way the swimming pool was built.

"The Maricopa Post Office serves a population of 1,800 black, brown, red and white residents scattered over some 140 square miles. The nearest swimming pools were at Casa Grande and Gila Bend," he said.

John E. Smith and Fred Enke prodded the Maricopa Rotary Club. The former University of Arizona athletes donated 3½ acres with highway frontage, a few hundred yards southeast of the town. All 25 members of the Rotary contributed money, time or equipment. Two dozen men spent most of their weekends for four months at the hardest labor.

At a cost of $22,404.90, Maricopa Rotary built a pool worth $50,000 and only $12,000 remained to be paid on the mortgage. Hundreds of Forty Mile Desert youngsters learned to swim the first year the pool was open. The pool was the largest body of water many had ever seen.

Broderick said the pool wasn't exactly a dream come true. It was more like a mirage, given substance.

In late April, 1959, Arizonans had to squeeze closer together.

The core of the Elario family arrived. Mama. Papa. Two sons. Their wives. Seven *bambinos*. Welcoming the new residents were four grownups and five children, all Elarios.

In 1945, there wasn't a single member of the Italian-American family to be found in Arizona. The closest Elario was working for the navy department in the State of Washington. He was Leo Elario, Jr.

"Doesn't it ever stop raining here?" complained Elario to a fellow worker. "I haven't had my overshoes off for four months."

The remark was overheard by an old Arizona Indian, nicknamed Chief. Chief spoke up:

"Why don't you go to Phoenix? I lived there all my life and the sun shines almost every day."

Leo Elario came to the promised land. He worked in Phoenix as a warehouseman, learned how to lay bricks, became a masonry contractor, and acquired his own general contracting firm, Century Builders.

Leo Elario's family, deeply rooted in Topsfield, Mass., thought he had gone soft in the head. Papa Elario had immigrated in 1912, married a Massachusetts girl, founded a building business, and fathered many children. All of the offspring sensibly settled in or near Topsfield—all but Leo Jr.

But as young Leo prospered, Topsfield Elarios came to visit. Mama and Papa began to spend some time in Phoenix every year. Once they brought an unmarried daughter, Barbara. An enterprising Sunnyslope gent, Richard Dawson, wooed and won Barbara, and returned with her to Topsfield.

"The desire to move to Arizona increased for many years," said Leo Jr. "I didn't think they'd reach the same decision all at once. This past winter did it. They all got fed up with slush and mush."

Dawson brought Barbara and their two children. Close behind were the elder Elarios, and their sons, Henry and Donald, their wives, and seven children. Three homes were sold in Topsfield.

There was promise the exodus would continue. There were three more large, second-generation branches in Massachusetts, and with Topsfield evacuated, the state was becoming downright lonely.

Chapter Thirteen

PRESCOTT—If Bill Stewart were politically inclined, he could probably win any election in and around this city.

He was one of those rarest of humans who is liked and respected by anybody you ask. He earned esteem by excelling at one of mankind's most exacting skills, and passing on his talent to anyone willing to learn.

Stewart was a marksman. Laid out on a table, his medals for rifle and pistol sharpshooting would fill a square yard. He had held the state small and big bore championships, and had gone back to the big league matches at Camp Perry, Ohio, 10 years. He and his teammates in 1940 beat out 50 crack civilian teams to win the VFW Trophy.

At 69, Stewart had lost little edge off his eye. A couple of years before he won a medal in the Coast Guard Match by shooting a big bore score of 99 out of 100 points from 200 yards, sitting position.

Stewart was so small you'd think a Springfield would kick him back to the ordnance shop. His short, slim build was wiry still, and he made up in technique what he lacked in size. That was nearly the story of his life.

Orphaned at 4 in Indiana, he was put in a home until he was 18. By the time he came to Prescott in 1922, he had held many hard-labor jobs. He worked in some of the Bradshaw mines, and then became fireman-engineer at Fort Whipple, where he stayed 25 years.

To two generations of Yavapai youngsters, Stewart became Uncle Bill. Any boy or girl willing to endure the disciplines of Uncle Bill got rifle, ammunition, and education free of charge. Stewart taught gun safety and basic rules by the book. After a student had the fundamentals, Stewart polished the pupil with lessons from his experience. For example, Stewart taught children to shoot the military .45 automatic with thumb and trigger finger only. That's the way he shot the piece; the method made flinching almost impossible.

Stewart estimated that Prescott High School students shot 35,000 hand-loaded rounds through rifles he supplied the school. He also dug into his retirement pay to buy rifles for favorite students. He received no salary as high school rifle coach.

Prescott parents came to entrust other teaching chores to Stewart. He held classes in hunting, camping, swimming, bowling, driving, and even tennis.

Stewart was remarkably capable in other ways. He lived west of Prescott in a two-story concrete home he built by himself. In 1952 Stewart packed his pickup truck, drove to Alaska and returned—no small adventure for a man in his 60s.

He never married, and he said he always wished he had a family. That may explain partially Stewart's affection for all children—but it went deeper than that:

"Teaching kids is the most important job there is," Stewart

said. "Pretty soon they are running this world. I want to help them do some things right."

PEACH SPRINGS—Kate Crozier had had the last laugh on many a friend and enemy, brown and white, which was one of the comforts of having survived 120 years.

Crozier was living with his son, Roy, a mile north of this Hualpai Indian center. A visitor to the rambling home was treated with all the ceremony of a 19th Century pow-wow.

"You sit here," said Roy, indicating a chair facing Kate, who was sitting on a bunk.

"Now you ask questions, and I'll interpret," said Roy.

I said, "I've heard Mr. Crozier was an Indian scout."

Roy addressed his father at length in the Haulpai tongue. The old gentleman listened. He made a striking picture. His gray hair hung to his shoulders, and it was gathered in a blue bandana. His brows were black. A white mustache framed a firm chin. Kate Crozier wore dark glasses, because he was blind.

He spoke to his son in Haulpai.

"My father says he was a scout for General Crook for a year. He was in his 40s when he enlisted as a private in 1882, and he once helped chase Geronimo into old Mexico."

There was another question in English and many minutes of Hualpai.

Then Roy said, "He saw three of Geronimo's band hanged at Fort Grant. Since he left the army he has worked with the white man as a prospector and cowboy. He has been an Indian policeman and a member of the tribal council, and now he is a cattleman. He is a full blooded Hualpai, and was born near here.

Kate Crozier smiled faintly and grasped his cane. Much Hualpai was exchanged, and Roy said in English:

"My father is one of the men who fought the railroad, and worked to establish the reservation for the Hualpai. For this he was given a herd of cattle by his people. He believes that his blindness was caused by brush hitting him in the face as he rode after his stock."

A man who has lived so long must have many relatives? Kate Crozier turned to Roy. Roy translated the question. Kate lifted his hand as he spoke for a long, long time. Roy then translated his father's speech:

"He has but one son and two daughters, but he can count 20 grandchildren, and he was never added up his great-grandchildren. They are so many, and they live from Los Angeles to Oklahoma."

How does the old gentleman spend his day?

More Hualpai.

"He used to get around by himself," said Roy, "Even after he went blind in 1922. But in the last few years he has had to rest in bed, and it is not often he can go by himself to the store or cafe. He says he is growing weak all over."

It was time to go. Kate Crozier had not spoken one word of English. I took his hand for a goodby shake.

"Listen, buddy," said Kate Crozier. "It's nice having people like you drop in for a visit. I'm getting old, and nobody pays much attention to an old Indian. Well, so long, pal."

OAK CREEK—Creel census taker has a brassy sound, but Minnie McFarland gave the job the tinkle of silver earrings in the moonlight.

Minnie said she wouldn't trade with any worker in the world. After all, she was paid to keep an eye on creation's most entertaining combination of critters—humans and fish.

Arizona's only woman creel census checker was hired in 1953. Before that Minnie already was a legend of the Colorado River. She came west from Missouri with her husband, a cook, and Minnie soon learned every channel, whirlpool and slough along the Colorado from Eldorado Canyon to Lake Mead. For seven years Minnie was a registered guide.

But when her husband died in 1954, Minnie needed steady work. She began to go around on a regular weekly schedule, counting, measuring and inspecting catches of fish. She watched for biologists' tags and signs of disease on the fish. She interviewed the fishermen—asked where they had their luck and what kind of boat or lure they used.

The information she gathered was sent to the state game and fish headquarters in Phoenix, where it was used in fisheries management. Not only did Minnie perform her required tasks well, she became "weatherman, news reporter, philosopher, and observer of human nature."

Ladylike, she kept a diary:

"No big fish today. Mostly 12 to 15 inches. One 20-inch and eight 18-inch."

"Stormy all day. Water temperature 52 degrees. Several of the fishermen sitting in their cars, fishing out of their windows. Three of them hooked big trout."

"Rained. Snow on the hills. A nasty day to even try, but some idiots never fail to show up."

"Fishing good. Two big channel cats came in and caused quite a stir at the dock. One at 10 pounds. One 6-pounder."

Minnie used three homes. She parked her house trailer at Temple Bar on Lake Mead. She traveled in a pickup truck outfitted for light housekeeping. And often Minnie would sleep in her boat, tied up in some quiet cove on the upper Colorado lakes.

The biggest fish she ever measured was an 18-pound, 6-ounce rainbow trout taken by a Nevadan at Willow Beach. Her biggest bass was caught below Willow Beach, and it weighed 10 pounds, 2 ounces. Once she saw a crappie which weighed 3 pounds, and a bluegill sunfish which reached a pound.

Minnie was not on the Colorado anymore. Her boss gave her a well-deserved change in assignment, to the high, cool stretch of trout stream above Sedona.

"I expect I'll be doing about the same work here," said Minnie, a trim brunette. "The fishermen will walk the creek looking for fish, and I'll walk the creek looking for fisherman."

So engrossed was she in her work, said Minnie, she had given up fishing: "Haven't wet a line in over a year."

Gabor Zsitvay, 29, lived in Budapest, Hungary.

He studied architecture at the technical university in that city. After the Hungarian freedom revolt was crushed by the Russians, Zsitvay crossed into Austria Nov. 20, 1956.

For a while he sought a new life in West Germany, but, encouraged by a brother who lived in Phoenix, Zsitvay came to Arizona in January, 1957. He took a brief vacation, was hired first by the architectural firm of John E. Stephens & Associates, and then by Frank R. Fazio & Associates.

Zsitvay decided that he would make Phoenix his permanent home, and that he would become a naturalized citizen of the United States. He also hoped to have his own office of architecture. To these ends, Zsitvay went to the state board of technical registration to begin work toward an Arizona architect's license.

Laszlo Sandor, 33, was born in Budapest, Hungary. He studied architecture at the technical university there.

After the Russians quelled the Hungarian revolution, Sandor fled with his wife and infant son. They crossed into Austria Nov. 11, 1956, and went to West Germany to begin anew in the booming free state. He did not know what had become of the others in his family until he heard from a brother.

The brother wrote to Sandor from Phoenix. Why didn't Sandor come to America, too? asked the brother.

The Sandors arrived in Phoenix in February, 1958. After a brief vacation, Sandor was hired by the architectural firm of Ralph Haver & Associates.

Phoenix and Arizona appealed to the Sandors. They agreed that they would make their permanent home in the city, and that they would become American citizens. Some day, Sandor thought, he might have his own professional office.

Sandor and Zsitvay had not met in Hungary, or in Germany, or in America. They had lived in Phoenix many months, each unaware of the other's strangely parallel education, travels, desires and adventures.

And they arrived at the Arizona architecture registration board not five minutes apart. In the explosion of happy Hungarian which followed, they nearly forgot their missions—to apply for state architect's licenses.

KINISHBA—There are those who tear down, and those who build up, and this is a monument to both.

Here the mark of genius is commingled with the scar of the vandal. Today it's a tossup which work, of good and evil, is the most impressive.

The old pueblo of Kinishba was largely ignored for 600 years. Its people had gone away, for unknown reasons, leaving sturdy stone apartment buildings sufficient to house some 2,000 persons.

Perhaps Kinishba was collapsed by the elements before the Apache took possession of the White Mountains around it. Soldiers from Fort Apache, 4 miles to the east, passed time hunting for pots and axheads, and as men of learning came to the state, a few surveys and modest excavations were made.

But not until the 1930s was the enchanting story of Kinishba revealed and rounded out. The work was one of the many major accomplishments of Dean Byron Cummings of the University of Arizona.

Through the summers of some nine years, Dr. Cummings directed the exploration and restoration of a large portion of Kinishba. Backed by the Arizona State Museum, Dr. Cummings painstakingly fitted together the evidence of a hard-working, artistic, peace-loving people. Archaeology students from U of A and Apache laborers rebuilt the walls and roofs of more than 100 rooms around a central patio.

Forty-five acres were tightly fenced. Interiors of the rooms were refurnished with tools and housewares unearthed at the site. Nearby, a museum was built. Dr. Cummings had great hopes and plans for the museum. In his book, *Kinishba*, Dr. Cummings wrote:

"As soon as display cases are obtained for the museum, the articles taken from the ruin will be put on display and will help complete the picture of these inhabitants of Kinishba.

"Visitors will then be able to climb over the rock piles representing the remains of the ancient apartments that still lie undisturbed, saunter through the uncovered rooms of Group I, sit on the bench in the old patio in the shade of the walls of the restored portion, and repeople Kinishba with its happy, industrious throng. . . .

"What is to prevent Kinishba from becoming a clearing house of ideas, information, and trade that will be profitable both to the Apaches and white people? It is sure to become an educational center which will be recognized as valuable in the general scheme of progressive uplift of native Indians and white immigrants.

"It will help the Indians to better appreciate the accomplishments of the older tribes who once occupied their land, and lead them to greater pride in their own race. On the other hand, we boasted 'Americans' will see that other Americans have accomplished something, too, and that the 'natives' are worthy of our respect."

Twenty years after Dr. Cummings wrote with hope and optimism the museum was still standing on the slope above the restored pueblo.

The museum doors had been hauled away.

The window frames had been smashed out, frame, sash and all. From lintels hung frayed strips of cloth—the ragged remainders of venetian blinds.

In the main room of the museum, a massive pine post which once supported the ceiling, had been sawed off at the base. The floors were littered with broken glass, splintered wood, and strips of linoleum. Toilet fixtures had been reduced to piles of white chips by rifle fire.

The flagpole had been pushed over, and it lay rotting on the ground a few feet from its concrete base.

Electrical fixtures were gone, and the wiring ruined wherever a human hand could reach. Plaster had been pried off in sheets. Roofing had been removed by sections. The chimney was toppled, the garage gutted, the caretaker's quarters smashed.

Here and there, the vandal had left his signature. There were Indian names. There were white names.

The fence which once protected Kinishba was broken, and the gate was gone. Cattle paths interlaced the grounds of the museum and ruins.

Of the treasure removed from Kinishba, not a single pot remained on the grounds for the enlightenment of the visitor. There was not a scrap of writing to explain the discoveries and deductions made there.

Whole walls had been pushed down in the restored pueblos. Rooms were crammed with debris and filth. Sewers designed to drain the restoration had been choked by rock.

In Whiteriver, headquarters of the White Mountain Apaches, the leaders expressed shame for what had occurred. But they said the Apaches did not restore Kinishba, and they should not not be held responsible for its care. The tribe could not police the place, and the Indian Bureau is not a branch of the National Park Service.

Besides, the White Mountain tribe had often expressed a willingness to turn over Kinishba to a responsible agency. But despite high-sounding promises, the white man's legislature of Arizona in 50 years had managed to establish a parks department that consisted only of a one-man office, and not a single park.

Whoever was to blame, Kinishba today stands as a mockery to the visions of Dr. Cummings, who wrote of his museum:

"But let the student and visitor then pass on into the museum and examine the things these people wrought."

Like the injured man in the old joke, Russell A. Wright only hurt when he laughed.

Wright underwent a surgical operation both painful and personal. He was sent to his home at 4839 E. Osborn to convalesce.

"I'm comfortable," said Wright, "until I have to cough, sneeze, or laugh. Then it's agony."

Wright received a fat package in the mail. Inside were about 20 get-well cards.

Seemed that Wright's youngest daughter, Mori, carried the story of her father's operation to her third grade class at Scottsdale's Ingleside School. The teacher, Mrs. Berta Whinery, encouraged the students to make the get-well cards.

It was a colorful and imaginative bunch of crayoned cards which Wright received, but the sentiments doubled him in pain.

"Operation do stink BUT Father you don't," was the message from Mori.

"I hope realy true you get out too, and that what men like," was unsigned.

"So get out of that bed before it throws you out," John R. admonished—and he drew a cartoon of a bed throwing a patient as the latter exclaimed, "Yipe."

"Sorry your in the Hospital. Roses are red, volets are blue, Operations stink, But I still like you. From Diane."

Wright wiped the tears from his eyes, gripped the edge of the bed before picking up the message from Betty. The card said simply, "TOO BAD."

"You had better get well right now!" ordered Jack.

"GET OVER IT," Scrawled Glenda H. "Roses are red Violets are Blue—Honey is Sweet—But Operations Stink! Poor you."

"Get well before I get sick," pleaded Jim R., who decorated his card with a graveyard.

A cheerful youngster named Bill pictured a corpse on a slab and several sizes of red crosses around the words, "Get well operation will you."

"Throw that hurt away," wrote Dave H., with love. He drew a picture of a hospital attendant kicking a star labeled

"Hurt" out of the emergency entrance and into the oleander hedge.

Jim Emery had some advice, "An apple a day keep the doctor away," and he included a "mixup game: BETTER WELL GET SEE SOON." The convalescent was supposed to rearrange those words into a sentence.

"You better get well your operation stank like a skunk," wrote Kirk.

"Get well soon, Mr. Write," Doris. "Bluebirds love," Marilyn. "Mori want you back," Carol. And so the sentiments went, until Wright was trembling between a chuckle and a groan.

By coincidence, Mrs. Whinery was hospitalized over the same weekend for more treatment of a slow-healing appendectomy. It hurt when she laughed. Last we heard, the third graders were thinking of sending the poor woman some get-well cards.

Mrs. William Ekstrom got a blue bike and a right-hand catcher's mitt for Mother's Day.

But it wasn't the way you think. Not at all.

She had two sons, Roland, 10, and Billy, 11. Both went to St. Francis School, and were members of the Little League. The younger boy played first base for the Kings, and Billy pitched for the Cardinals.

Until her boys began to play Mrs. Ekstrom didn't know a foul line from a take sign. But as the spring grew warmer, the boys began to teach her the National Game. She was dragged to the ball park at night. In the afternoons, she was impressed into games of catch in the back yard.

One problem. Mrs. Ekstrom was left handed. All she could find was a left-hand catcher's mitt. This meant that every time she wanted to catch the ball, she'd have to put the mitt on her pitching arm. She'd have to take off the mitt in order to throw.

So the catcher's mitt was from the boys, for her very, very own.

Now, about the bike.

The year before, the boys were given new bicycles. But Mrs. Ekstrom believed her boys were too young to travel far on the bikes without supervision.

This had been cramping another of the joys of the boys.

They liked to swim at the St. Francis pool, a mile and a half from the Ekstrom home at 931 E. Montebello.

The boys couldn't ride their bikes that far. It was a long, hot walk, and Mrs. Ekstrom had no car.

So the blue bike was also from the boys, for her very, very own.

Now, the boys hoped Mrs. Ekstrom could ride with them to the pool. The three of them would jump on their bikes and pedal to refreshing dips, which would be followed by rousing games of baseball pepper in the yard.

JOE SUN!

Look, ma, we're speaking Chinese, along with the sixth graders at Maryland School.

The man responsible is Fred Ong, whose home is behind his grocery at 6736 N. 19th Ave. Fred's daughter, Eileen Kay, is a sixth grader at Maryland School.

One day Eileen Kay returned gah (home) from hawk how (school) and told her fu chun (father) that the sin sung (teacher) was telling about the geography of Chung Kwock (China).

Fred, who earlier in his life spent 10 years in Canton, telephoned the teacher to ask if he could be of help. Miss Nancy Rumple invited Fred to be a guest lecturer.

To Fred, it was call of great responsibility. He made copies of a page of about 75 Chinese characters, their English meanings, and phonic equivalents.

JOE SUN—good morning. NEE HOW—How are you? JOY KEEN—goodby. LOOK NIN CUP—sixth grade. MING TIN—tomorrow. JAA JAA—thanks. MOE CHUN—mother. GEE—paper. NUIE—girl. GUM TIN—today. BUT—pencil. The sounds may be strange to other Phoenix Chinese, who speak in dialects different from Fred Ong's Cantonese.

The kids at Maryland School kept Fred 30 minutes overtime. Fred spoke of the history and geography of China, and passed out Free China magazines which he receives from Hong Kong.

A few days later Fred got a bundle of letters. They were mostly in English, but with a liberal sprinkling of tediously-drawn Chinese characters.

"NEE HOW MA? JAA JAA for coming and talking to us and telling so much about CHUNK KWOCK. When I went to GAH I called my MOE CHUN. She stared at me like I was crazy. JOY KEEN. Diane Bickerdyke."

"It was interesting to see how China's people write. Our NUIE SIN SUNG thought it was interesting, too. Thanks for letting us look at your magazies. I looked at one GUM TIN. The BUT they write with was neat. I wouldn't mind visiting CHUNG KWOCK, And thanks for the GEE." Russell Schmunk.

Fred got a special kick from the letter from his daughter, Eileen Kay:

"YAA YAA for coming to our HAWK HOW and giving a speech on CHUNG KWOCK. We are all speaking Chinese now. JOY KEEN."

Fred was pleased with how quickly the children picked up the phrases, and skill in drawing the complicated symbols.

"I was humbled and overjoyed to know what an hour's work with these brilliant youngsters of today could do for their regular school work," said Fred. "I think parents who have some special interest, hobby or rare experience should visit with their children's friends in their class room. I'm glad that I did."

Well, JOY KEEN until MING TIN, you all.

There has not been a blue Monday at Porter's warehouse in Phoenix since Mrs. Sue Shranko was hired in the labeling room.

Every Monday she has come to work with heaping platters of American and European pastries she has spent the week-end baking. It has been her practice to bake cakes for birth-days, for homecomings, for weddings.

"There's nothing special about it," said Mrs. Shranko of 2605 W. Van Buren. "It gives me pleasure."

Password at meetings of the Slim Lines or Bust Society was, "Hi, SLOB."

A short dozen women organized SLOBS as sort of a Cheesecake-aholics Anonymous.

"We all had been dieting, with little success, because we were too weak to resist temptation," said Mrs. Donald A. Mortimer of 7508 E. Minnezona. "Most of us are mothers who have to prepare big dinners and highly fattening desserts for large families. Few women have the will power to deny themselves with all of that food around."

Mrs. Armand J. (Ellie) Mattausch, of 5209 E. Virginia, thought up the name for the society, and was elected president. They met weekly for weigh-in.

Weights were registered at the chartered meeting. At subsequent meetings the women had to pay 25 cents for every pound gained. If they stayed even, they were fined a dime. All members brought 25-cent gifts to each meeting, and the woman who lost the most weight got all the loot.

The woman who gained the most weight between meetings was sentenced to wear a wooden pig around her neck. The pig, made by a SLOBS husband, was about 4 inches wide, and scratchy.

A SLOBS meetings was something between a session in group therapy and the Spanish Inquisition. Ridicule caused some members to kick their chocolate lusts. There was much talk about dieting, and occasionally the entire membership of SLOBS could be found exercising on a living room floor in time with recorded music and instruction.

Calorie-counting was a SLOBS cornerstone. One woman

lost 30 pounds, and most SLOBS lost at least 5 pounds, and several as much as 10.

The women taped magazine pictures of size 12 dresses to their refrigerator doors, and when temptation crowded them, they were supposed to call a fellow member and talk it out.

They gave one of the new achievement tests to a class at a Wickenburg elementary school.

One part of the test required that children match up words which seemed to go together.

As the matching word for "Credit," one youngster chose, "Frequent."

Missed the Ice Capades myself, and had to rely on the report of my 3½-year-old assistant.

"Skunks and a man sat down on the water and the queen and pretty ladies and all the men wore pants and bears and they didn't have NO trees."

Sounded like a heck of a way to run an ice show.

The Rev. Thomas Green, pastor of St. George's Orthodox Church, 4502 E. Indian School, lived in a monastery 10 years. As far as world events were concerned, Father Thomas was as isolated as the man in the moon.

Then he came back to a civilization that was to him strange and confusing.

Father Thomas was born in Boston, to a family of devout Episcopalians. In 1946 he made a retreat to the Episcopal Good Shepherd Monastery, which then was in South Carolina, and later was moved to Florida. After a year as a guest, Father Thomas dedicated his life in the service of prayer with the Order of St. Augustine.

He and his fellow monks lived simply. The furnishings of the monastery were functional, the food spartan. After chores, the monks spent hours in theological study. Unnecessary conversation was prohibited, and the brothers were allowed no money, no possessions, no decisions of importance.

Except through the citizens who made retreats to the monastery, the monks were without communication with the world about them. The monastery had one radio, and in 10 years Father Thomas heard it twice, each time a report of a happening of religious importance.

It was Father Thomas's intention to become an Episcopalian priest. But in 1956, after months of agonizing appraisal, Father Thomas decided to leave the monastery. He had come to believe that the Orthodox Church "was unchanged through the centuries since it was founded, and offered the only true way" for him.

He left the monastery on the best of terms with the Episcopal Church, and with the monks who had been his brothers.

"My first impression," said Father Thomas, "was that I had forgotten how to talk. My ability at small talk had just disappeared. People seemed to chatter incessantly. Also, I had grown no older, but everybody else had aged 10 years. This was hard to accept. My best friend from school days was married and had four children. I was like a child with money. It seemed that high school children were making fabulous salaries, and I hadn't had control over a dime for 10 years.

"I walked through my old neighborhood in Boston. I didn't meet a single person I knew. Once when I flew from Louisville to Boston, I took two tranquilizer pills."

Father Thomas had to learn worldly manners all over again. He was shocked at the informality, and baffled by the slang of teenagers. The world was reading less, moving faster, forgetting common courtesy.

And although Father Thomas never regretted his decision, he said, he sometimes longed for the serenity of the monastery.

Chapter Fourteen

TEMPE—Swede Swanson may have traveled more miles than any other living Arizonan—and he never got farther than 10 miles from home.

Swanson had been Tempe's ice man for 36 years in 1959. He had gone around and around, in the same general circle, and those who thought he hadn't gotten anywhere didn't know him very well.

He was given Harry, but his name was Swede since he came to Tempe from Chicago and El Paso in 1912. He shod horses and fixed cars until 1923, when he became a route man for Crystal Ice.

"I have never been beyond Phoenix, or past Mesa, in all that time," said Swede.

He was too busy toting ice. For 33 years, until 1956, Swede did not miss work for any reason. He made his route seven days a week, 12 months a year, through holidays, through bad weather, through times of crisis at home.

The record was fully documented by Swanson's company. When he finally took a rest, it was in Mesa's Southside District Hospital to recover from a fall in the ice plant. People at the hospital said they couldn't remember when a patient received so many cards and visitors.

At 69, he was a lanky 6-footer with still-black hair who could lift a 300-pound block of ice from his truck to the pavement. There were not many husky youngsters who could move ice alongside Swede.

His route stretched from the experimental farm on the Tempe-Mesa highway to 48th Street, and from Baseline to the Butte.

Times changed for ice men, said Swede.

The big seller used to be blocks. Now it was cubes and crushed. Refrigerators did that, said Swede, and where he used to call on homes, he now principally served taverns, restaurants, and other businesses. When electricity and refrigerators came to Guadalupe, his business in block ice was cut by 3,500 pounds.

Not only were Swanson's work days continuous, they were also long. It was not unusual for him to be up at 4 a.m. and to make his last call at 9 p.m. As an independent ice dealer, Swanson could set his own hours, as long as he didn't work more than 24 a day. As a worker, Swanson guessed, he was 405 years old.

"I haven't a thing to complain about," said Swanson. "It's been a good job. I never took a vacation because I didn't think anybody else could take care of my customers the way I do.

"Almost three years ago I was going to retire. My wife had put up with me and my long hours away from home for 41 years. Just before I was going to quit, and take her on a long trip, a heart attack took her away suddenly.

"Then there wasn't any reason for retiring."

At first, the teacher thought Linc was just shy.

Most of the 58 children were that way on the hot, humid September day at Abraham Lincoln School kindergarten.

They gripped tightly the hands of mothers and older brothers and sisters. They said little. They were wary of this new thing called school.

For some weeks, the teachers were busy matching names and places, and wiping tops and bottoms. One boy was crippled and needed special attention. A girl cried exactly one half hour every morning. As for Linc—the teacher was almost grateful for having a boy like him who demanded nothing, and gave her no trouble.

Soon the class relaxed. Once-timid children joined freely in the games, the dancing, the lessons, the singing.

And it was then that Linc slowly began to stand out. The teacher studied him. What was it that made him different? He was active. He seemed to be happy. The explanation was so simple, it was shocking.

Since joining the class Linc had not uttered a sound.

The children were vaccinated in October. Back in the classroom, they laughed and chattered about the frightful experience behind them.

Linc didn't say a word.

Thanksgiving came. Afterward, the children bragged, one to the other, about the size of their turkeys and numbers of relatives. Linc held his tongue.

Linc was an extrovert in other ways. At dancing, he swung his partner with graceful abandon. He clapped his hands the loudest in time to music. He even allowed himself to be chosen the Leader of Marching.

Yet after Christmas, when the other children were full of conversation, Linc was quiet.

At the beginning of the second semester, the teacher was deeply concerned. Despite her most thoughtful efforts, Linc had been silent for almost four months. The teacher asked for help from the school counselor.

Linc's mother was consulted.

"I can't understand it," she said. "He talks all the time at home."

The mother was questioned more closely. There was some trouble at home, she said, but nothing that would affect a 5-year-old. The parents had been arguing—had even spoken of divorce.

"That couldn't possibly be the reason," said the mother, and she would discuss it no more.

Toward the end of the school year, Linc's teacher thought she was given a glimpse of the truth.

One day she asked the children to draw pictures of their mothers and fathers. Linc, still silent, drew beautiful figures. But he omitted a detail from the faces of his parents.

Mouths.

Most of the first three years of his life he spent in prison.

Authorities came to his house one day and told his family to pack. They were forced to leave their home and business. Along with hundreds of others of their kind, they were put in concentration camps.

This did not happen in Europe or Asia. It happened in Arizona, in America.

James Mamoru Sagawa was born June 22, 1941. His father Kiichi, had been an Arizona resident since 1906. He was operating his vegetable shipping business in Tolleson when the family was arrested.

There were eight Sagawa children, four girls and four boys. James was the youngest.

After Pearl Harbor the Sagawa family was swept up in the relocation of Japanese-Americans. Loyalty had nothing to do with the arrests. One of the elder Sagawa boys became an intelligence officer for the army. Even as he served, his family, most of them native Americans, was locked up at Mayer, and later at Poston. James' earliest memory was of watching his father fly an artistic kite over the barbed wire fences of the Poston camp.

The war ended. The family was released.

Many California Japanese were dispossessed during their confinement. But the Sagawa family was able to return to the Tolleson farm. Kiichi Sagawa raised vegetables, and became a lay minister in the Japanese Free Methodist Church. He moved his family to a home at 4214 W. Indian School, in order to be close to the church.

James went through the grades at Alhambra School, and graduated from West Phoenix High, 10th in his class.

He was a member of the National Honor Society, of Parnassus, and of the Key Club. He was in the All-state Band four years. He held offices in student government.

"I never felt I had a second-rate chance," said James. "For me, it was first-rate. It was a stupid thing to do, to lock up the family, but we've never been bitter about it. If it had to happen to us, it's a good thing it happened here, where the government's gone a long way to correct the mistake."

Things worked out well for the Sagawas. James' three brothers graduated from college. One became an accountant, and the others engineers. Two sisters married ministers (Baptist and Holiness), another was a Phoenix housewife, and the other attended college in Long Beach, Calif.

During James' senior year at high school, he took competitive examinations for a General Motors scholarship. There were 20,000 applicants. He was the only Arizona winner, and in the fall of 1959, the boy whose life began with a false arrest, took an $8,000 scholarship to California Institute of Technology.

It was misting rain and growing dark when the cowboy wound his reins on the ranch house gate.

Water had gotten under his slicker, and he was tired and hungry. Between jobs, the itinerant cowboy and his drawn horse had been on the trail all day. The cowboy stomped onto the porch.

"Howdy, stranger," said the rancher as he swung open the door.

"Much 'bliged if you'd put up me and my horse for the night, mister." Such was the faith in hospitality in the West, before the Century of Progress.

"I'm sorry, son," said the rancher with sincerity. "There's no room. My wife's ailing, and all the in-laws are over here tending to her. Tell you what—I'll give you some chuck, and you ride out another 4 miles to a line shack of mine. It's a tight cabin. Has a fireplace. You can dry out there."

Soon the cowboy was on his way, with a jar of beans and a loaf of bread warming his saddlebags. He followed directions and before long he sighted the shack through the now slanting rain. He put the horse under a lean-to, and carried his saddle and gear inside.

The cabin was dank, and black as malapai. The cowboy groped his way to the fireplace. Then, in the flickering light of his fire, the cowboy tended his wet gear. When the chores were done, he moved to the fire with his supper.

That's when he heard it.

Laughter. It filled the little cabin. It was an unrestrained, shriek of a laugh.

From his frozen squat, the cowboy tilted his head to peer upward. There, perched on a beam, was the source of the laughter—a middle-aged woman with matted hair. She was dressed in black. Shadows of beams and posts moved across her pale features. She laughed again.

The cowboy ran, pausing only to grab his horse. He spent the night in the woods. He did not sleep. There was the rain. And through the long hours, the cowboy began to question his own sanity. Had he really seen, and heard?

Next morning he rode aimlessly bareback along the trail. He had to retrieve his possessions from the cabin, but he didn't dare. He met two deputies. He spilled his story, and his doubts about his own reason, to them.

They laughed, deeply, and long.

"You weren't imagining," said one. "That was probably the escaped crazy woman we're looking for."

The truth of the story was sworn by Clifton Egerton, longtime railroader of Bowie and Benson, and in his later years a resident of Las Cruces, N.M. The cowboy was a close friend.

If the historians are going to dredge up every tragic pistol shot of the Old West, asked Old Man Egerton, why don't they shake out a few laughs as well?

There were a-plenty.

A Florida boast of receiving the first delivery of mail-by-missile is as fishy as Miami Beach.

In 1947 a load of United States mail landed on Arizona soil. Elsewhere, rockets have been transporting mail since 1931. After a Regulus I guided missile carried 3,000 letters from a submarine to Jacksonville, even Postmaster General Summerfield called the experiment "of historic significance to the peoples of the entire world."

That, it may have been, but it was not a first.

Art Joquel II, of 8148 N. 12th St., Phoenix, was an eyewitness to the rocket mail flight from Winterhaven, Calif., across the Colorado River to Yuma in 1947. Joquel, history teacher at Sunnyslope High, was photographer, lecturer, and writer for the California Reaction Research Society.

"It was largely a group of scientifically-minded students of Glendale Junior College. They were old enough to have the know-how, and young enough to try anything wild," said Joquel.

Long before our government began crash programs of rocketry research, the California society was testing homemade missiles at its blockhouse and range on the Mohave Desert. The year 1947 was the centennial of the U.S. postage stamp. In celebration, the society brought two rockets to Winterhaven on June 28.

The rockets were 15 feet long, and 3 inches in diameter. In the noses were bundles of first-day covers for stamp collectors who had requested them from throughout the nation. Besides the centennial stamp, the letters bore an additional stamp for air mail, a rocket-mail sticker, and a cachet reading,

"Across the Colorado River, Winterhaven, Calif., to Yuma, Ariz., June 28, 1947."

The first rocket blew up. The nose section was hurled into the Colorado, and before the retrieving team could launch a boat, the mail was carried downriver toward Mexico.

"It's never been recovered, as far as we know," said Joquel. "The container was rust-resistant, and watertight, and might be on a sand bar or out to sea or gathering dust in a Mexican hut."

The second rocket wobbled, but it landed within 100 feet of its target on the Arizona side. Three hundred letters were delivered to Yuma Postmaster Eleanor McCoy. It was Saturday, and she kept her office open late to accommodate the rocketeers. The rocket mail flight was believed to be the first between states. Since the rocket mail flight in Austria in 1931, there have been many shoots between cities and across international borders. But the California-Arizona flight was supposed to be a United States first.

Collectors paid 50 cents for each rocket letter. Over the years the catalog price went to $15 and higher.

Florida can't even lay claim to the first ship-to-shore rocket mail delivery, said Joquel. A Swiss named Zucker posted some letters in this way from his yacht in 1935.

"No. Absolutely. Positively and finally," I had been saying. "We'll never keep a dog in the city."

The city is too confining and dangerous for dogs. Dogs ought to have room to roam, and leave sign, mate, bark, and chew up resistant objects. There are too many cars and property lines and rules in the city.

"Never," I swore. "There's no use arguing," said I, scratching the velvety ears of the newest member of the family.

Then there was the man who carried a cane in his parachute.

Capt. William J. Fenton, flight operations officer of the

4522nd Combat Crew Training Squadron at Williams Air Force Base was a jet pilot. But walking, for him, was a chore.

In 1949 he was a member of probably the first official air demonstration team, which jockeyed P-51s and AT-6s. Then he crashed, while he was a passenger in a cargo plane. He was in a hospital 2½ years, recovering from hand and ankle injuries. When he got out he learned to fly jets, despite lingering physical shortcomings which made it necessary for him to walk with a cane.

He was worried about walking home, in case of a bail-out, so he bought a telescoping cane and sewed it in the back of his parachute.

Carl Fletcher's claim that he owned the two happiest dogs in all the Sonoran Desert smacked of exaggeration.

Think about that brag. Between Hermosillo and Wickenburg there were, say, a half million dogs. Most of them, it would be safe to guess, were happy. You may not find a tick every time you scratch a dog, but you'll almost always lay hands on an optimist.

Anyway, I went out to see Carl Fletcher and his hounds at 535 W. Edgemont. The dogs were beagles, a male, 5 years old, and a yearling female.

I never did grasp the names firmly in mind. I think the male was called Fletcher's Skipper, and the female, Frisky Feathers, but they just as well could have been Skippy's Friskers and Feathers Fletchy. Somewhere Fletcher had papers which carried the pedigree names.

Until the spring of 1959, Fletcher had just the older dog. The dog had the run of the neighborhood. He could open a dozen gates in order to raid bowls set out for cats, and he developed a mooching route at the back doors of businesses. According to Fletcher, the dog always would go last to the ice cream stand and beg a cone for dessert. The rich diet almost killed the dog. He was 30 pounds overweight when Fletcher put a screen-and-latch combination on the fence gate that even the dog couldn't crack. The hound sulked. He acted as if he were the unhappiest dog on the Sonoran Desert.

Fletcher bought the female, which delighted the older dog, but gave Fletcher another problem: Where to keep them. Mrs. Fletcher suggested the back yard, and when the votes were all in, she was a majority. Fletcher put the hounds outside, but they seemed to suffer in the heat. They moaned, and tried to dig tunnels under the back door.

"C'mon outside and see what I've done," said Fletcher.

He led me to the side of the house, where an imposing duplex doghouse was standing.

Each compartment of the doghouse was carpeted with 3 inches of foam rubber and paneled in plywood. The 4-inch-thick walls and ceilings were insulated with cork, and the roofing and siding was of a quality grade of asbestos shingle.

"And here," said Fletcher, "is the crowning touch." He pointed to a small evaporative cooler attached to the rear of the doghouse. Air was drawn through excelsior pads which were moistened by a recirculating pump using water from a house line through a copper tube.

"Don't they look happy?" asked Fletcher.

I peered into the air-conditioned chambers. The dogs were grinning and you could almost hear their chuckling over the drone of the motor.

On the way back inside the people house, Fletcher let me in on a little secret. Frisky Feathers (or was it Skippy's Friskers) was expecting the happiest litter of hound pups in the whole Sonoran Desert, come September.

Every time the sideburn set beats up peaceful and aging Arizona citizens, mostly for kicks, the victims probably yearn for the good old days. Way back when, juvenile troublemakers were dealt with directly and forcefully. The times were uncluttered by soft-hearted judges, head doctors, and social planners.

Before World War I the town marshal of Benson was an uncomplicated soul named Bill Bennett.

He operated a thriving saloon, where a 2-ounce shot was 15 cents, and a man had to stand to drink it. Booze was all Bill dispensed. Customers who wanted company or conversation were directed across the tracks to the Hog Ranch, which was not a ranch and had nothing to do with raising hogs.

Bill served his hitch as the town's one-man police force as sort of a civic duty. He never got bogged down in a lot of legal thinking.

A case in point was when a rancher chased a dude down Benson's main drag. The rancher shouted accusations of wife-stealing, and he punctuated his remarks with shots from a Winchester carbine.

"That man's got a gun! Somebody stop him!" screeched a bystanding townswoman.

Bill, who was watching the fun, a pleased look on his face and his thumbs hooked in his gun belt, laughed. "Let 'im shoot the sorry bastard," he said.

But if Bill could honor the unwritten law, he could also uphold the old proverbs—especially the one about children, seen and heard. Bill couldn't spell rehabilitation, but he knew right from wrong.

Bill was sitting his horse in front of the depot small-talking with Jeff Milton, when a hulking, fuzzy-chinned child walked by. The boy had come into town the night before, got drunk, and tried to tree the town. Marshal Bill regarded the boy dourly and said: "I thought I told you to go home last night."

The chain of profanity which fell from the boy's lips would have shocked a section boss. Between the curses, the gist of his spiel was that no second-string tin badge from a hick railroad town was going to tell Hard Case what he could and couldn't do.

Bill stopped the speech.

He leaned down, and, swinging with all his might, he slugged the boy across the bridge of his nose with a blackjack. The boy crumbled, cold. When he came to, he was lying under the marshal's horse. His nose was fractured, bleeding and rapidly swelling.

"I'll go home. I'll go home," he whined.

"Not for a while," Bennett growled. "Now you're going to the 'gow." Survivors of that era recall that during the remainder of Bennett's term the juvenile delinquency rate in Benson fell to zero point zero zero, and that the town has stayed remarkably law-abiding ever since.

Like, man, all you creeps in Cubesville aren't tuned in.

I wasn't either, but now I'm hip. A friend gave me a beatnik dictionary. No more king's jive for this cat. Like wow! Beatalk is the grooviest, man.

Think I'll take my wife to the movies again? Get off the wall, square. I'll break a George squiring that plucked chicken to the flicks at the pucker palace. No Dullsville for us, Dad.

Ordinarily, before I was turned on, I'd have worn slacks and shoes and shirt with a bow tie. She'd have gone in a dress with high heels.

Cool it, Kookie. Now I'll cover with the rags and johns and leathers with the bent brummel, and Murgatroid, she will swing in a crazy quilt and twin trees. Maybe I'll raise a goat and lower the shades. Dig? Grow a beard and wear dark glasses.

That's not all I learned from the Goneville glossary.

Next time I turn off a light I'll blast the Edison. When a park my car, I'll stable the iron. I'll look at my wrist watch and consult the Mickey Mouse. When I take a coffee break, I'll make a short trip to Rio. And soon as the gang gets together for a party, I'll inform them they are a swings-like-16 galaxy at a wail.

Mama's going down to vitamin village, not the grocery store. She'll have to get used to living at a pad, not a house, and if she doesn't can the lip I'll knuckle the creep. Tough toenails.

The kid will have to change her ways, or fall out. Instead

of milk, that kitten will drink moo juice if she wants to grow up far out. If not, I'll fall on her, and she'll wind up in Germsville. Ol' St. Beatnik is coming to Nadaville.

The boss can quit paying me money for working in the office. I'm not telling a Cherry Tree. That high lama has to make with the bread for cave-time. Otherwise, later, monkey run.

If you all think I've gone ape (insane), call the fuzz rod (squad car) for a trip to the head-shrinkers' flat (psychiatrist's couch).

He'll tell you I'm not a juicehead. Just crazy.

Drop me off at Whistleburg (where the girls gather) and I'll pick up on (learn) the muscle sides (rock 'n' roll records) and smoke kick sticks (cigarets) and trade skin (shake hands) with a juiceman (bartender).

Turn up the stereo (listen). I Mazda (see the light). This snagged stag is ready to shake it, and blow his jets, and become bugged.

I'm tooling down to Beatsville, to feel high, to be a groovie, to find gas, to meet some hipsters, and fall out with Squaresville forever.

This is the end, man, the end.

Fifty years from now, I predict, Arizonans will still be writing and reading yarns about the last of the Indian scouts.

Some newsmen would not cross the street to meet the governor. But let any Arizona journalist hear of a doing or dying of a last Indian scout, and he will go 200 miles to record it.

Last scouts, without exception, are good copy. Their hair is likely to be long, and they have astounding numbers of great-grandchildren, and they probably breakfast on near beer and salted peanuts. Last scouts are the most colorful relics of the West's most romantic era.

Happily for all, last Indian scouts seem to be growing more numerous as the years wear on. The day a story is printed about the death of the very last Indian scout, chances are two more will turn up.

Cynics who suspect deceit, by either red man or white, will be disappointed.

I've written a half-dozen "last-of-the-Indian-scout" pieces, myself. The subjects, or their surviving kin, sincerely believed they represented the last of their sort. At the time, they seemed to be.

It was on the best faith a few years ago that I told of the deaths of four Apaches—the last of the Indian scouts who chased Geronimo.

Famous Sergeant Chicken died, then Lambert I. Stone, then John Chowbig, and finally David Declay.

"And then there were none," the last scout series ended.

Since then, there have been a good many more last-scout reports. Some originated in Arizona. Others came by wire from New Mexico. It was my pleasure to interview Kate Crozier, a 120-year-old Haulpai, the last of the Indian scouts who chased Geronimo. Until the next one comes along. And I hope I get to him first.

There were, to begin with, a lot of Indian scouts. Two hundred—some histories say 300—helped the army put away Geronimo. Not until 1947 were later-day generations of scouts permanently disbanded at Fort Huachuca. Records and scouts were scattered.

Apparently the reading public doesn't object to our inconsistent last-scout narratives.

I have in mind the image of a paleface reader. He glances at his paper, and his eye hangs on a headline, "Last Indian Scout Dies."

"Look here, Myrtle," the reader says, "this story tells how the last living link between Arizona's civilized present and its violent past was broken yesterday with the passing of—well, I can't pronounce the name. Makes you feel kind of sad, doesn't it?"

And this same reader is not in the least offended when,

a week later, the same newspaper boldly displays another last-scout story.

Perhaps deep down we white people, in honoring legions of last scouts, are trying to pay back something our forefathers swiped. The motivation experts might want to study this.

All I know—any old Indian who announces himself as the last scout is sure to get his name in the journals.

Okay?

The morning of Father's Day the Rev. Arnold Dockery was put to a critical test.

His sermon, appropriately enough, was about fathers, and the need for paternal patience. Dads would do well, he said, to be more tolerant of the misdeeds of their children.

Sitting in the first pew of the Church of Litchfield were Mrs. Dockery, and four Dockery boys, including Phillip, 4. Midway in the sermon, Phillip left the church and returned with a large paper bag.

The boy took his seat, opened the bag, and released a dozen frogs, which soon were hopping all over the church.

Displaying commendable fatherly patience, Mr. Dockery took little notice of the mischief, and delivered the remainder of his sermon.

Take it from Lim Yee, It's not easy for an American to act like a Chinaman.

Yee is as Yankee as yellow pop. He was born in Canton, but was brought to this country when he was 4. He was educated at Monroe School and Phoenix Union High and during World War II he was a United States sailor in the South Pacific.

For 10 years Yee operated a little neighborhood grocery at 1051 W. Glendale. He named his boys Reynold, Robert and Rudy.

So along came a big motion picture outfit from Hollywood to shoot a Chinese picture, "The Mountain Road," on an Apache Trail location.

A call was put out for Chinese extras. The pay was $1.25 an hour, plus lunch, plus permission to take snapshots of the stars. Several hundred Valley Chinese-Americans signed up. The Tangs and Ongs and Chins and Lees and Lus. Lim Yee thought it would be educational. He took his sons, and his father-in-law, Ma Wing.

Mostly the Arizona Chinese were used as refugees. For five weeks they plodded along sections of the Apache Trail, supplying background action. Reynold, 12, was given a part in which he snatched a bit of food from a Caucasian actor. Robert, 18, was a gate boy, and Rudy, 19, played a guerrilla.

The director seemed to be impressed with Lim Yee's broad Chinese face and physique, still solid at 40.

"You be a soldier," said the director.

So Yee shucked his coolie clothing and joined the Chinese army. Gen. Frank Dorne, technical adviser, assigned Yee to a speaking part. He was supposed to say, "Attention!" in Mandarin dialect.

"I only speak Cantonese," apologized Yee. The general spent a half hour teaching Yee to say the word in Mandarin.

Later Yee was given an important scene with the star of the picture, Jimmy Stewart.

Yee played a sentry. Stewart was to drive up in a Jeep. Yee was instructed to check Stewart's pass, and wave him on.

The scene was set. The cameras rolled. Stewart's jeep approached. Lim Yee's face broke in a great, genuine grin.

"Cut! Cut! Cut!" shouted the director. "No, no, Lim. You are a Chinese soldier. This is an American trespassing on your native soil. You are suspicious. You hate his guts. Now, try it again."

Again the actors were placed. Cameras. Action. A fierce Lim Yee suspiciously examined the pass of the trespasser whose innards he despised.

When the scene was done, the director wrung Yee's hand. "You were wonderful," said the director.

Yee, and the other Valley extras, took more stills than did Hollywood. Yee had snapshots of all the stars. Of Stewart, Yee said: "He is an all-around guy. The nicest person you'd want to meet."

Yee said he was sorry when the movie people finished shooting and moved to another location.

He was just beginning to get the hang of how to act like a Chinaman, said Yee.

The words were tediously printed on ruled tablet paper:

"Dear Sir: I came across the World War I Medal of Honor winners and found besides Frank Luke, Arizona had another hero. He was Corp. John H. Pruitt, U.S. Marine Corps.

"For conspicuous gallantry and intrepidity above and beyond the call of duty in action with the enemy at Mont Blanc Ridge, France, Oct. 3, 1918, Corp. Pruitt singlehandedly attacked two machine guns, capturing and killing two of the enemy. He then captured 40 prisoners in a dugout nearby.

"This Gallant Soldier was killed soon afterward by shellfire while he was sniping at the enemy.

"I know of many things honoring Frank Luke. But to my knowledge nothing to commemorate Corporal Pruitt. If there is not, why not? I think there should be a street or school named after him or at least a statue or plaque in his honor.

"Greg Stephenson, 12 years old, 4553 N. 56th Ave., Glendale."

The boy had a point.

John Henry Pruitt won not one, but two Congressional Medals of Honor, one from the army and one from the navy. He was the only Arizonan of the few Americans, so honored.

Pruitt was brought to Phoenix from Arkansas when he was an infant. He grew up in Phoenix, and enlisted in the marines. After sea duty aboard several vessels, he was assigned to the Sixth Marine Regiment. Pruitt fought at

Aisne, Meuse-Argonne, St. Mihiel, and Chateau-Thierry, and he was an army all by himself at Mont Blanc Ridge.

Friend Greg quotes from the official citation. The reports of Corporal Pruitt's buddies tell a more human story. The outfit was pinned down by a German gun. Corporal Pruitt set out alone, fought an hour, and returned to his lines carrying the machine gun. A few hours later he again went alone to the German lines, attacked a strong point, and took 40 prisoners. Next day Corporal Pruitt was rewarded with a relatively safe assignment: sniper. Ironically, the man who successfully made frontal assaults against machine guns, was killed by a stray German shell.

A grateful nation awarded him the Medals of Honor posthumously, and additionally, four Bronze Stars, four Silver Stars, two Purple Heart medals, clasps, and citations. High honors came from the French and Italian governments.

A navy destroyer was named for him. So was an American Legion post at Ray. But for one reason or another, Arizonans largely forgot about one of their greatest heroes. The bell from the decommissioned destroyer was mounted in the lobby of the U.S. Naval and Marine Corps Training Center at 2042 E. Thomas.

Three years ago his medals were put on permanent display at the state capitol. Cliff Carpenter, of Scottsdale, was perhaps Pruitt's most closely related survivor. Carpenter's deceased wife was Pruitt's sister.

"There isn't a statue," he said. "Not a street named for him. Not a school. To my knowledge, there is nothing.

"But maybe it's enough, that, after these years, a little boy should care."

Mrs. Avis H. Wilson had the answer to one of mankind's oldest frets. She knew how to pick a good watermelon.

Long before people became aware of the H-bomb and the traffic toll and juvenile delinquency, they were frowning over melons. Here men were about to fling themselves into space, and not one in a million could carry home a watermelon with confidence the thing would be fit to eat.

Mrs. Wilson for 38 summers had been selling watermelons under the chinaberry trees in front of her home at 3142 N. Seventh St. In later years a fruit stand was built, but in the old days, Mrs. Wilson had the harvesters dump melons in heaps on the shady lawn. Out back was a 10-acre patch which her husband, the late L. F. Wilson, leased and farmed. One summer Wilson mounted a silver dollar over the melons, with a sign saying that anybody who got a bad melon could have a replacement melon plus the dollar. The Wilsons sold 60 tons of watermelons that summer before a customer took the first dollar. They lost only three silver dollars all summer long.

Since her husband's death, in 1952, Mrs. Wilson had taken on a business partner, but she personally supervised the store during melon season, June to October. An arthritic, she got around in a wheelchair.

She had seen all kinds of self-styled melon experts.

One type she called The Scratcher. This person would peel the surface of a melon with his thumbnail. The melon was supposed to be sweet or sour, depending on how the melon peeled.

Then there was The Plunker, sometimes known as the Thumper. A musical note was supposed to mean the melon was green, and a dull thud, overripe. A noise in between: Ambrosia.

Mrs. Wilson had no patience with The Cruncher. This tester would either hug a melon, or bear down on it with his knee, in an attempt to determine the worth of it from the noise of destruction from within. Mrs. Wilson would allow crunching on her place, but The Cruncher had to take the melon, good or bad.

The Deviner called on supernatural powers. He balanced a broom straw crosswise on a melon. If the straw stayed put, the melon would taste like a cucumber. If the straw swung parallel to the longitudinal axis, Huckleberry himself would steal it.

Mrs. Wilson knew a Patter. He would heft a melon, pat it, and judge it by the vibrations it transmitted to his holding hand.

But of all the methods, Mrs. Wilson thought hers was best.

"Plug it," she said. "Plug it and taste it."

Chapter Fifteen

SAN DIEGO—Mysteries explained, or things you learn while traveling with a 4-year-old:

On every airplane there is a nurse who first gives you goodies, and then forgets to give you a polio shot.

The man who takes your baggage at Sky Harbor Airport has to run like the devil to hand your bags to the man who hands them to you at Lindbergh Field.

Fog is when the sun shines at night.

The ocean breakers at La Jolla are made by teenage boys slapping their surfboards on the water. The waves are big because God helps. The sand would be more fun if it were in boxes, like it is supposed to be. If grownups would all go down to the beach and gather sea shells, they wouldn't have to work.

Some of the horses at San Diego Zoo wear pajamas. Sea lions stay under water for long periods because they are ugly, and monkeys are the way they are because they sassed their mothers. Phoenix, as a cultural center, will never fully mature until it has some baby goats that the kids can play with, and a place where chicks can be seen hatching, and a 100-year-old turtle that lets youngsters sit on his back.

Every time Daddy cusses, a California driver does something foolish.

People who live in the biggest houses wear the fewest clothes.

At 433 W. Washington are two surprises.

One, the name, Phoenix Trunk Co. The other, the boss, Eleanor Bowen.

Mrs. Bowen is a graying, gregarious gal who has borne seven children. She has warm brown eyes and strong hands and a way of putting you at ease.

The building is something else. It is one of Phoenix's oldest structures. The late S. J. Doster founded a trunk factory there in 1895. The place hasn't been painted since. The wiring looks like an Edison experiment, the ceiling is stained with rain that seeped through 50 years ago, and the floor is cupped with wear. Except for a one-way path, it is filled with the darnedest assortment of oddities humans could assemble.

Here, Eleanor Bowen has found a happiness.

About five years ago she loaned some money to a friend who bought the trunk factory from the Doster estate. Within a year, the friend retired, and Mrs. Bowen became full owner of a trunk company.

She didn't know a hasp from a handle. Demand for new trunks had faded. Most of the repair business had been lost. Mrs. Bowen visited the railroads and airlines and said:

"If you'll bear with me, I'll learn the repair business. Give me some time."

Reluctantly at first, transportation companies brought damaged luggage to Mrs. Bowen for repair. Now repair of such damaged suitcases accounts for two-thirds of her business. After five years, Mrs. Bowen is willing to tackle any repair, and she rarely fails. She has repaired gun cases, built quivers for arrows and once she restitched the handle of a policeman's blackjack.

Mrs. Bowen has one part-time employe. Her husband, Jesse, a railroader, helps out in busy periods. Mrs. Bowen has had little time to put the shop in order, but she knows where everything is. In the loft behind the shop is a pile of oak stock used by the old trunk factory. On a roll-top desk are a 1909 typewriter, an adding machine of that period, and postage scales.

"While I was rummaging through the cubby locker I found a gallon jug of whiskey. It must have been there for years and years, and brother, was it mellow," she said.

Mrs. Bowen believes she has earned a small fame in the luggage repair business. A vice president of a sewing machine company visited her shop. He said he had heard about the lady luggage fixer in the East.

"I think I'll keep on for a long time," said Mrs. Bowen. "It gives me something to do, and one of these years, I may make some money at it.

"The name of the business is enough to keep me here. That's one thing I'd never change. . ."

APACHE JUNCTION—George S. Thompson was born in a dugout canoe, he cussed a president, and he chased the Apache Kid.

The cussing story is Thompson's favorite. June 24, 1898, during a lull in the Spanish-American War, Thompson gathered himself a tidy breakfast from the Cuban countryside. He filled his canteens with rum and syrup. He appropriated Spanish tobacco, which he traded for guinea hen eggs, flour, and bacon. Next morning he cooked and set a feast. His coffee was a trifle strong, so he went to a creek for some water.

"When I got back, my flapjacks, my bacon, my eggs, my coffee, and my syrup was gone," related Thompson. "Near my camp there was a short, stocky fellow with thick glasses and a mouthful of teeth. He had my breakfast in his arms."

As Thompson tells, he dressed down the breakfast thief with language that withered the papaya trees.

"I apologize," said the tubby man in the slouch hat and gaping puttees. "Here's $10 for the breakfast."

"Keep it, you good-for-nothing blankety-blank," Thompson answered. "I can't eat gold."

In 1905 Thompson was ordered to Washington to help interpret at a meeting of American and Latin diplomats. At a state reception Thompson was introduced to President Theodore Roosevelt.

"You look familiar," said the President. "Where were you in June, 1898?"

"Camping in a papaya grove near Santiago." said Thompson.

"And I took your breakfast, didn't I?" With that, the President turned to his guests and said for all to hear:

"I have heard the cussing of loggers in the Northwest. I have heard cowboys and mule skinners and roustabouts. But if any of you want a liberal education in cussing, here is the best teacher in the world."

Thompson said he entered the world with an oath. He said his father was a Union soldier who escaped capture by fleeing on a British ship to Brazil. There Thompson's father married his mother, an Indian. Thompson was born in 1865 in a canoe, on a tributary of the Amazon, while his mother was trying to reach her mother's home.

The Thompson family settled in this country after the Civil War. Thompson joined the army when he was 14. He served in Arizona as courier between Forts Apache and McDowell, and took part in a chase after the Apache Kid. Thompson was chief of scouts in the Philippines.

Army officials told Thompson he is the senior member of the Order of the Purple Heart. He was wounded 11 times, in five campaigns.

Thirty-five years ago, Thompson moved to Arizona to

homestead 320 acres. He lives alone. Children around Apache Junction know him as a kindly gent who buys chewing gum and soft drinks for them by the carton.

Older friends think of Thompson as the man who cussed the President.

(George Thompson died Sept. 9, 1960.)

PEARCE—This town is an island of regression in a sea of progress.

The rest of Arizona is booming. Multi-million-dollar buildings. Superhighways. New subdivisions. Growing industries. Population expanding.

And old Pearce rots and melts away, year by year, and fewer old dogs snap at flies in the sun, and the weeds take over the streets, and the dry desert winds find more hiding places for the red sand.

Now that the general store is closed, the post office is center of the town's activity, when there is any. July 1, 1959, Mrs. Gladys McLeod began her 26th year as postmaster, and the people in Washington didn't send her so much as a thank-you card.

But Mrs. McLeod said she had no complaints. In many ways, living in a town that's going to pot is more pleasant than chasing fortune in a beehive.

A native of the town, Mrs. McLeod went away with her railroader husband from 1918 to 1933. A year after they returned to Pearce, Mrs. McLeod got the post office work, which runs in the family. Her mother and a sister were Pearce postmasters before her, and Mrs. McLeod's son is a clerk in the Willcox post office. Mr. McLeod died in 1939.

Mrs. McLeod is also the town's telephone operator. Infrequently she crosses the dirt main street to sell gasoline from the pumps in front of the padlocked general store.

When Pearce was at its prime, 3,000 persons made homes on the talus below the Commonwealth Mining and Milling workings. The glory holes above the town gave up $45 million in gold and silver before they flooded out. Then the government pegged the price of gold, and Pearce went into a death rattle that Mrs. McLeod has heard for a quarter century.

In her tenure, Pearce population has dropped from 150 to 25. Children from neighboring ranches keep open a two-teacher school. Most of the townspeople are retired. One, Royal James English, is son of a famous lawyer of Tombstone's roaring days.

"I don't feel passed by," said Mrs. McLeod. "My nights are busy, with order of Eastern Star meetings—I'm a past matron of the Eastern Star in Willcox—and with St. Martha's Episcopal Guild. And days, I work."

She sorts outgoing mail from Pearce and Gleeson, and she oversees a star route to 25 mail boxes in the Chiricahua Mountains. One of the principal advantages of living in a town like Pearce, said Mrs. McLeod, is the elbow room. She picked up a city block for back taxes, and most of another was willed to her by a friend.

If Mrs. McLeod outlasts the town she might own it all when there isn't any left.

BEAR CANYON—Tonight we are camped west of Coronado National Memorial, within hailing distance of the Mexican Border.

The oaks are low and the grama grass is high. Supper early; moon late. Below us the brook talks to the owl, and the crickets applaud. Now and then a fox barks high and away on Miller Peak, and our brave dog stirs and paws at his ears. The blondes are asleep under mounds of sleeping bags and blankets and tarps.

I stay awake a while, pondering on a peace of mind that many other peoples do not have.

Here I am, camped in the open, defenseless on an international border, with my greatest treasures strewn around me. For all I know there is not a gun, American or Mexican, cocked from *Baja California* to the Gulf of Mexico.

No fortification stands between my camp and Mexican

Cananea, in the mountains to the south. No armor patrols against invasion. No electrified wires keep the peoples of two countries apart. Along most of the border, there isn't so much as a fence.

I look to the Milky Way, and try to choose a star that might represent the division between Mexico and Arizona. But the stars are not segregated, and neither are the clumps of grass in the country of Coronado.

We could take Mexico in three days. Well, two weeks, stealing time to drink the excellent dark beer which comes in the little bottle and at small price. But I don't believe that invasion by us is feared by a single Mexican—the finest politician to the poorest peon. Some of our tourists are overbearing, but not even the loudmouths with three cameras and many dollars would allow aggression.

And what of us? On what other international borders, besides Canada, could we camp noisily, and with a high fire? There has not been a serious border dispute since the days of Villa, beyond the memory of most men. I do not think that the miners who are now drinking their inexpensive, small bottles of dark *cerveza* in Cananea will cross the unguarded border and pillage my camp. A wetback may pass by, but he will not grasp for an illegal dollar until he reaches a cotton field at Casa Grande.

The moon comes out of El Paso and begins its journey to Tijuana. It will illuminate no official murders of refugees by men in uniforms.

Our countries have had, still have, differences. There are ethnic differences. Economic differences. Religious differences. But for a half century, the most powerful and most industrious nation on earth, and sleepy, agrarian Mexico, have gotten along.

I wonder.

Khrushchev, on which border would you camp tonight, without guard, with a probability of living to sunrise?

India? Poland? Hungary? Korea? Indochina? Yugoslavia?

And on that question, which seems out of place in such a peaceful setting, I close my eyes.

TRACY'S TRADING POST—I drove 100 miles to ask Goldie Richmond if it was true she killed a mountain lion with her bare hands.

"No," she said.

It was a lynx cat. It measured 42 inches from its broad nose to the tip of its stubby tail. Goldie keeps the skin of the brute among the souvenirs of a remarkable life.

She and her first husband, Marion F. Tracy, came to the Papago Reservation in 1928, to doctor a sick brother of Tracy's. The brother was too ill to move. And after he died, said Goldie, "We were too broke to leave."

The Tracys became miners and trappers, working the brushy mountains 4 miles north of Covered Wells, midpoint of the Papago Reservation, which was and is one of Arizona's more desolate regions.

It was a rough life for a woman. Water was so dear, Goldie said, she made a rack of ollas. The top pot held drinking water, which dripped into a second pot, her refrigerator. A catch pot at the bottom was for animals.

"We had 29 traps set out in a box canyon," she said. "One day my husband and I went to check the traps and set more above a water hole. The canyon narrowed down to the width of a room. My husband was leading, on the lookout for cactus patches. I was carrying rabbit meat in the bait bucket.

"My husband pushed through a big desert hackberry and I followed. Just as my husband came out of the brush, the cat jumped off the rock and landed on his back, and started to chew and claw. He gave Mr. Tracy some terrible wounds.

"I grabbed that cat by the throat and squeezed with all my might. It tried to claw me with its hind feet—ripped off my skirt and petticoat and stockings—but I held on because I didn't dare let go. When the cat became limp, I dropped him, and my husband bashed him with a rock."

Goldie bears scars from the fight to this day. One is 8 inches long, on her left wrist and forearm.

In 1932, the Tracys built their trading post 35 miles east of Ajo. Until 1959, when a state highway home was put at Tracy's, the nearest white neighbor was 15 miles farther east, at Covered Wells.

Mr. Tracy died in 1938. Goldie married James M. Richmond in 1941. The trading post has attracted a considerable Papago settlement. Two hundred Indians live nearby.

Richmond drives a peddling route two days each week, and he goes one day to Tucson for supplies. Goldie has no help while he is away.

"I've never had reason to fear my neighbors. The Indians are better than most white people," she said.

Goldie is huge. She is nearly 6 feet tall, and she weighs, I'd guess, 300 pounds, but maybe that's too high. Her curls have turned to a white frame for a round, smiling face. In her spare hours, the woman who strangled a lynx makes intricate quilts which win blue ribbons at the Arizona State Fair.

PINAL RANCH—The last time she showed me her mud floors, Mrs. Dudley I. Craig was slowly and surely going blind.

It was a great pity, and all her friends disliked to talk about her future, because Grandma Geraldine was animal-proud of her independence.

But there was no ignoring the dismal truth. Cataracts were dimming the eyes that has seen the gentling of a raw land with the blood of men and tears of women. She fussed with a magnifying glass over her newspaper, and, much to her embarrassment, began to bump into pieces of furniture that hadn't been rearranged for 80 years.

Her home is in the mountains back of Superior. It is a museum of pioneering ways, and a monument to a gracious and talented family.

"Come in," she said to us, flinging wide the plank front

door. "I guess you've come to see the floors again?"

She hadn't changed, that I could tell, in three years. Each white curl was in place. Still thin, still brisk, still sure.

For a person going blind, I thought, she was a remarkable guide. I resisted an impulse to take her arm, as she led us on a tour of the 14 rooms of Pinal Ranch.

She rolled back a corner of carpet and showed us the concrete-hard mud floor—where the cherry root makes a bump—where chair rockers have pressed ruts. She had us admire the adobe walls and juniper framing.

The Rochester hanging lamps. The chuck box used by her husband's pioneering parents. Black iron cooking pots. Coffee grinders. The curing room, darkened by corn cob smoke. Priceless pieces of Wedgwood. Ironstone china. An Estey organ, shipped around the Horn to Casa Grande, and packed by mule from Silver King, in '83. Native granite hearthstones in three adobe fireplaces. An 1850 Florence sewing machine.

The library, muslin balloon ceiling intact, is walled with first editions and autographed copies. Here Mrs. Craig's husband studied scientific ranching and fruit farming. He died in 1954, shortly after he received honors for his 60 years of service as U.S. Weather Bureau volunteer observer.

Mrs. Craig showed us her old wood stove, the penciled diary of the pioneer's journey, her turkey platter large enough for a 40-pound bird.

"Well," at last I had to ask. "Isn't it a hardship, a lady of your years, living alone, cleaning this big house, preparing your own meals, and . . ."

"Oh," she said, "I guess you don't know. I had operations on both eyes, three days apart. You ought to see me tootle around in my Volkswagen."

That dream of many a careworn housewife, an expense-paid cruise to Hawaii, is approaching reality for the Potluck.

Eight Phoenicians belong to the group.

Mrs. Ken (Mary Lou) Watson brought them together

22 years ago. There was little money then for doing the town, but Mrs. Watson figured she could afford a party at home. She invited three girl friends of the Phoenix Union High School class of '33 and their husbands. The dinner was potluck. And so have been succeeding dinners, every other week, except during World War II.

In the beginning, the couples chipped $1 per person into a kitty. Whenever the cat was fat, the four couples went to some fancy place and ordered the best. It was akin to winning a prize. No worries of shattered budgets spoiled the fun.

The Potluck was disbanded during the war, and re-formed in 1946 with three original couples: The Watsons, of 2635 N. 20th Ave.; Mr. and Mrs. Charlie Langford, of 915 W. Catalina; and Mr. and Mrs. N. D. McLeod, of 120 E. Tuckey Lane.

The fourth couple, Mr. and Mrs. Maurice Skiff, of 3909 E. Highland, also were from the Phoenix Union classes of the early 1930s. Fortunes of the families improved. Watson is superintendent and, with Langford, part owner of a printery. McLeod owns a string of optical stores. Skiff supervises a large district for a finance firm.

Friendship became a factor in work, as well as play. The men teamed up to paint their houses. The couples have had adjoining seats for Arizona State University games every year. Scarcely a hunting or fishing season goes unhonored by the men of the Potluck, and while they are tramping Kaibab or plugging Mead, the women hold a widows' night in Phoenix. The kitty was hard hit when the men took their wives on a deep-sea excursion off Guaymas in the Gulf of California.

"We never touch the pot unless we're all together," said Mrs. Watson, "and it seems the teasing never ends about some member or another taking advantage of the pot."

Around 1950 the twice-monthly ante was raised to $5 a couple. The Potluck has taken its members to Las Vegas twice, and paid all expenses except some modest losses at the tables.

"We all have many other friends," said Mrs. Watson, "and we go our separate ways in other activities. The Potluck hasn't limited us—not at all."

In fact, several similar societies have been formed by friends of members of Potluck.

Looking toward the 25th anniversary of Potluck, members declared the pot off-limits for minor raids. Barring some unexpected misfortune, the pot, which now stands at $1,000, will be sufficient for the Potluck's longest trip.

From time to time, at a football game or a Christmas party or a housepainting, a Potlucker can be heard chanting, "Honolulu in '62."

Best way to learn about a guy, they say, is to go hunting with him.

In recent years I've gotten to know one fellow pretty well. He is as old as the century and compact in build, and he is the stubbornest man allowed at large.

Old Country, we call him. Squareheaded Hunky. He was born in what is now, or was once, Czechoslovakia, the eldest son of a miner. The family ate boiled potatoes for breakfast, mashed potatoes for lunch, and fried potatoes for supper. Once a day a rich woman brought a priceless gift—one egg, for a sick girl in the family.

America was supposed to be different, but in 1908 the streets of Kansas were not paved with gold. They weren't paved at all.

This fellow and his brothers used to go down to the railroad tracks, where a grade slowed the huffing freights. The boys would throw rocks at the train crews. The crewmen retaliated by throwing coal. After the running fights, the boys would stuff the coal into burlap bags, and tote it home for the stoves.

Growing to manhood, this fellow held a series of the hardest jobs of the times. He farmed, he was a sawyer, he cut down and bucked out cordwood, and he spent a winter of 16-hour days tonging oysters off a Chesapeake Bay schooner.

Shortly after he married, and had two sons, the depression hit, and he was put out of work. To maintain payments on the home mortgage, he contracted to dig septic tanks. Once he agreed to make a tank for $50. A few feet down he struck solid rock. But a bargain was made, and he dug the hole for the agreed price. It took him three weeks of the meanest kind of toil.

No worthwhile future seemed open for an immigrant whose formal schooling had stopped at the eighth grade. So this man went back to high school. He attended classes three nights a week for seven years. On other nights and on weekends he did his homework. He whipped algebra, and added French to the three languages he already understood and spoke. He was nearly 40 when he graduated. The home town paper pictured him holding his diploma, and as far as I knew, that was the only time his mug has been in print.

Soon afterward, he got the raise in pay he expected. Right along with it came the first attack of arthritis.

Pain has walked with him, sat with him, slept with him, for the past 20 years. The doctors pulled his teeth, baked him in ovens, boiled him in water, hitched him to electric machines, stuffed him with pills, slurps, honey, citrus, and vitamins, and even purified his blood, one quart at a time. The wizards at Johns Hopkins gave him their tests.

Nothing helped, until a country doctor prescribed Arizona. His way of climbing stairs then was to lift up one leg with his hands and drag up the other leg.

He rarely complained; never stopped fighting. The Arizona sun loosened his joints somewhat, and today he can even go deer hunting with his sons. I'm one of them.

JACOB LAKE—The woman skipped up to the window of the checking station and proudly announced:

"I got a buck doe."

Gabby Blaser didn't even blink. In seven years of keeping track of one of America's most famous hunts, he has heard and seen just about all there is.

"Well, ma'am," said Blaser. "Usually deer are either bucks or does, not both. Could you describe yours, please?"

"It doesn't have any horns, and that means it is a doe," explained the woman, "but other places he was built like a buck."

Blaser noted the killing of a buck fawn.

How Blaser has kept his sense of humor these past several years is a wonder. Each fall he brings his trailer to North Kaibab Forest, where he lives from September through December. In prehunt surveys he observes the day-to-day habits of the Kaibab game, at home in the lovely woodlands north of Grand Canyon.

Then, bam! Come the hunters.

In 1959 there were 6,000 split into two sections. Each hunter who killed was entitled to a second bonus deer. In four days, 1,500 deer were checked through Blaser's station.

The hunt was rigidly controlled. Hunters were required to check in and out. Data was gathered on weight and condition of the deer, where and when the kills were made, and how hard and long the hunters worked to find game. Biologists use Blaser's figures in managing the Kaibab herd to produce the most possible deer, within food production limits of the range.

The toughest part of Blaser's job is commiserating with the luckless and feckless who fail to shoot a deer.

"Where are the deer?" is the question heard most. He tries to give useful tips. Once, while hundreds of hunters were crashing through Kaibab's isolated canyons, three deer, including a fork-horn buck, walked to within 100 feet of the checking station.

One woman accused Blaser of hiding the deer. She poked her head through the window and cursed him. She even used some words that were new to Blaser.

"I'm sorry, ma'am. Better luck next time," was all he'd say.

Despite such abuse, Blaser was convinced he is in the work he wants. During the hunts he puts in 16 hours a day. He had seen a hunter with "man" sewed in bright tape on his back. He had weighed a 250-pound buck, and measured a 38-inch antler spread. He was first-name friend to thousands —great-grandmothers who hunt for the table, Texans who seek a world's trophy.

Fond as he was of deer, said Blaser, he liked people better.

Aunty Bill is inclined to romanticize, but how else can she tell the story of the wren of Roosevelt Dam?

She was a young, pretty and curvy widow of World War I when she toured the West in 1920.

"Dressed up like Astor's pet horse, and wearing a little go-to-hell hat," she visited Roosevelt Dam and was smitten by the beauty of America's first reclamation project.

A year later she returned, determined to find a home in the Southwest. Something drew her back to the great masonry arch which dammed the Salt River. A rainbow followed her bus to the dam, and that's the day she met Ben Reynolds. He was vacationing at the old Apache Lodge, and volunteered to guide the other guests. Outside, as if by a miracle, Ben Reynolds produced a wren in his hand.

"I guess he had caught it somehow earlier," recalled Aunty Bill. "But I always wanted to believe Ben was like St. Francis, for whom the animals held no fear. I made Ben promise never to tell me where he got that wren. He put the bird on the railing outside the lodge, and it hesitated a moment before flying away."

Ben and Bill (her real name is Eleanor) fell in love, at first sight. They were married Jan. 21, 1922, at the fourth light from the north tower, on the Gila County end of the dam. Villagers and other friends from miles around came to the reception. The cowboys all dumped their moonshine into the wedding punch, and the ancient canyon at the confluence of the Salt and Tonto resounded with the whoops of celebration until dawn.

Uncle Ben and Aunty Bill had one extravagance—friends. He was successively chief clerk, head of commissary, and hydrographer at the dam. He was also the weather bureau's volunteer weather observer at Roosevelt. Aunty Bill became Roosevelt's hostess with the most. Their lives seemingly became inseparable from the workings of the dam, and the doings of the town.

On July 19, 1942, the Reynoldses' eldest son took his bride on the dam, at exactly the place where his parents were married 20 years before. That wedding was fancier; the reception more sober.

Aunty Bill still lives in the big house above the dam. Ben Reynolds retired in 1949, and died in 1953. One morning while visiting with friends in Phoenix, she told how it was:

"As he wanted, his ashes were scattered from the dam at night.

"The next day we had a memorial service on the concrete apron where the old Apache Lodge stood. The governor of Arizona came to speak, and friends crowded around, and the services began.

"A wren landed on the railing. Through the whole ceremony the wren walked and flew around the hotel point, and it seemed to have no fear of the humans there."

But then, said Aunty Bill, she has always been a romantic sort.

He was no stranger to toil.

He grew up on hard labor in Pecos, N. M., and his hands were calloused to the drill and shovel in the Jerome drifts. Phelps Dodge was pleased to transfer such a worker to the Bisbee mine.

At 41, he was stoutly muscled, and on those occasions when he bared his chest, a tattooed tiger could be seen leering through a forest of black fur. He was all man and a yard wide—this William (Tiger) Mares.

Nothing like hard work to take a man's mind off himself, he figured.

He would repair and enlarge his house in Don Luis. It was small and not modern. There lived his wife, two sons, Louie and Jimmie, and a daughter, Joan. Another son, William, might want a place to stay when his hitch was done in the navy.

Adobe was Tiger Mares's choice for walls. He mixed the clay, straw and water, poured the bricks, dried them, broke them from their molds, and stacked them by his front door.

He searched the corners of Tombstone Canyon for other building materials—salvaged or discarded, but still sound.

Tiger Mares had hardly begun when he was taken to Copper Queen Hospital for amputation of a leg. Quickly he learned how to get around on an artificial limb, and he returned to a fulltime schedule at the mines.

And during spare hours he pushed his work at home. Friends and family helped. The 'dobe walls rose to enclose a living room, a bedroom and a porch. All was well-thought-out and made. A large picture window was set in the living room, and a false ceiling was installed in the hall to accommodate air conditioning.

As the project neared completion, Tiger Mares again was forced to enter the hospital. He continued to plan and direct the improvements to his home from his hospital bed.

Mares probably never realized what a heroic figure he became to many of his neighbors. His story was circulated, but in whispers, so as to spare the feelings of the Mares children. Mares had a large, admiring audience, but no one dared to applaud.

A friend visited him, and later said:

"He is one of those strong and cheerful characters who put to shame the whiners and loafers among us. He is a builder."

William Mares died, and only then were the Mares children told:

The Tiger began the plans for the house the day he learned his death by cancer was inevitable.

Rain was whipping the earth to a fury when I arrived at the camp of Richard (Hobo Dick) Zimmerman.

He's the one that lives in a wheelbarrow.

The barrow was parked well off the highway a mile or so northwest of El Mirage. It is surely unlike any other wheelbarrow in the world. Thick handles join in a frame attached to a big rubber wheel. For foul weather Zimmerman's bed was on the frame, and tarp made a shelter over the whole contraption.

Nearby, over an open, sputtering fire, coffee steamed in a gallon fruit tin. A mongrel named Chief was curled under the wheelbarrow. On the side of the wheelbarrow was a wavering message: "If the Lord so will I shal push this rig from El Centro Calif to Bay City Mich." Drawn down into his parka, Hobo Dick looked like a snapping turtle at bay, but after a handshake he was as friendly as spaniel pups.

"I've been on the road since I was 15," he said, "and I'm 78 years old now. I'm known from coast to coast as the spokesman of the 'bos."

Years ago, he said, he was snowbound while logging alone in Alaska. He had seven slabs of bacon. As he ate the bacon, he wrote a fanciful story on the wrappings, and with the first thaw sent the manuscript to a publisher in Montreal. The story sold for $450, and Hobo Dick since has written hundreds of yarns about the knights of the road. Zimmerman now makes his living sharpening saws and scissors. The work is light, and he knows the tricks.

Nine years ago he dislocated both shoulders trying to catch a fast freight in Texas.

"My shoulders weren't put back right," said Hobo Dick. "I can't get on a train now unless it's standing still, and even then the vibration makes my shoulders hurt something fierce. I didn't want to give up traveling, so that's why I built this wheelbarrow."

Once he pushed his wheelbarrow from Amarillo, Tex., to Bay City, Mich., roundabout 2,360 miles. Hobo Dick often goes to Bay City, because there lives his mother, 101 years old.

The weight of the wheelbarrow, 120 pounds, has tended to relocate his shoulders, said Hobo Dick. He has grown fond of setting his own schedule, free of the limitations of railroad travel.

"Take this trip, for example," he said. "I started out in July. I only carry five gallons of water in the summer, and I ran out on the shores of the Salton Sea. A highway patrolman found me and got some food and water, and it's been easy sailing ever since.

"Those boys must have radioed ahead, because it seems I'm expected wherever I go. When I crossed into Arizona, one of your patrolmen was waiting with a box of chuck."

Zimmerman is a leisurely traveler. If pressed, and when Chief is in shape for the trail, he can cover 20 miles a day. But he said he kills weeks on end at favored camping spots.

There's no hurry, he figures.

One of Arizona's best-tended Thanksgiving traditions was begun 40 years ago in a raw copper town.

Four young couples gathered to swap their loneliness for plates of turkey. Every year since, there has been such a Thanksgiving dinner, attended by original couples, with additions of friends and family.

The town was Clemenceau, on the northern foothills of Mingus Mountain; the year, 1919. Unpainted buildings lined the primitive streets which converged on the new smelter of the United Verde Extension. The nearest picture show was 50 miles across the mountain.

Mr. and Mrs. C. N. Hagius had the first dinner. He was engineer for the power plant. They invited Dr. James R. Moore, company physician, H. V. Kuse, mining engineer, Alex Vaughn, garageman, and their wives. Although the families soon scattered to other Arizona towns, friendships that deepened at that first dinner have drawn them together year after year.

The Vaughns now live in Kingman. He is an oil products distributor who has operated service stations in Salome, Wellton, and Hayden.

Mr. Kuse died a year ago, after long service as consulting engineer for Phelps Dodge in Douglas. His wife moved to Louisiana.

The Hagiuses have a home in Tucson. He is retired. Mrs. Hagius has been to all 40 dinners. Hagius missed a few, because of his job as power plant engineer at Tucson.

The Moores, hosts for the 1959 dinner, live at 305 W. Granada. The Vaughns and Hagiuses were to come to Phoenix, along with a dozen other friends from early Clemenceau days.

Included are Mr. and Mrs. Harold R. Brisley—he is pathologist for Phelps Dodge at Douglas—G. L. Pritchford, employe of the Prescott post office, Mr. and Mrs. John Garrett of Cottonwood (he is a retired druggist), Mr. and Mrs. Max Anderson of Coolidge (he is an Indian service engineer), and Mr. and Mrs. W. R. Ryan of San Bernardino, Calif. (he is retired from army ordnance work). Dr. and Mrs. M. O. Dumas, of Cottonwood, Mr. and Mrs. T. G. Grieder, of Fontana, Calif., and Mr. and Mrs. J. B. Jordan, of Ajo also are regulars.

"Friends, in-laws, children, grandchildren—all have been welcome," said Mr. Moore.

First dinners in Clemenceau were potluck, and they were rotated from home to home, year to year. Guests traveling long distances these days cannot bring covered dishes, but they do give money to the hostess. This is a practical holdover from the old days, when the dinners would draw as many as 35 guests.

The original four couples had 12 children and 14 grandchildren. Most difficult times for the dinners were during World War II, when gasoline rationing curtailed personal travel. One year the central Arizona families saved rationing coupons and pooled them for a trip to Douglas.

"The friends you make when you're newly married are the friends who last the longest," said Mrs. Moore.

The J. K. Mowrys, married 14 years, had no children. They were sure they wouldn't need three bedrooms in their new home at 3030 E. Meadowbrook. They had two partitions removed to form an extra-large living room. This left them one bedroom.

Next year Mrs. Mowry bore twin sons.

GUAYMAS—We went fishing, but I had no faith.

This had been a bad season. The deer were plentiful during the turkey hunt, and turkey could be found when deer were desired. There were no ducks at any hour.

So I had no faith in the sign outside fishing headquarters at the hotel at Guaymas: "Fish guaranteed 365 days of the year."

These were the worst months of the year for fishing here, said our guide. No marlin or sailfish. Few yellowtail tuna were striking.

And the temper of the Gulf of California did not promise an exceptional day. An offshore wind was chasing whitecaps across the blue bay.

But the price for the charter boat was tempting. Ordinarily the charge is $6.50 per person, but the Dons Club of Phoenix had bargained for $4.50. On hand, too, was a Mexican game ranger selling fishing licenses at $1 per copy.

Our cruiser was a freshly painted red, white, and blue marlin hunter about 20 feet long. It bucked and wallowed northward to a chain of small islands where our Mexican guides dropped anchor and broke out tackle.

They supplied thumb-size hooks, steel snells and braided leader. Some of us fished with reels and rods from the fighting chairs at the cruiser's stern, and others used hand lines.

Crude sinkers carried the baited hooks 40 feet to the bottom of the sea.

"This is a good place for red snapper," assured our skipper, a young Mexican who said he was 12 when he decided to become a charter boat boss. The red snapper did not bite. I knew they would not bite.

"Mackerel!" exclaimed the skipper, "Spanish mackerel." He pointed to where, a half mile away, birds of prey were plummeting into the white caps. Bait rigs were quickly exchanged for feather jigs, which were trolled.

Slowly the cruiser drew the jigs across the school of mackerel. And then one struck. Osborn Foster, of Phoenix, brought aboard the first beautiful fish—silver and yellow spots, slim and streamlined, weighing a couple of pounds.

With the spell broken, fishing shortly approached perfection. At times four fish were being reeled in at once—and there were lulls to restore suspense.

Altogether, we caught 80 or more California and Spanish mackerel, which amounted perhaps to 150 pounds. For only 10 cents a pound, the boys on the docks cleaned and froze the catch for transportation home.

I became a believer.

MAYER—When a feller learns to judge the jump of a frog, just by looking, we'll show him Mrs. Martha Hickey.

Go ahead, we'll say. How far off the ground would Mrs. Hickey go?

She is a tall, long-limbed woman who is as old as the century. Her still-brown hair is bound up plainly, and her usual expression is a Fred Allen combination of gloom and devilment.

Mrs. Hickey manages the White House rooming and boarding house in this old mining town off Arizona-69, 70 miles north of Phoenix. The town went to sleep 35 years ago, but Mrs. Hickey is busier than ever, maintaining the hotel without a hired hand.

When she immigrated to Arizona from Switzerland,

Mayer and the country roundabout were booming. Martha was 19. She waited tables and helped cook for as many as 110 miners, cowboys, and laborers. Board was $1 a day, no limit on servings.

At about this time a towering smelter smokestack was erected on the butte down slope from the boarding house. The stack stands to this day. Most motorists who know the landmark believe it expelled the noxious gases from one of Arizona's great smelters. Truth is, the stack was never used. Construction was begun in 1917, after the Mayer ore began to pinch out. Weber Chimney Co., of Kansas City, Mo., insisted a contract was a contract.

Reinforced concrete was poured in five-foot sections by men earning 36 cents an hour. The walls were made to taper in thickness from 12 to 6 feet, and the inside diameter was drawn from 16 feet at the bottom to 10 at the top. The stack was guaranteed to withstand 100 mph wind and 1,300-degree smoke.

But the smelter closed, and the stack served no purpose other than to tilt the hats of awestruck visitors. The stack inside was like a vertical, black, smooth-sided mine shaft. The top, 129½ feet above its base, could be reached by a plain wooden ladder.

Martha eventually married a fireman from the ill-conceived smelter. She followed him to other towns, other mines. They had two children. After her husband died, she returned to the town that she thought to be home, to manage the old boarding house, to comb out her memories.

At times she can almost hear the rough talk of the boarders as she served the steaming dishes to the massive dining table:

"Takes a man with guts to climb up that stack," said one. "One look down, and you freeze. No place to hang on at the top, either."

Said another, "I know a girl who'll climb it."

"A dollar she won't."

"You're on. Martha, will you climb up the stack?"

A few more dollars were wagered, and Martha went over

to the stack, climbed it hand over hand, stood for a while admiring the view, and came down.

The winners probably knew little about frogs, but they believed in a girl from the Alps.

The talking animal story is not what it used to be, and that's a shame.

Not too many years ago, a horse that could recite the Lord's Prayer stood a fair chance for Page One. Reporters who specialized in such yarns were respected and rewarded as craftsmen and circulation builders.

"An' whur d'ye think yer headin', McCarthy?" the city editor might say.

"Off t'interview a talkin' German Shepherd dog."

"Yer a true son o' th' old Sod, me bucko, and be sure to get its views on the Kaiser, and take care th' Persian cat ain't no ventriloquist."

Times have changed so sharply I doubt that a menagerie of eloquent elephants and rhetorical rhinoceroses and loquacious lemurs would earn two paragraphs outside of a signed column.

The world is numb toward things which talk. We have telegrams that sing, and boxes of candy that speak sweetly. Talking machines dominate our dens, our cars, our desk tops.

All this came to mind the other day when some folks up Clarkdale way were telling me they have a dog which listens. Let me state it again. The dog does not talk. Does not speak words. This is a genuine listening dog.

Minnie, of mixed breeding and 2 years old, is the pet of the Joseph Goldfarb family. Timmy Goldfarb, 10, is Minnie's master.

About a half-block from the Goldfarb home lives the Perry Moore family. Moore is Mrs. Goldfarb's father.

Almost every afternoon it was Minnie's habit to trot over to the Moore residence, causing the families no end of trouble. After sunset Minnie refused to go home. Threats and noises would not budge her. Apparently she was afraid of the dark.

Walking Minnie back home become a bother.

Then Timmie and his Grandpa hit upon an idea that smacked of genius.

Timmie picked up the Goldfarb telephone and called Moore. Moore held his receiver against Minnie's ear, and Timmie clucked and whistled, and shouted:

"Here, Minnie! Minnie, Minnie, Minnie! Come home, Minnie! Here, girl. Here, girl!"

Without hesitation, Minnie dashed from the Moore home, braved the black night, and arrived moments later, panting and wriggling, at Timmie's side.

The trick worked night after night. It occurred to Moore that Minnie might respond to other suggestions. One day, when Minnie was at the Goldfarbs, Moore called there, and after the telephone was placed to Minnie's ear, he asked:

"Do you want to go for a ride, Minnie? Hurry, hurry, if you want to go for a ride."

Minnie raced from the Goldfarbs to the Moores', where she jumped into the car.

An amused witness to these carryings-on is Dinah Moore, 17.

"I think it is unusual when people are answering their telephones and taking calls for a little dog," she said. "The people turn to the little dog and say, 'It's for you, Minnie!' "

Chapter Sixteen

If I were a hatemonger, I wouldn't know what to scrawl in what color on the door at 716 N. Central.

Already written there is "Maricopa Mortgage Co., Inc." which gives no hint of the variegated gathering of the humans inside. They are joined in the base motive of making a buck, it is true, but more important at this season, perhaps, is that they get along.

Julian J. Blum, president and founder of the firm, is a Jew. Three years ago he set up the company with intentions of catering to people who might have trouble borrowing elsewhere. Half of Maricopa's business has been with Negroes and Spanish-Americans.

Helping to form the company with Blum was Rosario Cirincione, Catholic of Italian extraction, who is now executive vice president.

Along came Marlan Keith Edwards, an Episcopalian of Welsh-English background who had some cash and a law degree in his pocket, and he dealt himself in as secretary-treasurer.

The other directors, both vice presidents, were presidents of mortgage companies which merged with Maricopa. Carl Gutmacher comes from a family of German Protestants, and Joseph Martin's Spanish great-great-great-grandfather was the first mayor of Los Angeles, and is buried under the altar of the San Gabriel Mission.

In Tempe, the driver of a transit-mix concrete truck forgot to take his lunch pail to work. Later, on his way to deliver a load of concrete, he stopped at his home.

A shiny convertible was parked out front. The truck driver peeked into his house, and saw his wife in the arms of a stranger.

The husband tiptoed out, aimed his chute, and filled the convertible to the window sills with soupy concrete.

How's that for a compact car?

Fellow newspaperman Turk Smith believes he has discovered a significant difference between the cities of Phoenix and Scottsdale.

He occasionally borrows small amounts from the home office of the Valley Bank, located in downtown Phoenix.

Once he was in Scottsdale, and, needing some money for a trip, he applied for a $50 loan at a branch. The loan officer stared at the application form.

"Your chances would be better," he said, "if you'd ask for $100."

It was "Thirty" for Old No. 30.

After a quarter-century of the hardest sort of service, the faithful typesetting machine was sold by The Republic to a Phoenix printing plant.

Old No. 30 was what typesetters call an ad mill. It held

four different fonts of type, and was capable of setting the four sizes in one line. With a system developed by Rube Goldberg and the Intertype people, the machine also could redistribute its used matrices to the proper fonts for storage.

Somebody in the back shop thought William (The Deacon) Sutterlin ought to be notified. He went to work at The Republic in 1910, and retired just five years ago.

At that time it was estimated The Deacon had run 917 tons of type metal through his machines. Old No. 30 had been his last, and favorite. When he went to work in the shop there were four typesetting machines and 15 employes. Now the work force totals 200. When Old No. 30 was replaced, there were 33 machines.

Sutterlin set the stories of history's most tumultuous time. But to the day he quit, he didn't like to handle stories about crime. Give him a good school yarn—or the play-by-play of a tight World Series game. Those he enjoyed.

Sutterlin is a devout member of First Baptist Church, and his extra-curricular lectures to fellow workers about the evils of smoke and drink earned him his nickname. The Deacon's two sons became ministers.

Old No. 30's last day was spent in setting ads.

Early in the morning a white haired, 76-year-old man wearing the familiar round spectacles entered The Republic composing room. He went over to Old No. 30, stared at it a few moments, and then put a fancy greeting card on it.

Read the sentiment:

Thinking of you often
And of all the fun we've shared
Remembering it's nice to have
A friend who really cared,

And thoughts of you mean wishes
That are really warm and true,
Because it means so much to know
A nice someone like you.

". . . And now with a heavy heart we must part forever but memories will linger always. The Deacon."

Then, William Sutterlin stuck on the front of Old No. 30 a red, red rose.

The experiences of Mrs. Al Thomas with a duck named George should bring a sweat of sympathy to the brows of thousands of Arizona parents.

Children in the neighborhood of the Thomas home at 3216 E. Orange brought ducklings home from the Arizona State Fair one November. The baby ducks were prizes in coin-pitching games.

Leslie, 9, younger of the two Thomas daughters, just *had* to have a duck. Her parents, city folks, couldn't see anything wrong in Leslie's having a duck, too.

George came to live at the Thomas home. At first the Thomases were afraid George might die, as did other pet ducks in the neighborhood. Then there emerged a haunting fear that George might live forever.

When in the cuddly, downy state, George lived in cardboard boxes, and was moved from room to room, according to the needs and whims of the family. He thrived. He learned to leap over the sides of his cardboard prisons, and, in the words of Mrs. Thomas, "soon convinced us that there is nothing messier than a duck." A friend supplied a parakeet cage, which made George a suitable home for only a few weeks. He simply outgrew the cage.

By this time Mrs. Thomas was buying poultry feed by the sack, and the man at the feed store suggested that as soon as George grew white feathers, he might be released in Phoenix's Encanto Park. Man said there were lots of happy ducks out there.

George was moved to an outside storage room. Daily one Thomas or another mopped out.

That got to be a drag, and George was given the run of the fenced back yard. But George did not want to run. He took up station at a glass door, where he could keep an eye on the family. Naturally, his pacing place on the patio was well defined by duck droppings.

"He will be happier with his friends," said Mrs. Thomas. "It is time for George to join his own kind—to paddle around on the beautiful lagoon—to do the things that ducks do."

Leslie reluctantly submitted to her mother's decision. But the girl insisted on going along to Encanto Park to bid George goodby. Mother, daughter, and duck approached the bank of the lagoon. The happy Encanto ducks were swimming, quacking, and diving. They paddled over and begged for chunks of bread.

"Go on, George," said Mrs. Thomas. "This is your new home and these will be your new friends."

George would not budge. Mrs. Thomas gently picked up George and set him down in the lagoon. The duck flew out of the water as if it were flaming gasoline. Mrs. Thomas again got a grip on the duck. She pitched him out into the lagoon. George sank for a moment, then clumsily clawed his way back to Mrs. Thomas. Again and again she heaved the duck far from shore.

"Mother, he's scared," cried Leslie.

Mrs. Thomas and Leslie and George angrily stalked together back to the car and went home.

Jet airliners were being discussed at Sky Harbor.

"Just think," said one man. "Before long you'll leave Chicago after breakfast and arrive in Phoenix before breakfast."

Mal Hernandez saw his opening: "What'll the stewardesses do then? Pump stomachs?"

Feb. 10, 1960 the Eldon Randall Chapter of the National Honor Society was chartered at Fort Thomas High School.

A sophisticated world might judge Randall a dedicated, if unimportant, master of a little high school in Arizona's Upper Gila Valley. But folks there wouldn't trade him for a John Dewey, with a Robert Hutchins and a James Conant to boot.

One of 12 children of the Frank C. Randall family of Pine, Eldon Randall nearly finished college at Brigham Young and ASC Flagstaff before World War II. He served three years as a medical corpsman in such places as Guam, the Philippines, Bougainville, and New Caledonia.

While completing his senior year at Flagstaff he established himself as one of the school's all-around star athletes. In the winter he was a high-scoring basketball player, and in the spring he won the turkey calling, sawing, and log chopping championships.

The big guy was hired as coach at Thatcher High. From the start, he led with imagination and loyalty. One of his teams was dispirited before the game with a powerful opponent. Randall turned his back on his solemn charges, removed his dentures, and gave his boys his most toothless grin. Thatcher won.

When one of his football players was seriously hurt, Randall gently massaged the injury an entire day. In 1951 the Thatcher High annual was dedicated to him.

In summers at ASC he earned a master's degree and an administrator's certificate. He became principal of Thatcher High. He was given the school's coveted "Most Loyal Parent Award."

In 1955 he moved down the road to Fort Thomas. Luring him was the challenge of a 55 per cent Apache student body, and a substandard school plant. His untiring efforts to improve the school brought him the dedication of that school's annual, also.

Then at 6 a.m. March 25, 1959, Randall awakened to the news that his school was afire. He led the fight, but smoke damage was extensive, and the vocational shops and home economics rooms were destroyed. At inflated costs, insurance was insufficient to replace the two school services that Randall considered most important to his unusual student body.

"Let's rebuild it ourselves," said Randall to his town.

He threw his muscle into concrete work, in raising walls, in laying tile, in roofing, in painting. He worked through the summer daily until 10:30 p.m., and toward fall he set his quitting time at midnight. His wife brought his meals to the construction job. His own four children nearly forgot what their father looked like. From the entire summer, inventory and vacation time for many principals, Randall stole five days for himself—and those he gave to his family.

Classes came to order in a school better than the old.

"How do you thank a man for living the kind of life that most of us just *try* to live?" asked a townsman. "Usually you can't. But the students are giving the biggest honor they have for a teacher, counselor, principal, and most importantly, a friend."

Half a century before Sperry was a leading name in Arizona industry, a Mesa schoolboy sat down to write the most important letter of his life.

It was to his parents.

"School will be over very soon, as you know," he began.

"Almost ever since I came here I have been thinking what I shall want to do after I leave. In making my decision, you can just wager that I have tried to consider your wishes and I know that you will agree with me when I tell you what I want to do. . . .

"I want to enter the aeroplane business. I know you have no objections to this save that you think the game has a poor future. As for me, I have utmost confidence in a brilliant one, and I think that is near at hand. . . .

"If you doubt the future of aeroplanes, you are simply placing yourselves in the unmagnanimous position of those who doubted the future of the automobile. The aeroplane is bound to become safe and practical.

"Already they know that if they have a certain relation between the rear elevator and the main supporting plane, longitudinal stability would take care of itself.

"Where would aeronautics be today if the Wright brothers and others had not had implicit faith in the future of it? Then should we, who have seen what can be done with the crude, unscientifically designed machines of today, be afraid to plunge in?

"The first thing I want to do is finish the plane.

"You should not condemn aeroplaning as a dangerous pursuit because a few reckless and, in fact, ignorant men, wholly incompetent save simply as pilots, are taking reckless, fool chances to make large financial returns. These men . . . bear no relation to sane flight. . . .

"I am very determined to go into aeroplanes and I think that you should help me get started, as you promised to do last fall, when you said that if I returned still strong for aeroplanes you would help me."

Son of an inventor, the boy had grown up in a home filled with machines and gadgets. He built a glider, and had to tear down part of the house to move it outside.

Later he installed an engine, and flew it often from the fields around his Cleveland home. But the boy's health and education suffered. His parents made a bargain. The boy was to go to Arizona for a year—to study at Evans School at Mesa, which preceded the more famous ranch school at the foot of the Tanque Verde Mountains outside Tucson.

At the end of the school year the boy was more determined than ever on a career in aviation. His parents gave the support they had promised.

His first work was development of gyroscope instruments. An automatic pilot of his invention brought him a prize of 50,000 francs. He made a drift indicator, and contributed ideas to speed and altitude instruments. He made the first United States night flight. He invented the turn-and-bank indicator for blind flying.

In 1923, a stalled engine caused an airplane to settle into the English Channel, and its pilot, Lawrence Burst Sperry, drowned in an attempt to swim ashore.

He lived just one decade after he made his decision on the desert.

No matter how big a man is, the size of his funeral usually is determined by the weather.

A raw wind was rolling gray snow clouds across the White Mountains, and still 1,000 people gathered to bury J. Rufus Crandell. It was the biggest funeral Snowflake ever had, and possibly ever will have.

Freshest memories of Mr. Crandell were of an old man's mannerisms. In recent years he had a way of telling a joke, and taking a little side step, and slapping his thigh, and saying, "Don'tcha see now, don'tcha see?"

But among the grownups at the funeral were those who remembered when J. Rufus Crandell hiked from his family's farm to Snowflake. He was 15. He wore all the clothes he owned, and in a flour sack slung over his back were his greatest treasures, a violin and a bow. He borrowed books at the Snowflake Stake Academy, and soon was acclaimed the town's best scholar, and best baseball pitcher. How the boy found time to practice his fiddle, folks wondered.

In 1910, with his own high school diploma scarcely dry, he began to teach. Only three times did he leave his plateau-and-mountain country for any length of time. He went to Brigham Young University to study music. He went overseas with the AEF. He went to the Mormon Temple in Salt Lake City to marry Laverne Richards.

Music, believed Uncle Rufus, should be taught children in their earliest years.

"I remember him coming into our first grade room," recalled a student. "He didn't have a pitch pipe—just that violin under one arm and the bow in his hand, and he would limp to the blackboard on baseball-scarred legs. He didn't waste time with ear-training.

"On Fridays he would come around with a square, spring-driven phonograph, and fill a music-appreciation hour with *The Whistler and His Dog* and the marches of Sousa."

Friends and colleagues applauded Mr. Crandell's accomplishments when he retired in 1936.

Some bragged that because of Mr. Crandell, Snowflake had twice as many musicians per capita as any other town in the nation. The president of Arizona State College called him "the dean of music in Northern Arizona."

World War II depleted the faculty at Snowflake, and Mr. Crandell came out of retirement to teach without pay. He held classes in Taylor, Heber, and Clay Springs, and in other communities that couldn't afford a teacher. If he had charged for all his private lessons, he'd have died a millionaire.

Grand words were said over Mr. Crandell by bishop and stake president, patriarch and school principal.

But more appropriate were the efforts of a vocal soloist, a quintet, a women's chorus, and a 90-voice choir, with ASC Music Director Harold Goodman in a violin obbligato.

Uncle Rufus was put away with the music he created.

A Phoenix lady anesthesiologist received a letter from an insurance company, asking her to send in her report on the insurance examination for Mr. So-and-so. Her prompt answer was:

"There must be a mistake. I have not examined Mr. So-and so."

A few days later the company sent another letter, rather sharply worded. Would she kindly send along the examination report, which was overdue?

The answer was testy, too.

"I did not examine Mr. So-and-so. I do not do any insurance examining. I am in an entirely different field of medicine. Please refrain from bothering me with any more silly questions."

That should hold them, the doctor was thinking, when the third communication from the insurance company was put on her desk. She opened it, and out fluttered the company's check ($2) as payment in full for the examination of Mr. So-and-so.

The doc has intended asking Mr. So-and-so, whom she happens to know, just who in the heck did examine him.

But she is filled with the chilling fear that he might say, "You did."

After 31 years of unbending loyalty to his industry, a Phoenix man took his first airplane ride.

"It was a grand experience," grudgingly admitted T. C. (Tommie) Osborn, general agent for Santa Fe.

Mrs. Edith Slaughter of Eagar had as a guest in her home a brother who enjoys an astounding reputation as a weather prophet.

His name is Robert Peach. As Mrs. Slaughter told it:

"Bob makes his forecasts from how much his arthritis hurts him. He predicts the weather every day, and almost without exception he is wrong.

"The other day he woke up and said, 'Sis, I seem to feel pretty good this morning, and I believe we're going to have at least three clear, warm days.' "

Mrs. Slaughter said that the words were scarcely out of Robert Peach's mouth when a three-day snowstorm began. There was a foot drift against her back door.

But Mrs. Slaughter had compassion for her brother and, indeed, for anyone who tried to foretell the weather in Arizona in winter, 1960. As even the desert dwellers were aware, the state's weather map too often looked like a plate of Gianelli's spaghetti.

"I have spent more than 70 winters in the Arizona mountains," said Mrs. Slaughter, "but I have seen things so different this winter that I wonder about the cause."

Daughter of a pioneer Tonto Rim family, Mrs. Slaughter was born in Strawberry and has lived the past 50 years in the White Mountains.

"Since early fall," she said, "the skies have been so very blue and the sunshine brilliant. It never happened before, but the sun shining through a south window made dishes on a table hot. A few days ago the sky near the horizon was a light blue, but farther above it was several shades darker. The last week in October brought us a wet snow which caused power lines and crossarms to break. In December, usually one of our most wintry months, it rained as well as snowed.

"On the afternoon of Christmas Day a black cloud hung in the north, and between it and our valley was a long, narrow, perfectly white cloud near the horizon. After midnight a terrible blizzard came up. A young man saw a most brilliant flash in the southwest sky. Thinking a power line had parted, he drove off the road and damaged his car. Later we learned lightning had struck the power poles during this snowstorm."

Mrs. Slaughter said at times she thought the heavens were afire, so vivid were the colors. For an hour one day a little cloud transmitted sunlight as a spectrum. Twice sunsets have been red to the point of being weird. Usually the smokestack of the sawmill south of Eagar is her barometer, "but not once all winter has the smoke risen straight up into the sky."

Paul Kangeiser, weather bureau climatologist, agreed the phenomena observed by Mrs. Slaughter were unusual, if explainable. But Kangeiser admitted he did not know why Mrs. Slaughter's past-spring's pullets were moulting in the middle of February, instead of in the summer, when they were supposed to.

Brother Bob didn't know, either, but perhaps nobody would believe him if he did.

The thought came to me, while a horse named Bingo was polishing his saddle in the same old place, that the Verde Vaqueros must make an amusing sight for spooks.

You have to accept the possibility that there are ghosts out in the Mazatzal wilderness. Shades of Spaniards and Indians and mountain men drape themselves about the shrubbery, and blend into the shadows. Not much of interest happens in that neck of the woods these days, and I suppose the spirits must become bored to life of death.

And along ride the Verde Vaqueros—94 members and

guests making a hundred-mile loop through some of the most spectacular landscape the Creator ever put together.

The trailride is new. Out Wickenburg way the Caballeros have been making an annual cavalcade, and other clubs organize yearly excursions through the White Mountains, Sycamore Canyon, and Bill Williams county. Route of the Vaqueros was across the Verde River at Fort McDowell, along the faint Reno Pass Road to the Dos S camp of Bernard Hughes, up Screwtail Hill to Sunflower, then westward down Alder Creek to Bartlett Reservoir, around the lake, across the Verde, and on to Fort McDowell.

Ectoplasm of the Mazatzal spooks must have turned green at the sight of so much well-bred horseflesh. The old mountains probably never have held such a collection of fancy animals and riggings. For that matter, many of the Vaqueros are expert horsemen. Also, their heart is in the right place, for sure. Their fee for the ride includes $50 from each man for the Scottsdale Boys Club.

But what must have given the ghosts a case of chortles was the way the Vaqueros kept themselves supplied with all the conveniences of home, and then some. Under the direction of Otto Gaare, Phoenix hardwareman, there followed the Vaqueros into the mountains a mixed-drink bar; a kitchen capable of producing a meal of three entrees and all the trimmings, even to strawberry shortcake; portable toilets; and an outdoor mess hall of tables and benches. There was a compressed air machine for blowing up camp mattresses, gasoline lights that made the blackest night day, an around-the-clock coffee counter, a sound truck for broadcasting messages, music and entertainment. When you arose in the morning the juice bar was open, not far from the drum of hot water for shaving and face washing. If you wanted to, you could give your horse no more care than you would a car, because there were wranglers for that sort of thing, and Gaare's retinue had rations of hay and grain. There was even a farrier, if your horse should throw a shoe.

Camping was made convenient so that the Vaqueros could

divert their energies into the ride. The day from Sunflower to Bartlett would have tuckered even the Indians and pioneers.

But the mountain ghosts must have rocked with laughter when they saw that mixed-drink bar bearing down on them.

Or that truckload of steel cots.

I got out my pencil and paper, and after a while Walt Ditzen said something printable.

"Luckiest guy in the world—that's me," he growled. The big guy meant it, too.

He is better known as a funny man. Millions of newspaper readers laugh along with his syndicated cartoon strip, "Fan Fare." In three panels, he has to be quick. Ditzen's hopeful little characters also have wandered onto Valley sports programs, billboards, brochures, ads—even onto T-shirts.

A round of golf with Ditzen is like a year in the monkey house. A sought-after master of ceremonies, he can wreck a party with his crusade against the evils of drink.

"Shame on you," I've heard him chide the Elks, "for openly guzzling booze at football games. Think of the horrible example you make for children." Then Ditzen would pause dramatically and open his coat, displaying a plastic squeeze bottle slung in his armpit, and a tube running up under his collar to his mouth. "These will be on sale at the door at the conclusion of the program."

But it was the new Ditzen I saw.

He was propped up in bed in Good Samaritan, which, because of his Catholic tendencies, Ditzen had nicknamed St. Sam's. Three weeks before he had a heart attack that nearly killed him.

His room ran wild with humor. A woman friend brought him a mink covered bedpan, and Ditzen said he wouldn't swap for anything the stack of cards and letters he received from friends and fans. A whole side of the room was hidden by blooms, and a near wall was decorated with colored pictures drawn by fellow cartoonists of the likes of Reg Manning and Bil Keane. Ditzen's corpselike visage appeared in the paper the week he felt the worst. A friend clipped it and scrawled: "Sorry you're ill. I didn't know you died."

"Yeah," said Walt Ditzen. "I love it all. I'm a big ham, and I lap it up.

"But I'm a changed man now that I've joined the Coronary Club. I've had my warning. Some people didn't have a warning.

"I'll tell you boy, 46 is no age to go if you have a choice. There are too many things to do. After 16,000 deadlines it is no time to feel a ball of lead like the cigaret foil you used to save when you were a kid building up in your chest, and to lie in bed afraid to go the sleep because you know if you do you won't wake up. I was scared yellow. I still am.

"I could have died, and had more than I deserved. I got a real lump in my throat at the Soap Box Derby last year, and in October I was the first civilian to fly twice the speed of sound, in a Lockheed Starfighter. You don't get those things in Crackerjacks, and I want to try for more.

"Ain't nobody going to fuss me again. No trivia. Not even a missed putt. What the doc says, I do. I used to read my own horoscope. Now I read them all. I love everybody."

Outside on McDowell, buses went by. On the side of the buses were placards with a cartoon character saying, "Be Smart. It's Your Heart," by way of advertising the Heart Fund.

From his bed Ditzen, suddenly a believer, could see the signs he drew.

After a 10-year battle with empty beer cans, R. R. Riley retreated farther into the hills.

Riley didn't win. He didn't lose.

Riley closed out a decade as ranger of the Mesa district, Tonto National Forest. His stretch of forest was 20 miles long. At one end was the city. At the other, the wilderness, the rivers, the lakes, the desert.

Until Alaska with its great woodlands joined the union, Riley could brag that he was boss of the most-used district of the nation's biggest national forest.

Folks who keep track of such things say that Mesa district was drawing 170,000 visitors a year when Riley took charge in 1950. In 1960 Canyon and Saguaro lakes alone were expected to be visited by 800,000.

In the decades before Riley took charge, fire consumed an average 40,000 acres of watershed cover. During Riley's decade, Mesa district lost only 2,000 acres to fire.

The first years of Riley's tenure saw a series of tragedies on the Salt River and Verde lakes. As many as 30 and 40 persons drowned a year. Despite redoubled usage, the drownings in 1957 were reduced to 9. In 1958 there were 2. In 1959, 3.

Riley was the first one to dodge acclaim. He said that he couldn't have improved recreation facilities much without help from his own supervisors, and through co-operative programs with Maricopa County. He was proud of his control of fire, in a decade of critically dry weather, but he said, "It was a matter of horseshoe luck, and getting on the fires fast, and the assistance of ranchers and townspeople." As for the reduction in drownings, Riley gave unqualified credit to the Maricopa Sheriff's Water Posse. "Those boys do the work," he said. "They're the ones who give their work and their money, and they are the ones who keep the law."

But many who know him well, said Riley was the right man at a bad time.

Together with Assistant Supervisor Perl Charles, he got the water skiers to shake hands with the swimmers, and the fishermen to unite with the speedboat drivers. Life-saving regulation of the rivers and lakes was initiated by the people who use them.

Riley was a career forester. After college in Colorado, he went to work for the forest service 28 years ago. He was stationed all over New Mexico, and was district ranger near Silver City before coming to Mesa. In a profession where frequent transfers are expected, Riley said he was glad he could put his two boys through Arizona State University. One son is a college teacher; the other, an army officer.

"Now I have a feeling I stayed too long and ate too much," said Riley.

He was being sent to the supervisor's staff of Apache Forest, with headquarters in Springerville.

And Riley's unsettled issue with beer cans and other litter fell to a younger man, Bob Wier, from the Coconino Forest.

For a while there, A. C. Ruebush was the only service station operator in the world who feared the words:

"Fill 'er up."

He never knew which gallon of gasoline he sold might bring a hulking black monster leaping from the bowels of the earth.

Ruebush and his wife run the service station at Concho, 30 miles northeast of Show Low on Arizona-61. The gas pumps are in front of a mostly-adobe store which is sparsely stocked with groceries and sporting goods.

At the rear of the store, defined by pigeonholes and a partition, is the post office of Concho. Villagers come there every day to get their mail, to draw warmth from a log-burning stove, and to gossip.

In February, 1960, Concho had a new conversation piece.

Ruebush looked out of his store one minute, and everything was fine. When he looked again, the 2,000-gallon storage tank had risen out of the ground. The tank, 12 feet long, 6 feet in diameter, and black as soot, had pushed up through a two-foot layer of Concho clay and rock, and was fully exposed.

A. C. gave the situation some thought. The winter in Arizona's high country had been unusually wet. Under his place, A. C. had always believed, was an underground stream, and this year the water accumulated around the tank. When A. C. pumped nearly all the gasoline from the tank, it became a big, buried bobber. Up it came.

Considerable labor went into reburying the tank. Overburden was cleared away, the tank removed, the excavation drained and cleaned, the tank replaced and the fill added. Ruebush put a telephone pole across the tank to hold it down.

Some weeks later Mrs. Ruebush noticed the ground was cracking in a perfect outline of the tank. The clay seemed to be rising. Apprehension of the Ruebushes and the town rose with the hump. Each sale of gasoline increased the pressure.

"I parked my car on the hump," said Ruebush. "I didn't think it would hold it, but I thought it would slow it down."

The bulge increased.

"Then he made me go out and sit in the car," said Mrs. Ruebush. "He didn't ask me. He just said, 'Go out and sit in the car.' "

The combined heft of Ruebush's Buick and Mrs. Ruebush was enough to stop the rise of the tank. Pretty soon the man came by with the tanker truck and filled Ruebush's underground tank. The added weight of the gasoline sank it back to where it belonged. The hump receded. The Buick was driven off. Mrs. Ruebush went back to tending her post office.

The tanker driver agreed to keep the Ruebush tank filled near to capacity until Ruebush's latest program was completed.

He was going to build a concrete block addition to the store over the tank. In order to come out of the ground again, the tank would have to lift the store, the post office, and, of course, Mrs. Ruebush.

In the home of Mrs. Florence D. Moll at 56th Street and Virgina is a stout hall gate.

The gate divides the house into a people part and a dog part.

Only a human skull stays in the people part. Mrs. Moll, 75, lives in the dog part, with five dogs, and she said the longer she lives, the more reasons she finds for liking dogs better than people.

Her home is a cozy adobe built in 1927. Roof poles protrude from the exterior, and the windows and doors are deep-set in the thick walls. There is no lawn; the desert engulfs the house as the sea an island.

First Mrs. Moll showed me the people part of the house. Paintings adorn the walls. Living, dining, and sleeping rooms are furnished with antiques. The skull reposes in a cabinet a few steps from the front door.

"My husband was a physician and surgeon," she said in her brisk outline-of-history manner. "That's how I acquired the skull. Husband got it for me. I used it in my painting. Study bone structure, that sort of thing. These are my portraits. None of this modern stuff. My people all look like people. Been a widow since 1936. Came out here for my health. Stayed at the inns. Love to ride. Used to stop here in this grove of mesquites because it was the only cool place on the ride. Decided to buy the whole 15 acres. Place was a mess. Hauled out 12 trailers of trash, auto bodies, and tin cans. It had been a desert dump."

Then she took me to the dog part of the house.

Boston Blackie and Pinto have private rooms. Each room has its own fireplace, and sleeping rags, and french doors leading out to privately-fenced romping yards. Each bedroom also has a private toilet, but I could not bring myself to ask Mrs. Moll about them. The other dogs share quarters with Mrs. Moll. One, a wooly mother sheepdog, sleeps on Mrs. Moll's bed.

Everywhere in the house are the products of Mrs. Moll's artistry. Here are wood carvings, there canvases; in cupboards are miniature portraits. She displayed a humidor-match bowl-ash tray set she made, when a girl, by pasting cigar bands in involved patterns under glass.

"Why aren't kids doing these things these days?" she asked. "Instead of robbing stores? Throwing their beer cans all over the place? Keep hands busy, I say. Keep out of trouble."

Mrs. Moll has other possessions which seem to set her apart from the ordinary. She owns five Jersey milk cows and a 1936 Lincoln Zephyr V-12. She keeps the cows because she happens to prefer raw milk and fresh butter. She hasn't driven the car in years, but she refuses to sell it because they are not making them so strong anymore, and anyway, it has only 27,000 miles on the speedometer.

"Everything out here is antique," she said. "Including me. But we do as we please. Do you?"

Excuse (Yawn!) my sleepy mug and dreamy demeanor, but I am not in the habit of horseback riding at 2 a.m.

At first I thought Frank Honsik, MD, had acquired a wrinkle in his diploma.

"Come on out and go riding with us," he said. "We'll hit the trail after dark, and I'll show you raw and beautiful scenery that is within sight of downtown Phoenix. It will be an experience you'll never forget." Then he threw in a promise of a glass of smiles and a fried chicken dinner, and I was hooked.

The Honsik place is at Tatum Boulevard and Mockingbird Lane, north of Paradise Valley Country Club. Frank, his wife, A.G., and their two robust sons live in a multilevel ranch house, and out back four horses reside at a multilevel hay shed, stable, and corral unit.

The horses, Smokey, Chico, Bravo, and Golden Nugget, are his companions in relaxation, said Frank. Some men race boats. Others hit a ball around. Honsik rides, almost every day or night.

After a wearing day at his office or in surgery, he said, he can change into denims and boots, strap on a hawgleg pistol, gouge Nugget with a spur, and tell the world and all of its trouble to go straight to hell. Then as he rides through the dark desert he feels a hope and purpose in the day ahead.

We rode out the driveway at 10:30 p.m., under a full

moon. The Honsik home is about 50 blocks east of Central, and a westward course quickly put us into the Phoenix Mountains. Where Frank and the horses were trailwise, we galloped, spreading sparks and hoofbeats, and in short order we were climbing a narrow draw.

The animals labored for half an hour in a steady walk. But for a few winking signals from the direction of Cactus and Cavecreek, we could have been in a wilderness.

"Get set for the shock," shouted Frank, who in his 40 years has been a polo player, a ship's doctor, a cavalry trooper, and marksman.

Abruptly, Phoenix, and the Valley burst before us. At a flat on the pass under Squaw Peak we dismounted and admired the view.

"The Biltmore under us," said Frank. "Those red lights, 24th Street and Camelback. Those very bright lights in a string way out there are on S. Central bridge, and the red lights above, very faint, are the towers on South Mountain. And somehow I always enjoy sighting it all through the ears of a horse."

A. G. spoke: "Like every gem in the jeweler's case, spread out on a tray of black velvet."

She said it at a time I was inventing a description, that the Valley looked like the aftermath of throwing a great big stick of dynamite into a great big bonfire, but the allusion was inadequate for the moment, and I did not utter it.

We rode down off the mountain, and I must admit the day dawned hopefully and purposefully, if a trifle early.

Chapter Seventeen

Mondays and Tuesdays, Tommy Reese hikes from his home at 1517 W. Yavapai to the Salt River bottom where "cane-with-a-tossle" grows high and straight.

Reese is a tall, thin, black man, 60 years old. His field shoes are weather-checked, and his overalls and cotton shirt are faded. His tall-crown felt hat is full of holes.

With the ambition of a man killing snakes, Reese falls to cutting cane.

On other days of the week Reese packs the cane to a big salt cedar tree on the west side of S. 19th Avenue, across from Arizona Livestock Auction. He sits himself down on a chunk of discarded concrete. He spreads a heavy cloth on his left knee for protection, and with a keen butcher knife he whacks the cane to length and splits it to size.

The sun rises and warms him, and the pile of cane strips grows. Trucks blast by; the steel slides through the brittle wood. Motorists stop and chat. Tommy Reese goes on splitting cane, stopping only to twist his Bull Durham cigarets, which he smokes down to butts as short as pencil erasers.

The sun is overhead when the pile of cane is ready. He binds a cross of cane strips, and spreads them like wagon wheel spokes. Then he begins the weaving of thinner strips through the radiating cane.

"Louisiana was my home," he said. "Came West in 1930. Still a bachelor man. Been a pickin' cotton, been a choppin' cotton in California and Arizona. Times like these when I can't find no laborin' job, I fall back on my trade."

He learned his craft from his father, who picked up the skill from Cubans while serving in the Spanish-American War.

By 3 o'clock Reese's basket is of heroic size.

"Maybe I'll go to El Mirage one of these days. That's what I want to do. I have it in mind to buy me a little piece of land and put up a little house, and have me a vegetable garden and raise a few chickens."

The basket grows. It becomes a cylinder two feet in diameter and several feet high. Reese secures the final tier of cane, and begins to make a top for the basket.

"I have it in mind to take my trade to the big highway at El Mirage. Mornings I'd tend my garden and feed my chickens and fix my house, and during the day I'd sit out on the highway makin' baskets."

By 4 o'clock, the basket is finished. A woman stops. She says that she has been needing such a basket for a clothes hamper, and Tommy Reese says that is what he made it for. The price is $5.

That's the life of Tommy Reese. He makes one basket a day out of cane he cuts himself, and he sells the basket, and the money keeps him alive to make more baskets.

And he has a dream.

"Antique collectors are funny people," says F. Verne Peck, a funny person.

Presently Peck is a collector of old cars. He used to collect guns, and once had a fondness for rocks. But in the past six years Peck has gathered up a 1912 Krit, a 1913 Cadillac touring, a 1926 Model T, and a 1915 Ford speedster. Needless to say, he is a pillar, or more properly a main bearing, of the Phoenix Chapter, Veteran Motor Car Club of America.

"One enterprising fellow in Vermont buys up old cow sheds, outhouses, and so forth, and uses the lumber to build antique wash stands, and the dealers sell all he can build," relates Peck.

"There is no limit to the kind of things that are collected. Tommy Manville for instance collects wives and his wives in turn collect alimony. Old cars, guns, dishes, salt and pepper shakers, buttons and numerous other items are collected. Button collectors have a national organization and their own publication. An aunt of mine is an avid button collector and her prized possession is a button from Lew Wallace's coat. To secure it she had to prove to the museum people that he was a cousin before they would give it to her. All this trouble for one button."

Peck, a state highway engineering aide of 1603 W. Adams, said that a collector must acquire stories to go along with his hobby.

"If you do not have a story to go with a valuable item," he advises, "just make one up. It will enhance the value considerably." He said a religious sect in Europe "has sold enough splinters of wood from the true cross to build a two-story hotel."

Peck said that "buying antiques is an art and never to be taken lightly. The seller must be made to feel he is hooking you good."

A person has to be a little "tetched" to be a collector, but there are compensations. For example :

"Recently near Safford I spied what looked like an old car in a feed lot. There was a large dog lying by the door step. When I knocked on the dilapidated kitchen door, it almost fell off its hinges.

"The old dog cocked one eye open and gave me a contemptuous look, yawned, and showed his long yellow fangs. Dogs seem to have a sixth sense that tells them when a person is not quite right. A vicious dog that would have absolutely no scruples about chewing the mayor himself will allow the village halfwit to kick and abuse him without resentment. All this goes to show that while it's not absolutely necessary to be crazy to be a collector, it helps."

Once Peck visited a widower in Gilbert who had collected so many things his house was filled from floor to ceiling, except for a network of tunnels. The man wouldn't part with so much as a Model T axle, and worse, said Peck:

"He insisted on playing me a tune on his violin, and I could well understand why his wife had preceded him in death."

You can take the girl out of the city, but blamed if you can stop her complaining.

At least that's been my experience. For seven years I have been attempting to educate one of those painted up town women to the joys of primitive camping.

"Boil the coffee," say I, the expert. "Take a big ol' handful of coffee grounds and pitch it into the pot, and bring it to a boil over hardwood coals. Best coffee in the world. Warsh the pot in the crick with sand and a hunk of sod."

And just about the time I think I've passed on a bit of my outdoor lore, she says, "As long as I can take my electric percolator, I'll go."

My hopes aren't too high, but I may have the answer—one of those flashy camping trailers with most of the comforts of home built in.

It is 14 feet long, white, with gold and silver trim. A tall man can walk into it and stand without ducking. At the front under a picture window is a dining booth about as big as those found in cocktail lounges. Along one side is the kitchen, with a three-burner butane stove. A hand-pump draws water from a storage tank to a miniature sink. The end of the trailer has a sofa-bed, and an overhead canvas bunk for Miss Fourandahalf. The other side is a wardrobe and cubby lockers.

We couldn't afford to buy one. Not as an experiment. They cost something over $1,000. The $35-per-week rental seemed more our speed, since the renter pays for insurance and butane and reasonable wear and tear.

I've seen such rigs on the highways and along the creeks and thought they were more trouble than they were worth. No free-roaming dog wants a tin can tied to his tail. I figured a trailer would be a bother to tow, a drag on the gasoline mileage, and a problem in parking and maneuvering. I may decide I was right, which has happened before.

The outlandish contraption won the immediate fancy of milady.

"Now this is more like it," she said, running a finger along the fashionable copper-tone range. She brought out her vacuum cleaner and pail and soap. She hasn't cleaned a place so cheerfully and thoroughly since her honeymoon apartment. She fluffed pillows and polished the brightwork, and bless me, Jesse, if she didn't scour the floor.

"Don't let me ruin anything for you," said I, "but I consider it a duty to point out to you that in all my many years of roughing it, I have never scrubbed the forest floor or wiped the black out of a firepit or turned my mattress of pine needles. Did it ever occur to you that this kind of camping is more work than mine?"

She gave me that secret smile, and a little later I could have sworn I heard her whistling a tune. But then, she never had before.

TUCSON—An Arizona dairy farmer left his two fine mules at the barn, and harnessed his prize bull to the plow. A passerby asked why.

"For two years this bull has been tearing down fences to visit my neighbor's cows," said the farmer, "and today I am going to teach the sonofagun there is more to farming than romance."

Charles U. Pickrell tells that story, and thousands of others. He is a living library of Southwestern lies, some of which are true. He prefers to call them essences.

"Facts are like cows," he says. "You can't pick the best until the whole herd is in the pen."

Pickrell was brought to Arizona when he was an infant. He rode the ranges before they were fenced. His life as cattleman-educator earned him the directorship of the University of Arizona Agricultural Extension Service. Most of his yarns were drawn from the fountain-head of Western legend, the campfire.

"I always like to credit my sources," said Pickrell. "Now, Pop McKale says he once woke up and saw a rattlesnake curled up on his chest. He didn't dare move, so he went back to sleep, and when he woke up again, the snake was gone."

Bill Ridgway, of Willcox, told one about an old wrangler nicknamed Cyclone. Once a territorial judge introduced Cyclone by his alias, and Cyclone exploded: "Everybody calls you a dignified old goat, judge, but nobody introduces you that way."

Ed Echols, longtime Tucson constable and champion rodeo roper, claims he found a gold nugget in the craw of a turkey, and his family ate nothing but turkey for a whole summer.

Johnny Bixler, rancher of the Bill Williams country, was bragging about a horse: "He's only got two little faults. He's hard to catch, and not worth a damn when caught."

A Tucson cowboy heard his mother was dying in Los Angeles. He couldn't afford public transportation, so he borrowed a bike. When he arrived at his mother's side, she was almost gone, but at that moment a tire on the bike exploded, filling the sick room with healthful Tucson air, and the old lady lives to this day.

Ben Perkins, another Bill Williams rancher, used to say

he had a horse that was so touchy to ride, a cowboy didn't dare shift his chaw of tobacco from one check to another.

The aforementioned Cyclone was supposed to have owned a couple of highly trained dogs. At roundup one dog would hold down a calf and the other would apply the brand and chew the earmark. Once Cyclone accused the dogs of mismarking a dogie, and the dogs fetched him the mother cow to prove they were right. Cyclone had to get rid of the dogs, because they finally insisted that they do the roping, and Cyclone do the branding.

A Mesa prospector set off on what was supposed to be an extended trip, but he returned to town within a few days, and said:

"My jacks were newly shod, and I had hobnails in my boots, and we got stuck on a field of magnetic iron. Lucky for me, I was able to untie my laces and step out of my boots and walk back to town. Now if some of you fellers will help me pull my animals free, I'll be much obliged."

PORTAL—It is sad to think that this hamlet will have to get along without Mr. and Mrs. George Newman, but they both insist that soon it will.

They have been saying so for 10 years, true enough, but now there is a ring of resignation in their statements. They carry their years with grace, but the chores of Newman's store are about to get them down.

Portal is at the mouth of Cave Creek Canyon, long a favorite playground for Cochise County, and lately a discovery of other Arizonans and Easterners.

Cleanliness alone sets Newman's apart from most country stores. At any time since the Newmans opened in 1935, a marine major could have passed it in a white glove inspection. Geraniums in painted gallon cans fill the front windows. The enameled shelves are dusted daily.

Newman retired as railroad engineer before bringing his wife, a registered nurse, to Portal. They built the cracker-box store and behind it a tiny apartment they called the icebox. Mrs. Newman, accustomed to sterile rooms and white uniforms, found herself battling dirt in a drafty store at the edge of a dusty street.

"Besides that, I had to put up with kerosene lamps and a little old put-and-take wood stove," said Mrs. Newman. "Later we got an electric plant. Every year we supplied power for the Christmas trees at the school."

Electricity from the valley changed Portal and Newman's. Soda pop is sold from fancy change-making machines, and the beer is chilled in large refrigerators. In fact, Newman's store is air-conditioned. Yet there are reminders of Newman's modest beginning. In stock are lamp wicks and tire boots and cold patches.

George Newman remains the titular head of the store. Two strokes and a near-fatal attack of pneumonia have dulled his hearing but not his wit. He prowls the store, waiting for a stranger to ask, "Are you George Newman?" giving him a chance to answer:

"Yes, what is left of him."

The major burden of running the store has fallen to Mrs. Newman. She is a beautiful woman, in a stout, gray, grandmotherly way. She dips up Polish sausages and pumps gasoline and punches open beer cans and rings up orders with the self-assurance of a woman who has not only whipped her enemy, dirt, but has managed to get the street paved out front. She has delivered 14 babies in Portal, including a set of twins.

"I don't know where we'll go, or what we'll do," she said. "We simply do not have the energy and means to put in the improvements that the store needs, and yet, after the way we started here from scratch, it doesn't seem right to sell out just when the boom is beginning.

"Sometimes I think my husband wouldn't last two weeks anywhere else, so maybe we won't leave after all."

PIMA—Nearly every morning Fred A. Williams, who

was born in 1880, runs around the block for his constitutional, he feels so good.

He is a man of many happy talents. All his life he has played the violin. A couple of years ago he decided to take up the cello.

He went to a Safford music store and determined the dimensions of a cello. Then for a month, he whittled sycamore and Graham Mountain fir, and he warped and glued it all together, and he strung it up, and he made a bow—and Fred Williams had a cello.

Williams made two violins of similar material. On the instruments he plays from "Songs of Praise," a publication of the Seventh-Day Adventist Church. Williams is a devout member.

"I have been an Adventist for 56 years," he said cheerily. "When I took the vows, my father said, 'You now have no more religion than a hog has,' but my father was wrong."

Besides his church, Williams has many interests. He has a rock shop on the highway. He also makes keys there, and sharpens saws. Next door is the Mexican food restaurant of the Alec Rodella family.

"We get along fine," said Williams. "I run the rock shop, and Alec owns the rock. Alec runs the restaurant and I own the restaurant. Ain't that funny?"

Saturday, the Adventist sabbath, the rock shop is closed. Williams goes to Safford where there is an Adventist church with a minister and some 50 members. Williams said there are plenty of regilions prospering in the Upper Gila Valley and they get along as harmoniously as the strings of his cello.

Williams was graduated from Pacific Union College, an Adventist school in his native California. He qualified as several kinds of engineer, and for a quarter of a century before he retired, he was chief engineer at an Adventist hospital.

He attributes his perfect physical condition to his Adventist diet. He eats no bread and little meat. Rather, he devours whole wheat biscuit by the carton, and vegetable cakes by the case. Keeps the arthritis away, he claims. The sight of Williams is enough to make a man switch to his feed. His skin is ruddy and clear, his eyes bright, his gray hair lustrous, his body straight and muscular. He said he doesn't have a single ache.

Frequently he takes time off to visit a son, J. D. Williams, who has a ranch at Aravaipa. On other occasions, the elder Williams joins another retired Pima man who owns a station wagon, and "we travel all around together."

It is William's belief that the grief of the world can be traced out to individual men and women. Before nations can live in peace, humans must quiet their own mean feelings for others, and that, said Williams, is the way he tries to live.

"I think there will be more Catholics in heaven than Adventists," he said, "simply because there are more Catholics to begin with."

CAVE CREEK CANYON—Some people come here to watch birds and some to watch the birdwatchers. It's a tossup as to who has the most fun.

Called "The Yosemite of Arizona," Cave Creek Canyon is carpeted and draped in grass and trees, and walled in by lichen stained cliffs. It is the habitat of a great variety of birds and insects and humans.

A couple of adults dashed through our camp. They wore binoculars on straps around their necks. They had the intent look of people who are late for a show. When they returned an hour later, they walked slowly, and their chins were on their chests.

"Coppery-tailed trogon," said Harlan E. Eckler. "We've been coming here 12 years in hopes of seeing it, and this is the first time we have so much as heard it. But it eluded us again today."

Mr. and Mrs. Eckler have a little house in Santa Monica, Calif., but they seldom occupy it. They live in their trailer, which they take all over the West in search of birds. In

Arizona they camp at Patagonia, in the Huachucas, at Pena Blanca Lake, in Organ Pipe National Monument, at Boyce Thompson Arboretum, and at Cave Creek. Eckler is a retired master aircraft mechanic who had his hands in production of planes for two world wars.

Since he retired 15 years ago, Eckler has devoted nearly all of his time to bird photography. Once he put on telephone pole climbers and walked 50 feet up a tree to photograph a nest. He began with a Graflex and now uses a 35-millimeter color camera with five lenses. The largest is a Big Bertha of 40-inch focal length, whose components were taken from a military aerial camera. Eckler built the tubes and mounts. Also in his kit of tools is a flash gun which can be triggered by a photoelectric circuit breaker.

Eckler commonly will set up a feeding tray, a couple of perches, an 18-foot stepladder, a beach parasol, his camera and flashgun—and then, if he is fortunate, he will get one picture. The game is so tedious that Eckler failed for 14 years to take a decent picture of a robin. Last year he succeeded, and the transparencies of a nesting robin were put with Eckler's collection of 18,000 color slides of birds, flowers and scenes.

"I know we are the butt of a good many jokes," said Eckler. "When we started studying birds in Cleveland, our friends thought we had gone soft upstairs. Now there are 5,000 members of birdwatching clubs in Cleveland. At first our trips were just for camping. Then we began to keep lists of birds. But the lists bored us. We found a challenge in photography. Nothing puts a photographer to a greater test. Our first pictures we colored by hand and preserved between sheets of glass.

"No matter how much a man knows about birds, he always wishes he knew more: Where they nest, how they nest, when they nest, how long they are on the eggs, how long the young are in the nest. And in order to produce consistently good work, the photographer must know these things about 700 species."

The Ecklers occasionally show their slides in towns along their trails, but they do not make a business of it. Their hobby is for their own pleasure, and if they snap the coppery-tailed trogon, no one else need know.

PUNKIN CENTER—One time I told a Phoenix operator I wanted to telephone Frankie Toot of Punkin Center, and the operator thought I was drunk.

"Punkin Center is a store, bar, and service station at Tonto Basin, north of Roosevelt Lake," I said, a little miffed. "Frankie Toot is the wife of Gyp Toot, who runs the place. That's right, Frankie Toot is a woman. Toot. T-o-o-t. Now put the call through or I'll report you to the supervisor. S-u-p-e-r-v-i-s-o-r."

In a few minutes Frankie Toot and I were chatting about the subject of my call. It seemed that Punkin Center year after year has led Arizona in per-capita collections for the March of Dimes.

Mrs. Toot, a grandmother of three, said the community of some 60 souls spontaneously adopted the National Foundation as its favorite charity. Every year a Texas-size pumpkin was picked from a nearby field and put on a shelf behind the bar.

Folks would come in to buy beer and take a 25-cent guess at the weight of the pumpkin. After the dimes drive, the person who guessed the weight of the gourd got it.

Anyway, the story was so backwoodsy I invented a Mammy Yokum mental image of Frankie Toot. I figured she would have a hair bun, a feed-sack dress and maybe a lump of snuff in her cheek .

"Hello!" said I to a genial, compact fellow at the Punkin Center store. "Are you Gyp Toot?"

"I'm him," he said, extending a strong, rough hand.

"I'd like to see your wife."

Toot cranked the proper combination on the wall telephone and asked his wife to come from her house over to the store.

While I was waiting for Frankie Toot, a beautiful woman entered the store. Her Marlene Dietrich figure was niftily displayed in a fashionable blue, ribbon dress. Dark ringlets framed a classic face. She walked toward me, and in a voice as soft as Miss Monitor's, said:

"I'm Frankie Toot."

Whatever little speech I had planned fled from my head, and about all I could say, was:

"The folks with the March of Dimes made you this plaque for hanging over the bar, and since I was coming this way, they asked me to give it to you."

Frankie Toot took the plaque, shaped like a map of Arizona, and read the inscription, "Highest Per Capita Award 1960 March of Dimes Special Recognition to the Community of Tonto Basin for Help in Bringing Dignity and Usefulness to Lives Impaired by Crippling Diseases."

Punkin Center raised $802.66 in 1960, said Mrs. Toot, batting her exquisite lashes. Tonto Creek was so high they couldn't bring the pumpkin to the bar, but the dance, cake sale, and auction at the school house was especially successful.

Frankie Toot said they knocked down a goat for $38.40 and sold a snip of the goat's tail for $1.50.

I wonder what the telephone operator would think about that?

CAMP VERDE—The most active businessman-outdoorsman in this country is dark-haired, 28-year-old Wayne Barnes.

With his mother he is partner in a cafe, service station, and trailer park at Cienega Creek, 11 miles south of Camp Verde on the Black Canyon Highway.

Down below the old Fort Verde parade ground and museum is his neat frame home, where lives his wife, Shirley, and 7-month-old daughter, Glenda. As do most young working men, Barnes keeps the lawn mowed and watered, and the weeds hoed.

Most of Barnes' spare time is spent hunting and fishing.

He has taken deer every year since 1952. He hunts with bow and arrows. Hanging over the counter at the Barnes cafe is a huge buck head and rack. The deer three years ago won the Arizona heavy deer archery contest for Barnes. He hunted for the deer four days in the area south of Grand Canyon. He stalked to within 30 yards of the deer, and killed it with a single shot. The buck, field dressed, weighed 174 pounds.

Four years ago Barnes also won the heavy deer archery contest. Two years ago, he placed second.

Last year Barnes didn't go hunting with the bow. Archery season conflicted with turkey and antelope dates. Barnes got his turkey and pronghorn, and then went out into the Dugas country with his rifle. He knocked down a fat buck, and had to pack the animal through a rockchoked canyon after dark.

When he isn't hunting, he's fishing. He counts among his trophies a 13½-pound catfish from the Verde River, a 4-pound trout from Montana, and a 6½-pound bass from Lake Mead.

Barnes has two cars, a pickup and a Jeep, and keeps all four in repair. He goes into the rough rimrock and collects Indian artifacts. His arrowhead collection, which he began a year and a half ago, has 2,000 specimens. Arrowhead gathering led to another hobby. Barnes developed a method of sawing flint and obsidian into thin sheets, which he then chips, Indian fashion into matching arrow points for earrings.

Barnes comes from a family of Arkansas natural musicians. Since he was big enough to lift a fiddle he has known the feel of taut strings under his fingers. Barnes has come to specialize in the steel guitar. He has had his own country dance band, and as soon as the summer tourist season matures, he intends to play at the Cornville barn dance.

"I can't seem to stay still," he said. "A long time ago I decided nothing was going to keep me from doing things I want to do, and it's true that I've had to work like the dickens, but I've won out."

A stranger would never guess that the graceful dancer and

hardy mountain climber of Camp Verde lost both his feet in a farming accident when he was 13.

COTTONWOOD—Harrison (Buck) Barbee has a little lot and house in Cottonwood, down the slope toward the Verde River.

It was his hope to make his property bloom. He asked for water from a nearby irrigation ditch, and was refused, on grounds he had no water rights. Then Buck Barbee figured that if he watered from the town system, it would cost as much as $10 per month. That was too much for a retired man, at least for Barbee.

Barbee went down to the Verde and cut a willow log. He carried it to his place and anchored the big end to the ground. Barbee propped the other end of the pole in a couple of braces made like sturdy stepladders. In the crotch of the brace the pole rested on an automobile coiled suspension spring.

Then Barbee fixed a chain to the protruding, small end of the willow pole, and to the chain, a steel drill bit of his own invention.

Barbee hauled down on the chain.

The drill scratched the soil.

The willow pole snapped back, lifting the chain and bit.

Off and on for two years Barbee drove the bit into the earth, and the pole pulled it up. The bit chewed through sand and river gravel, boulders, red sandstone, and even a four-foot stratum of copper rock.

At 54 feet Barbee struck water. The willow pole had lost some of its spring, and so had Barbee. He was glad the job was done. Then the chain broke, and Barbee lost his bit at the bottom of the hole.

That was the state of things now. Barbee, 72, had given up fishing for the bit until cool weather set in.

Meantime, he was going on with his dreaming. He is a short man of perhaps 125 pounds. He wears a full mustache and beard. His old gray hat is ventilated with holes snipped with his wife's shears.

"I've drilled 300 holes like this back in Kentucky, testing for coal. I'd have used hickory if there was any around, but this willow will do," he said. "I spent half my life behind a yoke of steers, and when I set to eat, it was on table. There wasn't anybody a-running off to a store with a little old paper sack to fetch the vittles."

Despite Barbee's unfulfilled plans for free water, his lot was indicative of his intentions. Chickens pecked under peach and apple trees Barbee started from seed. Vegetable and flowers grew in neat rows. Here and there were reminders of Barbee's Blue Grass loyalties: pole beans, damsons, and a black walnut seedling.

Barbee had it in mind that the middleman grips this country by the throat.

"Now, I raised tobacco for more years than I can remember, and the most I ever got for it was $18 a hundred. If you are a cigaret smoker, chances are you never weighed one. Well, I did. A cigaret smoker pays $700 a hundred pounds for his tobacco. I chew, myself. I buy it by a big box, at the cheapest price I can find, and I still pay $250 a hundred, and I have no doubt I am chewing some I raised myself."

Barbee said when his well comes in he is going to grow tobacco.

In June, 1960, the Ancient Mariner from the South Bank of the Salt sailed away on the Last Great Voyage.

I lost more than a dear friend. He was the best doggerel poet in Arizona, and for more than five years I had depended on him to brighten a corner of the column now and again. His genius was brevity. He could spank the world with a couplet.

Lt. Cmdr. Ray Duus (USNR Ret.) of 1040 W. Sixth Pl., Mesa, steadfastly clung to anonymity. I don't believe he was modest. He hungered for an audience. But he wrote his little pieces and published them, as purely proud as a child launching a shingle-sailboat. The art, yes. The person, no.

The funeral was brief, unadorned: An honor guard of sailors, white in the hot sun, a bugler, a post-size flag unfurled on the casket under a canopy. Roundabout were his widow, Sammie, a few close friends, his championship basketball team (the Mariner had been a high school coach before he went to sea), and a pair of bland undertakers. The Mariner was not of an organized faith, but a Mormon bishop said he was honored to speak words over Lieutenant Commander Duus.

It was a grand talk. It made real the Mariner's quest for education; his gallant service in two wars; his terminal years of pain and preposterous humor.

I tried to decide, of all the things he had written, which I liked best. And remembering it, I nearly burst out laughing while the minister was summing up. There came to me an image of the Mariner confronting an unsuspecting Davey Jones:

"You see, when I was down at Kwajalein some years ago, I went reef-crawling for cowrie shells on the island of Loi. I noticed a pretty tropical fish, colored seal brown and striped black. I had him flown to the States.

"Keeping him over on the Pacific Coast was no problem at all since a constant supply of sea water was available. But when we decided to move to Arizona, the question of a proper environment arose. I took a long chance, gradually replacing the salt water. By the time we moved here, he was completely at home in fresh water.

"Well, sir, the thought occurred to me if I could wean him from salt to fresh water, I might be able to get him to live on ordinary air. It actually worked. Got so he would follow me about the yard and even down the street.

"But tragedy struck. While passing the post office here in Mesa, that fish and I got caught in a line squall. Having lost his former sure-footedness (or should I say sure-finnedness?) he slipped into the gutter and drowned!"

The End

Index

INDEX (Continued)

INDEX (Continued)

INDEX (Continued)

INDEX (Continued)

INDEX (Continued)

INDEX (Continued)

INDEX (Continued)

INDEX (Continued)

This book was manufactured in Phoenix, Arizona. It was set in 12-on-13 point Linotype Caslon, composed to a design of several collaborators, and printed on a Miehle letter press, in the shop of McGrew Printing and Lithographing Co. Stock is fifty pound Garamond text. The 17 india ink chapter drawings were engraved on zinc by the Republic & Gazette Engraving Co. The book was bound in Joanna Book Cloth by Arizona Trade Bindery.